T0139201

Intrusion Detection Networks

A Key to Collaborative Security

Intrusion Detection Networks

A Key to Collaborative Security

Carol Fung and Raouf Boutaba

CRC Press
Taylor & Francis Group
Boca Raton   London   New York

CRC Press is an imprint of the
Taylor & Francis Group, an **informa** business
AN AUERBACH BOOK

CRC Press
Taylor & Francis Group
6000 Broken Sound Parkway NW, Suite 300
Boca Raton, FL 33487-2742

© 2014 by Taylor & Francis Group, LLC
CRC Press is an imprint of Taylor & Francis Group, an Informa business

No claim to original U.S. Government works

Printed on acid-free paper
Version Date: 20131009

International Standard Book Number-13: 978-1-4665-6412-1 (Hardback)

Visit the Taylor & Francis Web site at
http://www.taylorandfrancis.com

and the CRC Press Web site at
http://www.crcpress.com

Contents

List of Figures

List of Tables

Preface

The Internet has experienced explosive growth. Along with the widespread deployment of new emerging services, billions of computers and devices are connected to the Internet and are accessible worldwide. At the same time, the growing size and complexity of computer software leave thousands of software vulnerabilities exposed for malicious exploitations. Millions of attacks and billions of dollars of loss are reported every year as the result of cyber crimes. In this context, cyber intrusions are becoming an increasingly global and urgent problem. As a countermeasure, Intrusion Detection Systems (IDSs) are designed to identify intrusions by comparing observable behavior against suspicious patterns, and notify administrators by raising intrusion alarms. An IDS can be broadly defined as software or a device capable of monitoring network or computer activities and raising alerts when suspicious activities are observed. Examples of IDS can be antivirus software, network-based IDS (e.g., Snort, Bro), host-based IDS (e.g., OSSEC, Tripwire), honeynets, and firewalls.

Traditional IDSs work in isolation and can be easily compromised by threats that are new or unknown to their providers. An Intrusion Detection Network (IDN) is an overlay network composed of a number of IDSs. It intends to overcome the weakness of isolated IDSs by allowing them to share their intrusion information and detection knowledge with others, this way improving the overall accuracy of intrusion assessment. However, building an effective IDN is a challenging task. For example, adversaries may compromise some IDSs in the network and then leverage the compromised nodes to send false information, spam, or even attack other nodes in the network, which can compromise the efficiency of the IDN. It is, therefore, important for an IDN to detect and isolate malicious insiders. Another challenge is how to make efficient intrusion detection assessment based on the collective information and knowledge from other IDSs. Appropriate selection of collaborators and incentive-compatible resource management in support of IDS interaction with other peers are also key challenges in IDN design.

This book presents the IDN concept and discusses IDN design with an emphasis on the following questions: Why build intrusion detection networks; what are the problems underlying the design of intrusion detection networks; and what are the solutions to those problems? We present an overview of existing IDN designs and elaborate on the underlying challenges, including privacy, malicious insiders, scalability, free-riders, collaboration incentives, and intrusion detection efficiency.

Privacy is important because IDN users may be discouraged to participate in IDNs if there is potential information breaching during collaboration. We categorize existing IDNs into information based, consultation based, and knowledge based. We then analyze the privacy concerns in each of them.

In an IDN, participating IDSs can be malicious. A trust management framework is required to identify dishonest or malicious insiders. In Chapter 4 we discuss the Bayesian learning based trust management model where each participant IDS evaluates the trustworthiness of its collaborators through past experiences with them. A Dirichlet model is presented as a means to integrate past experiences and calculate trust values as well as the confidence levels in the trust estimation.

While IDSs provide intrusion detection opinions of their own, how IDSs use the collective opinions to make a decision whether an intrusion is detected or not is another challenge. Chapter 5 first discusses how Bayesian decision models can be used to make optimal intrusion decisions that have minimal false decision cost, and how sequential hypothesis models can be used to decide the minimum list of collaborators to consult in order to achieve a decision satisfying a given confidence level. The optimal decision model is used to compare the expected cost of whether or not to raise an intrusion alarm, and choose the decision which bears the lowest cost. The sequential hypothesis model is used to find the minimal number of collaborators to consult before a confident decision is made, which can effectively reduce the amount of communication overhead between IDSs.

Once collaboration connections are established, how much resource to allocate for each collaborator in order to maintain a fair, incentive-compatible, and with no-free-rider collaboration environment is the main topic discussed in Chapter 6. The nodes in the IDN are modeled as a set of uncooperative game players and all the nodes follow a predefined strategy to play the game. The game strategy is for each node to decide how to allocate resources to their neighbors fairly. It is proved that the game has a Nash Equilibrium (NE), and under the NE the amount of help received by each node is proportional to the amount of its contribution to others. Free-riding is thus not practical under this resource allocation design. In Chapter 7, a collaborator management model is discussed to allow each IDS to select a best combination of collaborators that minimizes cost. Because the optimal selection of collaborators is an NP hard problem, heuristic approaches are sought to find near-optimal solutions.

As discussed above, this book not only discusses efficient IDN design, but also provides a collection of problem solutions to key IDN design challenges and shows how various theoretical tools can be used in this context. Another highlight of this book is the evaluation of IDN designs, including comprehensive validation methodologies and evaluation metrics (e.g., efficiency of intrusion detection, robustness against malicious insiders, fairness and incentive compatibility for all participants, and scalability in network size).

Carol Fung and Raouf Boutaba

About the Authors

Carol Fung is an assistant professor of computer science at Virginia Commonwealth University (USA). She earned her bachelor's and master's degrees in computer science from the University of Manitoba (Canada), and her PhD in computer science from the University of Waterloo (Canada). Her research interests include collaborative intrusion detection networks, social networks, security issues in mobile networks and medical systems, location-based services for mobile phones, and machine learning in intrusion detection. She was the recipient of the best dissertation awards in IM2013, the best student paper award in CNSM2011 and the best paper award in IM2009. She has received numerous prestige awards and scholarships including the Google Anita Borg Scholarship, NSERC Postdoc Fellowship, David Cheriton Scholarship, NSERC Postgraduate Scholarship, and the President's Graduate Scholarship. She has been a visiting scholar at POSTECH (South Korea), a software engineer at Google, and a research staff member at BlackBerry.

Raouf Boutaba is a professor of computer science at the University of Waterloo (Canada) and a distinguished visiting professor at POSTECH (South Korea). He served as a distinguished speaker of the IEEE Communications Society and the IEEE Computer Society. He is the founding chair of the IEEE Communications Society Technical Committee on Autonomic Communications, and the founding editor in chief of the *IEEE Transactions on Network and Service Management* (2007–2010). He is currently on the advisory editorial board of the *Journal of Network and Systems Management*, and on the editorial board of *IEEE Transactions on Mobile Computing*, *IEEE Communication Surveys and Tutorials*, *KICS/IEEE Journal of Communications and Networks*, *International Journal on Network Management* (ACM/Wiley), *Wireless Communications and Mobile Computing* (Wiley), and the *Journal on Internet Services and Applications* (Springer). His research interests include resource and service management in networked systems. He has published extensively in these areas and received several journal and conference best paper awards such as the IEEE 2008 Fred W. Ellersick Prize Paper Award, the 2001 KICS/*IEEE Journal on Communications and Networks* Best Paper Award, the IM 2007 and 2009, and the CNSM 2010 Best Paper Awards, among others. He also received several recognitions, such as the Premier's Research Excellence Award, Nortel Research Excellence Awards, a fellowship of the faculty of mathematics, David R. Cheriton faculty fellowships, outstanding performance awards at Waterloo and the NSERC Discovery Accelerator Award. He has also received the IEEE Communications Society Hal Sobol Award and the IFIP Silver Core in 2007, the IEEE Communications Society Joe LociCero Award and the IFIP/IEEE Dan Stokesbury Award in 2009, and the IFIP/IEEE Salah Aidarous Award in 2012. He is a fellow of the IEEE and the EIC.

INTRODUCTION

In November 2008, a new type of computer worm started to spread quickly. It used three different types of attack on Windows® hosts: exploiting vulnerabilities, guessing passwords, and infecting removable devices [20]. In three months it took over about 9 million Microsoft® Windows systems around the world and formed a massive botnet [5]. The estimated economic loss brought by this worm was USD 9.1 billion [33]. The worm was named "Conficker," and it was only one of the thousands of worms that appear every year.

Nowadays the vast majority of computers are connected to the Internet. A number of applications used by billions of users on a day-to-day basis including email, Web browsing, video/audio streaming, social networking, online gaming, e-commerce, and online chatting rely on the Internet. At the same time, *network intrusions* have become a severe threat to the privacy and safety of computer users. Each year, millions of malicious *cyber attacks* are reported [64, 145]. Attacks are becoming more sophisticated and stealthy, driven by an "underground economy" [65]. By definition, *network intrusions* are unwanted traffic or computer activities that may be malicious or destructive, including viruses, worms, trojan horses, port scanning, password guessing, code injection, and session hijacking. The consequences of a network intrusion can be user identity theft (ID theft), unwanted advertisement and commercial emails (spam), the degradation or termination of the host service (denial of service), or using fraudulent sources to obtain sensitive information from users (phishing). Network intrusions are usually accomplished with the assistance of malicious code (a.k.a. malware). In recent years, network intrusions have become more sophisticated and organized. Attackers can control a large number of compromised hosts/devices to form *botnets* [5], and then launch organized attacks, such as distributed denial of service.

As a countermeasure, *intrusion detection systems (IDSs)* are used to identify intrusions by comparing observable behavior against suspicious patterns. Based on the technology used for detection, IDSs can be categorized as *signature-based* or *anomaly-based*. Based on the targets they are monitoring, they can be *host-based* or *network-based*. Examples of IDSs include antivirus software [26, 4], Snort [24], Bro [7], Tripwire [29], OSSEC [19], and HoneyNets [27]. Traditional IDSs monitor computer activities on a single host, or monitor network traffic in a sub-network. They do not have a global (i.e., Internet-wide) view of intrusions and are not effective in detecting fast-spreading attacks. In addition, traditional IDSs acquire detection rules only from their corresponding *vendors*. Various security vendors usually employ distinct intrusion detection technologies and knowledge. In practice, not a single security vendor has the entire knowledge to detect all types of intrusions. Therefore, traditional IDSs are not effective in detecting unknown or new threats. In turn, they can achieve better detection accuracy through collaboration. A good example of this is antivirus software, where it is common knowledge that a malware file that has not been detected by one antivirus software may be detected by another. However, if IDSs are allowed to communicate with each other and exchange intrusion information, each IDS can benefit from the collective expertise of the others. Therefore, collaboration between IDSs is envisioned to be a promising approach to improve intrusion detection.

Some early works on IDS collaboration include Indra [84] and DOMINO [149], where IDSs shared information to prevent fast-spreading attacks. However, their collaboration was limited to selected nodes that followed predefined communication protocols such as DOMINO. Later, in 2008, standardized models and communication protocols provided a method for various IDSs to communicate with each other. The two important standards are IDMEF (Intrusion Detection Message Exchange Format) [15] and CIDSS (Common Intrusion Detection Signatures Standard) [9]. IDMEF provides a communication standard enabling different intrusion detection analyzers from different origins (commercial, open-source, and research systems) to report to a managing entity for data analysis, aggregation, correlation, etc. It is XML based and includes two types of messages: heartbeat messages sent periodically to state that an IDS in the distributed system is still alive, and alert messages sent when a suspicious event occurs. Those events can be augmented with additional information in the form of XML compound classes such as the scanner type, timestamps, and classifications in the case of an alert, or even self-defined attributes (see Appendix A). The IDMEF is specified in RFC4765 [22] and implemented by many IDSs such as Snort and OSSEC. CIDSS defines a common XML-based data format for storing signatures from different intrusion detection systems and shares the signatures among them. In this way, it is primarily aimed at IDS administrators to exchange, evaluate, and criticize signatures. Also, a future scenario is considered in which independent contributors exist, enabling the provision of signatures independent of a particular product or software.

The standardization of communication protocols between different IDSs allows each IDS to obtain intrusion information and detection knowledge from other IDSs in the network. An *intrusion detection network* (IDN) is such a collaboration network, allowing IDSs to exchange information with each other and to benefit from the collective knowledge and experience shared by others. IDNs enhance the overall accuracy of intrusion assessment as well as the ability to detect new intrusion types. There are two types of IDNs in the literature: information-based and consultation-based. In an *information-based IDN*, nodes share observations and detection knowledge with other nodes in the network, such as knowledge related to new attacks. This type of IDN is effective in detecting fast-spreading attacks such as worms. However, it may generate large communication overhead, and all exchanged information may not be useful to others. In a *consultation-based IDN*, when an IDS detects suspicious activities but does not have enough confidence to make a decision, it may send *consultation requests* to others in the network. *Feedback* from the collaborators can be used to make a final decision as to whether or not it is an intrusion. Consultation-based IDNs have much lower communication overhead, are more effective in terms of communication efficiency, and are the focus of this book.

Although communication and collaboration among IDSs is feasible, building an effective IDN is a challenging task. For example, adversaries may compromise some IDSs in the network and then leverage the compromised nodes to send false information and spam, to free-ride, or even to attack other nodes in the network, which can compromise the efficiency of the IDN. It is therefore important for an IDN to detect and isolate malicious insiders. Another challenge is how to make efficient intrusion detection assessments based on the collective information and knowledge from other IDSs. Appropriate selection of IDN participants and incentive-compatible resource management in support of IDS interactions with peers are also key challenges in IDN design.

This book focuses on the design of IDNs leveraging effective and efficient collaboration between participant IDSs. We emphasize "collaboration" from the perspective of an IDS to provide a systematic approach for determining who to collaborate with and how to make intrusion detection decisions based on collective knowledge. The book will answer the following questions: why build intrusion detection networks; what are the problems underlying the design of intrusion detection networks; and what are the solutions to those problems? We overview existing IDN designs and discuss the underlying challenges, including privacy, malicious insiders, scalability, free-riders, collaboration incentives, and intrusion detection efficiency.

Privacy is important because IDN users may be discouraged to participate in IDNs if there is potential information breaching during collaboration. How to design communication protocol among IDSs to minimize information breach during collaboration is also a challenging problem. This is particularly true when some participants are malicious. A malicious IDN participant can not only gather information from other peers and turn it against others, but can also send false information or spam to other IDSs to compromise the efficiency of the IDN. Therefore, a trust management framework is required to identify dishonest or malicious insiders. Research results [69, 72, 74] show that an efficient trust management system can effectively identify malicious/dishonest or incompetent IDSs in the network, thus improving the quality of collaboration by eliminating the impact of malicious IDSs. In particular, we present in Chapter 5 a Bayesian-learning-based trust management model where each participating IDS evaluates the trustworthiness of its collaborators through past experiences with them. A Dirichlet model is presented as a means to integrate past experiences and calculate trust values as well as the confidence levels in the trust estimation.

Another important problem pertaining to IDS collaboration in an IDN is how IDSs use other's opinions to make a decision. The problem for IDSs in the IDN is to determine whether or not to raise an intrusion alarm, based on the feedback from collaborators. Two types of false decision cost are considered in the literature [75]: false positive cost and false negative cost. Bayesian hypothesis modeling can be used to model the risk cost of decisions and to choose the decision that has the lower risk cost. An interesting question here is how to determine the minimum amount of feedback an IDS needs to achieve a low enough cost [159]. Chapter 6 first discusses how Bayesian decision models can be used to make optimal intrusion decisions that have minimal false decision cost, and how sequential hypothesis models can be used to decide the smallest list of collaborators to consult in order to achieve a decision satisfying a given confidence level. The optimal decision model is used to compare the expected costs of raising or not raising an intrusion alarm, and then to choose the decision that bears the lowest cost. .

Once collaboration connections are established, determining how much resources are required for each collaborator in order to maintain a fair, incentive-compatible, and with no-free-rider collaboration environment is another interesting research question. Game theoretic approaches can be used to model the resource allocation strategy of IDN participants [162, 163]. Specifically, as shown in Chapter 7, the nodes in the IDN can be modeled as a set of uncooperative game players, and all the nodes follow a predefined strategy to play the game. The game strategy is for each node to decide how to allocate resources to their neighbors fairly. It is proved that the game has a Nash Equilibrium (NE), and under the NE the amount of help received by each node is proportional to the amount of its contribution to others. Free-riding is thus not practical under this resource allocation design.

In a dynamic IDS collaboration environment, participating IDSs may join, leave the network, or become compromised. How to select and maintain collaborators effectively is of paramount importance. This is referred to, in this book, as the acquaintance selection problem, which can be formulated as an optimization problem [70, 71] where an optimal collaborator set should lead to minimal false decision and maintenance costs. In Chapter 8 we describe a collaborator management model that allows each IDS to select the best combination of collaborators to minimize its cost. Because the optimal selection of collaborators is an NP-hard problem, heuristic approaches are sought to find near-optimal solutions.

In addition to the design of a consultation-based IDN, we also discuss the design of a knowledge-based IDN. Knowledge sharing and propagation is an important feature for knowledge-based IDNs because IDSs can effectively exchange intrusion detection information such as new intrusion alerts, black lists, emerging intrusion detection rules or malware signatures, etc., in a collaborative environment. Chapter 9 discusses effective information propagation mechanisms for IDSs in knowledge-based IDNs to select appropriate peers to propagate their knowledge to. For instance, a two-level game-theoretic formulation for the knowledge propagation control is employed, leading to a prime Nash equilibrium solution that provides a scalable, incentive- compatible, fair, efficient, and robust outcome. The chapter also presents an analysis, at equilibrium, of the macroscopic knowledge propagation properties on a large collaborative network.

To demonstrate the applicability of collaborative intrusion detection to real-world scenarios, we also use a study case to show the effectiveness of collaboration in malware detection, which is described in Chapter 10. In the collaborative malware detection network (CMDN), participants send suspicious files or their digests to their acquaintances for consultation. We especially focus on the decision algorithm design where possibly correlated feedbacks are aggregated to make a final decision. We show that the decision algorithm is efficient and robust to malicious insiders compared to many other existing collaborative decison methods in the literature. We use real malware and goodware data to evaluate the efficiency, scalability, flexibility, and robustness of the collaborative malware detection network.

As discussed above, this book does not only discuss efficient IDN design, but also provides a collection of powerful solutions to key IDN design challenges and shows how various theoretical tools can be used in this context. Another highlight of this book is the comprehensive evaluation of IDN designs, including various evaluation metrics (e.g., efficiency of intrusion detection, robustness against malicious insiders, fairness and incentive-compatibility for all participants, and scalability in network size).

This book is organized as follows. Chapter 2 presents an overview of network intrusions, their potential damage, and corresponding detection methods. We then have a survey of existing intrusion detection systems and intrusion detection networks in Chapter 3. Chapter 4 discusses our decentralized IDN topology design and architecture design. Chapter 5 and Chapter 6 are, respectively, dedicated to trust management and intrusion detection decision making. Resource management and collaborator management are discussed in Chapter 7 and Chapter 8, respectively. We also discuss knowledge propagation mechanism design in Chapter 9 and then we have a IDN study case in Chapter 10. Finally, we summarize and conclude this book in Section V.

CYBER INTRUSIONS AND INTRUSION DETECTION

Chapter 2

Cyber Intrusions

CONTENTS

2.1 Introduction

Since the first computer virus *Creeper* appeared in 1971, cyber attacks have been growing explosively and became a serious problem these days. Throughout the 1990s, the rise of commercial interest on the Internet has propelled information infrastructure as the core component of a global economy. Government agencies and businesses have become increasingly dependent on information technology for daily operations to increase their productivity. However, the increasing number of cyber threats and attacks has become a serious issue for the entire economy and government systems. Millions of attacks have been reported and hundreds of millions of nodes are compromised every year [32]. Sophisticated cyber attackers not only compromise the connected Internet computers for identity theft and information harvesting, but also use the compromised computers for criminal purposes, such as launching distributed denial-of-service (DDoS) attacks on some businesses or agencies. *Cyber wars*, as defined by Richard A. Clarke "...actions by a nation-state to penetrate another nation's computers or networks for the purposes of causing damage or disruption" [47], have become frequent and caused significant damage in recent years.

"America must . . . face the rapidly growing threat from cyber-attacks.."

—U.S. President Barack Obama
February 2013

Cyber attacks, by definition, are computer activities generally seen as targeting vulnerable computers and making them malfunction or resulting in disrupted flows of data that disable businesses, financial institutions, medical institutions, and government agencies. For example, cyber attacks can alter credit card transaction data at e-commerce websites and can cause the altered information to spread into banking systems. They can also disrupt the normal operation of information systems and bring down critical infrastructures. Cyber attacks can cause tremendous economic damage at a relatively low cost of initiating the attacks.

There are many different ways to launch cyber attacks, including malware infection, software/service vulnerability exploitation, denial of service, and phishing. In this chapter we discuss different cyber attacks based on their propagation properties, types of crime, and magnitude.

2.2 Overview of Cyber Intrusions

2.2.1 Malware

A network intrusion accomplishes its goal by executing malicious software/code on the victim machine. *Malware* is a term for all software or code designed to cause damage to a device or a network. There are many different types of malware, such as computer viruses, worms, trojans, and spyware.

A *computer virus* is a computer program that can insert/copy itself into one or more files without the permission or knowledge of the user, and then perform some (possibly null) operations [41]. Malicious viruses may cause a program to run incorrectly or corrupt a computer's memory, while nonmalicious viruses may do no harm. A computer can be infected with a virus when copying data from other computers or when using an infected external drive such as a flash memory or removable disk. As their name suggests, viruses can replicate themselves to infect other hosts, but typically do so after user interaction. For instance, a virus received as an email attachment infects the user host when opened by the user and eventually spreads to other hosts by sending the same email to contacts in the user's address book.

In general, most computer viruses do not actively search for victims through a network. Malware that actively searches for victims is known as *worm*. A computer worm is a program that propagates itself through the network automatically by exploiting security flaws in widely used services [143]. Worms can cause the most extensive and widespread damage of all types of computer attacks because of their automatic spreading capability. A large number of different worms have been documented over the years. Some of the most famous ones include Morris (1988), CodeRed (2001), SQL Slammer (2003), the Witty worm (2004), the Conficker worm (2009), and Stuxnet (2010).

A distinguishing characteristic of computer viruses and worms is their ability to self-replicate and spread within networks. There are some other types of harmful software/code which do not self-replicate, such as trojan horses (trojans). A *trojan* (also called a backdoor) is a program with an overt (documented or known) effect and a covert (undocumented or unexpected) effect [41]. For many years, trojans have been the most widely used source of malware by hackers [115]. Trojans appear to perform desirable functions, but in fact facilitate unauthorized access to users' computers. A typical trojan requires interactions with a hacker. Hackers can access the infected hosts and manipulate them using commands.

The most difficult to detect type of malware is Rootkit, which is designed to hide the existence of certain processes or programs from normal methods of detection and enables continued privileged access to a computer. Once a Rootkit is installed, it becomes possible to hide the intrusion as well as to maintain privileged access. The key is the root/administrator access. Full control over a system means that existing software can be modified, including software that might otherwise be used to detect or circumvent it. Rootkits are usually malicious and allow attackers to access and control the compromised system.

Finally, *spyware* is a type of malware that is installed surreptitiously on a personal computer to collect information about the user without their informed consent, such as their browsing habits. Spyware can report user information to the attacker, such as email addresses, credit card information, bank account information, passwords, and other sensitive information. The difference between spyware and trojans is that spyware aims at collecting information from users and a trojan allows hackers to access the infected host.

2.2.2   Vulnerabilities Exploitation

In the past few years, a plethora of services and applications has become available online and accessible by users worldwide. However, due to the increasing size and complexity of these services and applications, design and implementation flaws are commonplace, making them vulnerable to attackers. A *software vulnerability* is a weakness in a computer program that can be exploited by an attacker and used to gain unauthorized access or to degrade service performance. There are thousands of software vulnerabilities discovered and documented each year in vulnerability databases such as the National Vulnerability Database [18] and US-CERT [30]. An exploitable vulnerability is the combination of three elements: a system flaw, attackers' access to the flaw, and attackers' capability to exploit the flaw. To exploit a vulnerability, an attacker must have at least one applicable tool or technique that allows him to connect to a system weakness.

A vulnerability that is unknown or freshly discovered and not yet patched by system developers is called a *zero-day vulnerability*. Attacks that are targeted at a zero-day vulnerability are called *zero-day attacks*. Zero-day attacks occur during the vulnerable time window that exists between the time the vulnerability is known to attackers and when software developers start to patch and publish a countermeasure.

A typical example of a vulnerability is the *buffer overflow*, where attackers can manipulate an already-running program to overrun the buffer's boundary and overwrite its adjacent memory, and eventually cause the program to execute the attacker's code. A buffer overflow can be triggered by injecting malicious code through inputs when running the program. Attackers can take advantage of the buffer overflow vulnerability of a service to crash the service or run malware.

2.2.3   Denial-of-Service Attack

A *denial-of-Service attack* (DoS attack) is a type of cyber attack with the intention to render a machine or network service unavailable to its intended users. Although there are various attack techniques, motivations, and targets of a DoS attack, it generally consists of efforts to interrupt or suspend the services of an Internet host, such as banking services. A *distributed denial-of-service attack* (DDoS attack) occurs when multiple computers launch a DoS attack against a targeted Internet host simultaneously, usually under the control of the same attacker. These attacker computers are usually compromised nodes from a botnet. They flood the victim with intense traffic or service requests. When a host is overloaded with connections, new connections can no longer be accepted. The damage resulting from a DoS/DDoS attack is typically measured in time and money loss due to service downtime and loss of productivity.

There are typically two types of DoS attacks: operating system (OS) attacks and network attacks. In the former, attackers exploit the OS vulnerabilities and bring down the service using techniques such as buffer overflow. In the latter, attackers overwhelm the target host with an excessive number of external communications requests or amount of traffic, so that the victim cannot respond to legitimate requests, or responds too slowly to be acceptable. Such attacks usually lead to a server or bandwidth overload. In general, DoS attacks either force the target to reset, or consume enough of its resources so that it cannot provide intended service to legitimate users, or obstruct the communication media between the legitimate users and the victim so that they can no longer communicate adequately. For example, in a SYN flood attack, the attacker sends a large number of TCP/SYN packets, often with a forged sender address. Each packet initiates a connection request, causing the server to open a connection by sending back a TCP/SYN-ACK packet (Acknowledgment) and wait for a response from the sender address (response to the ACK Packet). However, because the sender address is forged, the response never comes. These half-open connections saturate all the available connections of the server, keeping it from responding to legitimate requests.

Early occurrences of DoS attacks include the DoS attacks in February 2000, where the attackers managed to bring down the websites of large companies like ebay, Yahoo, and Amazon after a series of DoS attacks [10]. A recent well-known DDoS attack occurred in late 2012, when a series of DoS attacks were launched against the American financial sector, leading to a cost of $30,000 per minute when the attacked websites were down [12]. A more recent DDoS attack in March 2013 targeted the largest spam filtering system, Spamhaus, was considered the largest DDoS attack in history. It generated 300 Gbps of traffic which slowed down the Internet around the world for about a week [11].

2.2.4 Web-Based Attacks

Although malware is a very popular way to attack computers or devices on the Internet, it usually requires victims to receive and run malicious code [53], which can be avoided by careful Internet users. Web-based attacks are another type of attack on Internet users and Web services. Typical examples of Web-based attacks include *SQL-injection* and *cross-site-scripting*.

SQL-injection is a way to exploit a type of vulnerability known as a *command injection vulnerability*. Typically, SQL-injection arises when untrusted data is inserted for malicious purposes into a query or command to a Web service. SQL-injection attacks can be used to retrieve information from compromised Web services and thereby cause information breaches. Information such as social security numbers, dates of birth, and maiden names are collected by hackers as part of *identity theft*. Another popular target of this type of attack is unprotected credit card information. Massive credit card information loss can cause significant damage to an organization's most valued asset, its customers. Solutions to mitigate the impact of SQL-injection attacks include applying data validation, encrypting sensitive data in the database, and limiting privileges [53], among others. SQL-injection attacks can be detected through anomaly detection methods (see Section 3.1) employed by intrusion detection systems (IDSs).

Cross-site-scripting (XSS) lies in the category of cross-domain security issues [53]. This type of attack takes advantage of security vulnerabilities found in Web applications, such as Web browsers. It allows attackers to inject client-side script into Web pages and retrieve the session data of the user. A cross-site scripting vulnerability may be used by attackers to bypass access controls such as the same origin security policy. Cross-site scripting carried out on websites accounted for roughly 84% of all security vulnerabilities documented by Symantec, as of 2007 [136]. Solutions to prevent XSS attacks include input validation and output sanitization, the usage of HTTP-only cookies, and binding session cookies to IP addresses [53].

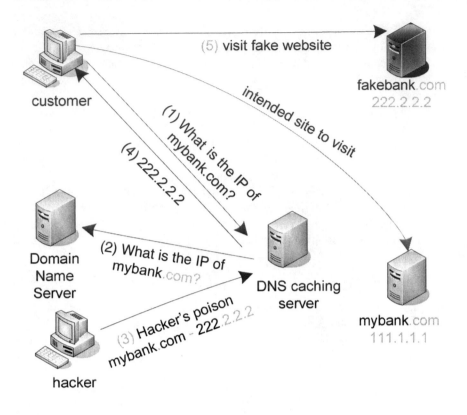

Figure 2.1: The DNS spoofing attack.

2.2.5 DNS Attack

A *DNS attack* (or DNS spoofing) is a cyber attack targeting a Domain Name System (DNS) server's cache database, causing the name server to return an incorrect IP address, and thereby diverting traffic to another computer (often the attacker's).

A domain name system server translates a human-readable domain name (such as example.com) into a numerical IP address that is used to route communications between nodes. Normally, if the server does not know a requested translation offhand, it will ask another server, and the process continues recursively.

As shown in Figure 2.1, to perform a DNS spoofing attack, the attacker exploits a flaw in the DNS software and fakes the response from a legitimate DNS server to a DNS cache server. If the DNS cache server does not correctly validate DNS responses to ensure that they are from an authoritative source (for example, by using DNSSEC), the server will end up caching the incorrect entry locally and serve them to other users and lead them to fake websites.

This technique can be used to direct users of a website to another site of the attacker's choosing. For example, an attacker spoofs the IP address DNS entries for a target website on a given DNS server, replacing them with the IP address of a server he controls. He then creates files on the server he controls with names matching those on the target server. These files could contain malicious content, such as a computer worm or a computer virus. A user whose computer has referenced the poisoned DNS server would be tricked into accepting content coming from a nonauthentic server and unknowingly download malicious content.

2.2.6 Organized Attacks and Botnets

Recent network intrusions have evolved to be more sophisticated and organized. Attackers are able to control a group of compromised computers/devices to launch distributed attacks; for example, the DDoS attack. Compromised nodes that are infected with malware communicate with a master through a command and control (C&C) server [141] or a peer-to-peer network. A group of compromised nodes and a master together form a *botnet*. The compromised nodes are called *"bot nodes,"* and the master is called a *"bot master."*

The life cycle of a bot node is shown in Figure 2.2. In the beginning, the victim machine was infected by malware. At this stage, a bot seed is planted into the victim machine. In the next step, the infected machine sends a request to a bot code host server and downloads bot binary and executes it. At this stage, the victim machine turns into a bot node. The bot node then initiates contact with the bot master and receives control commands from the bot master. Bot nodes can be used to commit cyber crimes such as DDoS attacks, spam propagation, ID theft, or phishing.

2.2.7 Spam and Phishing

Spam is the activity of using electronic messaging systems to send unsolicited bulk messages indiscriminately to users, especially for advertising products or services. While the most well-known spam is email spam, the term also applies to similar abuses in other media, such as instant messaging spam, social network spam, and spam in blogs.

Spam is a widely used method for spreading malware, delivering advertisements, and posting phishing links. For example, the famous "Love Letter" computer virus (2000) was spread by sending emails with the subject line "I Love You" and the attachment "Love-Letter-For-You.txt.vbs". When the receivers opened the attached executable file, it then activated the attached script and infected the host machine. The "Love Letter" worm infected more than 50 million users in 10 days and caused at least a USD 2 billion loss worldwide [82].

Another usage of spam emails is to post phishing weblinks. *Phishing* is a criminal activity consisting of stealing users' personal identity data and financial account credentials. Phishing attacks typically use two mechanisms. The first mechanism, known as social engineering, makes use of spoofed emails appearing to be from legitimate businesses and agencies in order to lead consumers to counterfeit websites designed to trick recipients into divulging personal data such as usernames and passwords. The second mechanism, known as technical subterfuge, plants crimeware

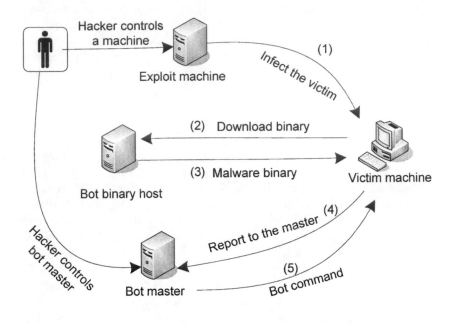

Figure 2.2: The life cycle of a bot node.

onto user computers to steal credentials directly through intelligent keyloggers and/or by corrupting browser navigation in order to mislead customers to counterfeit websites. Gartner estimated an increase in the cost of identity theft from USD 2 billion to USD 3.2 billion in 2007 in the United States alone [83].

Like any large-scale online service, large-scale phishing websites rely on online availability. Phishing sites, however, may be relatively easy to bring down if they use fixed IP addresses. This is not only specific to phishing sites. In fact, any illegal online organization that targets victims on a large scale requires high availability for the continuation of its operation. Recently, *Fast-Flux Service Networks* [34] have appeared to fulfill this requirement, ensuring a high availability yet evasiveness of illegal sites. Fast-Flux Service Network (FFSN) is a term coined by the anti-spam community to describe a decentralized botnet used to host online criminal activities. FFSNs employ DNS techniques to establish a proxy network on the compromised machines. These compromised machines are used to host illegal online services, like phishing websites, malware delivery sites, etc., with very high availability. An FFSN generally has hundreds or even thousands of IP addresses assigned to it. These IP addresses are swapped in and out of flux with extremely high frequency, using a combination of round-robin IP addresses and a very short Time-To-Live (TTL) for any given particular DNS Resource Record (RR).

Website hostnames may be mapped to a new set of IP addresses as often as every 3 minutes [34]. This makes it extremely hard to take down the actual service launcher, as the control node (mothership) is not known. The proxy agents do the work for the control node, and they also change rapidly. ATLAS is a system from Arbor Networks that identifies and tracks new Fast-Flux Networks [110]. In an investigation conducted in 2008, ibank-halifax.com was the largest detected fast flux domain, with a size of 100,379 hosts and a DNS entry life of 2 months. When an FFSN is detected, the domain registrars can be contacted to shut down the corresponding domain, hence removing the FFSN. Although this mitigation technique sounds doable, it is often a tedious and time-consuming task given the fact that not all registrars respond to abuse complaints [1].

2.2.8 Mobile Device Security

With the rapid advances in the so-called "Internet of Things," desktop computers are no longer the dominant form of computing. For example, smartphone usage has been growing exponentially and is replacing desktop usage to become the next popular tool for email, news, chatting, and Internet access. Following the growth of smartphone use, smartphone exploitation techniques are also growing. A key feature of modern smartphone platforms is a centralized service for downloading third-party applications. The convenience to users and developers of such an "app market" has led to an explosion in the number of apps available. Apple's App Store served nearly 3 billion application downloads after only 18 months [35]. Many of these applications combine data from remote cloud services with information from local sources, such as a GPS receiver, camera, microphone, or accelerometer. Applications often have legitimate reasons for accessing this privacy-sensitive data, but users may not be aware of whether or not their data is used properly. Many incidents have occurred where developers relayed private information back to the cloud [54, 108], and the privacy risks illustrate the danger [63].

In addition to the risk of downloading malware, mobile phone vulnerabilities are also targets for exploitation. Hundreds of vulnerabilities were discovered in the years 2009 and 2010. While it may be difficult to exploit many of these vulnerabilities successfully, there were two vulnerabilities affecting Apple's iPhone iOS operating system that allowed users to *"jailbreak"* their devices. The process of jailbreaking a device through exploits is to install malicious code, which can gain the user root privileges through exploiting a vulnerability in the iOS.

2.2.9 Cyber Crime and Cyber Warfare

Computer crime refers to any crime that involves a computer and a network. The computer may have been used in the commission of a crime, or it may be the target. *Cyber crimes* are defined as "Offences that are committed against individuals or groups of individuals with a criminal motive to intentionally harm the reputation of the victim or cause physical or mental harm to the victim directly or indirectly, using modern telecommunication networks such as Internet (Chat rooms, emails, notice boards and groups) and mobile phones (SMS/MMS)" [80]. Issues surrounding this type of crime are usually high profile, including cracking, copyright infringement, child pornography, and child grooming. They also include problems of privacy invasion when confidential information is lost or intercepted, lawfully or otherwise.

Some cyber crimes may threaten a nation's security and may be used as attacking tools for military purposes across nations. Cyberwar, also known as "information warfare," became known first in 1994 when Winn Schwartau published a book entitled *Information Warfare* [123], when the computer security community was just starting to wake up to the fact that the critical infrastructure we have built was vulnerable to certain attacks that could potentially lead to loss of life or tremendously expensive damage. Cyber warfare involves the actions by a nation-state or international organization to attack and attempt to damage another nation's computers or information networks through, for example, malware or denial-of-service attacks. The objectives of cyber wars are usually political (e.g., to bend the other side to one's will) by causing damage. It is not inconceivable that a successful cyberwar can overthrow the adversary's government and replace it with a more malleable one. A few well-known cyber warfare incidents in recent years include the StuxNet (2010), the Titan Rain (2005), and the Georgian cyber war (2008).

2.3 A Taxonomy of Cyber Intrusions

In this section we summarize the above-mentioned cyber intrusions and provide a taxonomy based on their malware types, attack targets, and attack methods. The taxonomy is shown in Figure 2.3.

2.4 Summary

Cyber intrusion has become an increasingly serious and global problem. This chapter provided an overview of cyber intrusions and categorized cyber intrusions based on their propagation properties, types of crime, and magnitude. Many types of cyber attacks and their corresponding defense techniques are described. We then provided a taxonomy of cyber intrusions based on the type of used malware, attack target, and attack method.

To protect computers from cyber attacks, intrusion detection systems (IDSs) are used to monitor computer/network activities, and detect and terminate cyber attacks. An intrusion detection network is an overlay that allows IDSs to communicate and make collaborative intrusion detection. In the next chapter we provide a survey of intrusion detection systems and intrusion detection networks.

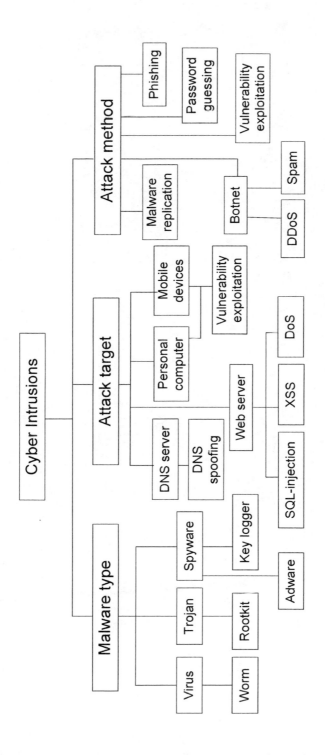

Chapter 3

Intrusion Detection

CONTENTS

3.1   Intrusion Detection Systems

Intrusion detection systems (IDSs) are software/hardware systems designed to monitor network traffic or computer activities and emit alerts/alarms to administrators when suspicious intrusions are detected. IDSs are different from firewalls. A *firewall* is a device that filters all traffic between a protected or "internal" network and a less trustworthy or "external" network, while IDSs sniff or monitor network traffic or computer activities but do not drop or block them. A firewall can be used along with an IDS to block identified malicious traffic in order to protect internal computers from being further exploited. Based on the technology used for detection, IDSs can be divided into signature-based and anomaly-based types. Also, based on data sources, they can be host-based or network-based.

3.1.1   Signature-Based and Anomaly-Based IDSs

Signature-based IDSs compare data packets with the signatures or attributes of known intrusions to decide whether or not the observed traffic is malicious. A signature-based IDS is efficient in detecting known intrusions with monomorphic signatures. However, it is not efficient in detecting unknown intrusions or intrusions with polymorphic signatures. *Anomaly-based IDSs* observe traffic or computer activities and detect intrusions by identifying activities distinct from a user's or system's normal behavior. Anomaly-based IDSs can detect unknown intrusions or new intrusions. However, they usually suffer from a high false positive rate. Most current IDSs employ both techniques to achieve better detection capability.

3.1.2   Host-Based and Network-Based IDSs

A *host-based IDS* (HIDS) runs on an individual host or device in the network (Figure 3.1). It monitors inbound/outbound traffic to/from a computer as well as internal activities such as system calls. A HIDS views an individual device only, and may not be aware of the overall network environment. Examples of HIDSs include OSSEC [19] and Tripwire [29].

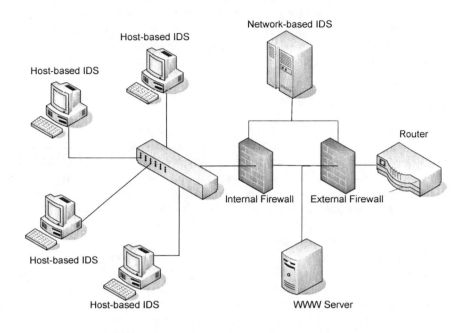

Figure 3.1: An example of host-based IDS and network-based IDS.

Tripwire is a brand of software used to ensure the integrity of critical system files and directories by identifying all changes made to them. Tripwire configuration options include the ability to receive alerts via email if particular files are altered, and automated integrity checking. Using Tripwire for intrusion detection and damage assessment helps in keeping track of system changes and can speed up the recovery from a break-in by reducing the number of files that must be restored to repair the system. Tripwire compares files and directories against a baseline database of file locations, dates modified, and other data. It generates the baseline by taking a snapshot of specified files and directories in a known secure state. After creating the baseline database, Tripwire compares the current system to the baseline and reports any modifications, additions, or deletions.

Network-based IDSs (NIDS) monitor network traffic to/from the network. A NIDS contains sensors to sniff packets, and a data analyzer to process and correlate data. Alarms are raised whenever suspected intrusions are found. However, a NIDS does not have knowledge about the internal activities of individual computers. Examples of NIDSs include Snort [24] and Bro [7].

Snort is a free and open-source NIDS, created in 1998 and developed by Sourcefire. Snort has the ability to perform real-time traffic analysis and packet logging on IP networks. Snort performs protocol analysis, content searching, and content matching. It relies on a set of predefined policies called "Snort rules" to detect suspicious traffic. The rules specify the patterns of potential attacks, including IP addresses, port numbers, protocols, and pattern strings. Snort rules need to be updated frequently to keep up with new attacks. Snort can also be used to detect probes or attacks, including but not limited to operating system fingerprinting attempts, common gateway interfaces, buffer overflows, server message block probes, and port scans.

3.1.3   Other Types of IDSs

Early intrusion detection systems, such as [55, 57] and [98], relied on logging the system activities to spot potential misuses that had occurred. The administrator reviews the outputs of the IDS to find attacks, remove threats, and patch vulnerabilities of the system. Modern IDSs analyze network traffic and/or system logs and perform correlations in real-time before sending alerts/alarms to administrators. Besides the traditional IDSs we listed in previous sections such as Snort, Bro, and OSSEC, other applications/devices can be used as intrusion detection systems. In this section we briefly describe honeypots and antiviruses.

Honeypots are systems set up for the purpose of trapping attackers/hackers and collecting traces for security analysis. A honeypot generally consists of a computer, data, or a network site that appears to be part of a network but is actually isolated and monitored, and which seems to contain information or a resource of value to attackers. Based on their level of interaction with attackers, honeypots can be divided into low-interaction honeypots and high-interaction honeypots [128]. Low-interaction honeypots are usually emulated services that are frequently requested by attackers. They have limited interaction with attackers because they are not real services. Most emulated services are only restricted to the first few interactions. Examples of such honeypots include Honeyd [14], Spector [25], and KFsensor [13]. High-interaction honeypots imitate real operating systems that host a variety of services and applications. Therefore, an attacker may be allowed to perform many types of attacks on this type of honeypot. An example of such a honeypot is Honeynets [27].

Antivirus systems are software systems that monitor, prevent, detect, and remove malware such as computer worms, viruses, adware, trojan horses, rootkits, and keyloggers. A variety of strategies are employed by antivirus systems. There is signature-based detection, which involves searching for known patterns of data within executable code, and heuristic-based detection, which can identify new viruses or variants of existing viruses by looking for known malicious code, or slight variations of such code, in files. Some antivirus software also uses anomaly detection techniques to identify malware by running it in a sandbox and analyzing the behavior of a file under execution in order to detect any malicious actions. Examples of antivirus software include Symantec [26], Avira [4], and Avast [3].

3.1.4   Strength and Limitations of IDSs

Intrusion detection systems are constantly evolving. Research on IDSs began in the 1980s, and products appeared in the 1990s. As new vulnerabilities and attack types become known, IDSs evolve and become more and more sophisticated. Indeed, IDSs are improving continuously and are able to detect an ever-growing number of attacks by including more and more attack signatures and attack models. Recall that IDSs look for known vulnerabilities and weaknesses, either through patterns of known attacks (signature-based) or models of normal behavior (anomaly-based). Whenever new attacks are discovered, the corresponding detection rules/signature are created by the IDS manufacturer and distributed to users' IDSs. Many commercial IDSs are quite effective in identifying new attacks.

However, it is difficult for IDSs to detect all potential attacks. Indeed, attackers only need to evade the IDS once to successfully compromise the system, while IDSs need to know all possible attacks to guarantee a successful defense. In practice, an IDS vendor has knowledge about some attacks, but no single one knows all.

Another limitation of IDSs is their sensitivity control. It is typically the case that a sensitive IDS raises too many intrusion alerts (most of them are false positive alerts), which makes it difficult for administrators to handle. However, when an IDS is less sensitive, it may miss critical attacks (false negatives) and hence fail to protect networks and hosts. Determining the optimal sensitivity of IDSs is a difficult problem.

3.2 Collaborative Intrusion Detection Networks

A *collaborative intrusion detection network* (CIDN) is an overlay network that connects IDSs so that they can exchange information, such as intrusion alerts, blacklists, signatures, suspicious files, and intrusion detection rules. Several IDNs have been proposed in the past few years. In an IDN, IDSs collect data from distributed peer IDSs and use it to achieve better intrusion detection. In this section we categorize IDNs using three features, namely cooperation topology, cooperation scope, and specialization. We also provide a taxonomy of some of the most prominent IDNs.

3.2.1 Motivation for IDS Collaboration

Isolated intrusion detection systems rely strictly on security updates from their respective vendors and are vulnerable to new or unknown attacks. Collaboration between IDSs allows each IDS to use collective knowledge from other IDSs to achieve more accurate intrusion detection, which is particularly useful for preventing new attacks. For example, when one IDS detects a new attack, it can alert its collaborators, which then can block similar attacks when they occur. Through knowledge-sharing, collaboration between IDSs intuitively benefits each participating IDS and allows the creation of an IDN with a much stronger intrusion detection capability. Building an effective collaborative IDN, however, raises a number of challenges, which we will discuss next.

3.2.2 Challenges of IDS Collaboration

Collaboration among intrusion detection systems has the potential to improve the effectiveness of intrusion detection, as IDSs leverage the collective intrusion detection information received from their collaborators. As such, participating IDSs are less likely to be compromised by threats unknown to them. However, IDS collaboration introduces communication overhead in the network. Because collaboration is based on information exchange, each participant receives help from others in the network but also has to spend resources (e.g., CPU, memory, network) to help others in return. Therefore, IDSs with low resource capacity may be constrained in collaboration.

Another challenge for IDNs is that the participant IDSs may become the target of malicious attacks. For example, adversaries may compromise some IDSs in the network and then leverage the compromised nodes to send false information or spam, or even to attack other nodes in the network, which can compromise the efficiency of the collaboration network. Therefore, it is important for an IDN to detect and isolate malicious insiders in order to eliminate their negative impact. In addition, how to make efficient intrusion detection assessments based on the collective information and knowledge from other peers is another challenge. In the following we discuss some of the key challenges in IDN design including privacy, malicious insiders, free-riders, scalability, incentives, and intrusion detection efficiency. Then we overview some of the most prominent IDN designs in the literature.

Privacy is a primary issue, as IDN users can be discouraged from participating in the IDN if there is potential information breaching during collaboration. To address this issue, a trust management model can be used to identify dishonest and malicious nodes. An effective trust management model should be able to distinguish honest nodes from dishonest ones, and high-expertise nodes from low-expertise ones. Free-riding the IDN is another important problem, where selfish nodes (a.k.a., free-riders) exploit the network seeking knowledge from others but do not contribute themselves. To handle this problem, an incentive-compatible resource allocation design can reward active participants and discourage free-riders. A scalable IDN can accommodate a large number of nodes in the network without overburdening any single node. A scalable IDN architecture design is necessary for a large-scale collaboration network. Although IDS collaboration can improve overall intrusion detection accuracy, its efficiency is limited by the quality of the individual intrusion detection systems. Collaboration cannot detect an intrusion that no single IDS in the network can detect. Therefore, improving the intrusion detection accuracy of each IDS is still an essential problem to solve. In our work, we will demonstrate the effectiveness of IDS collaboration and the amount of improvement in terms of detection accuracy over individual IDSs.

3.3   Overview of Existing Intrusion Detection Networks

In this section we give a survey of existing intrusion detection networks in the literature and summarize them based on their topologies, scopes, specializations, and technologies.

3.3.1   Cooperation Topology

The cooperation topology of an IDN can be centralized or decentralized. In a centralized system, all the intrusion data from end nodes is forwarded to a central server for analyzing and processing. In general, a centralized system (e.g., DShield [137] and CRIM [49]) has the advantage of having complete data and can potentially make more accurate detection. However, the disadvantage is that it may cause traffic clog close to the analyzing center, and the server is a single point of failure. On the other side, in a decentralized system, intrusion data is sent to different places for processing and analyzing. A decentralized system can be fully distributed or partially decentralized. In a fully distributed system (e.g., Indra [84], NetShield [44], and HBCIDS [72]), all nodes in the network play equal roles in cooperation as both data contributors and analyzers. The failure of a single node will have little impact on the functionality of the cooperation network. However, the lack of full data in each analyzer may lead to less accurate intrusion detection. In a partially decentralized system, some nodes may take the responsibility of analyzing data, and therefore have heavier workloads than peers which only contribute with data. The network structure may be clustered (e.g., ABDIAS[77]) or hierarchical (e.g., DOMINO[149]). A partially decentralized system targets to find a balanced solution between the centralized system and the fully distributed system.

3.3.2   Cooperation Scope

Another feature that can be used to categorize IDNs is the cooperation scope. The cooperation scope of a IDN can be local, global, or hybrid. In a local-scope IDN (e.g., Indra[84] and Gossip[52]), peers in the IDN are usually assumed to be fully trusted. The privacy concern of exchanging packet payload is usually neglected because all nodes lie in the same administrative boundary. Therefore, data packets can be in full disclosure and exchanged freely among peers. In a global IDN (e.g., DShield [137] and NetShield [44]), peers exchange intrusion information with other IDSs outside administration boundaries. Therefore, only limited information can be shared because privacy is a concern. In this case, data payload (or IP addresses, etc.) is either digested or removed in the exchanged information. In a hybrid system (e.g., DOMINO [149] and ABDIAS [77], the network is divided into different trust zones. Different data privacy policies are applied inside different zones, depending on the level of trust inside the zone.

3.3.3   Collaboration Type

Divided by collaboration type, existing IDNs can be *information-based*, *knowledge-based*, or *consultation-based*. In an information-based IDN, IDSs share intrusion observations with others, such as intrusion alerts, source IPs, ports, suspicious attack strings, or traffic volume, with other nodes to assist other IDSs in the network for intrusion detection. Examples of information-based IDNs are DOMINO [149] and NetShield [44]. Information-based IDNs are particularly effective in detecting epidemic worms and attacks, and zero-day attacks. In a consultation-based IDN, suspicious data samples are sent to expert collaborators for diagnosis. Feedback from the collaborators is then aggregated to help the sender IDS detect intrusions. Examples of such IDNs include CloudAV [114] and CMDA [122]. Consultation-based IDNs are designed for collaboration among different security vendors and are effective in detecting some intrusion types such as malware and spam. In a knowledge-based IDN, peers share intrusion detection knowledge such as intrusion detection rules, malware signatures, firewall rules, and black lists with other peers. Compared to the other two types of IDNs, knowledge-based IDN has the least privacy concern because observations are not shared with others.

3.3.4 Specialization

An IDN can be dedicated to a specific intrusion such as worms (e.g., NetShield [44], Gossip [52] and Worminator [97]), Spam (e.g., ALPACA [154]), Botnet detection (e.g., FFCIDN [155]), malware (e.g., CloudAV [114] and CMDA [122]), or can be used to detect general intrusions (e.g., Indra [84], CRIM [49], and HBCIDS [72]).

3.3.5 Cooperation Technologies and Algorithms

There are several components essential to IDNs, namely data correlation, trust management, and load balancing. In this section we briefly describe each component and give some examples of solutions.

3.3.5.1 Data Correlation

IDSs are known to generate large amounts of alerts with many false positives. In practice, it is not uncommon to have several thousand alerts per day in a reasonably sized organization. With the sheer number of alerts to deal with, it becomes hard to decide in a timely way about which alert to deal with first. Tuning IDSs by individually tuning their detection thresholds to reduce the overall number of generated alerts down to human scale is, however, not a solution as it may lead to the non-detection of some important attacks. Moreover, recent attacks have become more complicated and make use of a number of phases before carrying out the actual attack. The early phase of a multi-phase attack may appear to be benign but when correlated with later-stage alerts, can have a strong input in detecting the actual attack. The need for alert correlation becomes more apparent in the presence of cooperative attacks as it helps in linking together different alerts that may be spaced in time and place. *Alert correlation* is hence about the combination of fragmented information contained in the alert sequences and interpreting the whole flow of alerts. It is the process that analyzes alerts produced by one or more IDSs and provides a more succinct and high-level view of occurring or attempted intrusions [139]. In doing so, some alerts may get modified or cleared, and new alerts may be generated and others delayed, depending on the *security policy* in use.

Alert correlation techniques can be put into three broad categories. *Alert clustering* is used to group alerts into clusters (or threads) based on some similarity measure, such as IP addresses or port numbers [138]. The second category relies on the pre-specification known attack sequences [56, 109]. The third category uses logical dependencies between alerts by matching prerequisites (of an attack) with its consequences [49, 113]. Attack graphs [126] are used in this regard to simplify the identification of attack patterns that are made up of multiple individual attacks.

3.3.5.2 Trust Management

Trust management is an important component for intrusion detection cooperation, especially when the participants cross administration boundaries. Without a trust model, dishonest nodes may degrade the efficiency of the IDN by providing false information. A trust management system can help to identify dishonest nodes by monitoring the past behavior of participating nodes. Some existing IDNs that have trust management system are simple voting model [77] and simple linear model [72].

3.3.5.3 Load Balancing

When an IDN needs to deal with a large amount of data and over the capacity of a single IDS processor, it is necessary to distribute the workload into multiple servers to speed up the detection. Load-balancing algorithms help to distribute workload evenly on each IDS processor, and therefore improve the overall efficiency of the system. Some examples of load-balancing algorithms are signature distributing among collaborative IDSs group [96], data flow distributing among an IDS group [92], and data packets distributing among distributed IDSs [44].

3.3.6 Taxonomy

Based on the features provided above, we categorize a list of selected IDNs using a taxonomy as in Table 3.1.

3.4 Selected Intrusion Detection Networks

In the previous section we have described several criteria that we use to distinguish different IDNs and their taxonomy. In this section we select some aforementioned IDNs in the literature and describe in more detail their designs, purposes, and which categories they belong to.

3.4.1 Indra

Indra [84] was one of the first to propose a cooperative intrusion detection system. In the proposed system, host-based IDSs in a local area network take a proactive approach and send warnings to other trusted nodes about the intruder through a peer-to-peer network. For example, as shown in Figure 3.2, if an attacker compromises node B and then launches attacks from B to hosts in the trusted network, then node C detects the attack from B and multicasts a security warning to its trusted neighbors. Subsequently, if B tries to attack other nodes in the network, it will be repelled right

Table 3.1 Classification of Cooperative Intrusion Detection Networks.

IDN	Topology	Scope	Type	Specification	Technology and Algorithm
Indra	Distributed	Local	Information	Worm	—
DOMINO	Decentralized	Hybrid	Information	Worm	—
DShield	Centralized	Global	Information	General	Data correlation
NetShield	Distributed	Global	Information	Worm	Load-balancing
Gossip	Distributed	Local	Information	Worm	—
Worminator	—	Global	Information	Worm	—
ABDIAS	Decentralized	Hybrid	Information	General	Trust management
CRIM	Centralized	Local	Information	General	Data correlation
CIDS	Distributed	Global	Knowledge	General	Load-balancing
ALPACAS	Distributed	Global	Information	Spam	Load balancing
CDDHT	Decentralized	Local	Information	General	—
SmartScreen	Centralized	global	Information	Phishing	—
CloudAV	Centralized	global	Consultation	Malware	—
FFCIDN	Centralized	global	Information	Botnet	Data correlation
CMDA	Decentralized	Local	Consultation	Malware	—

away by the forewarned nodes. Indra is a fully distributed system that is targeted toward local area networks.

3.4.2 DOMINO

DOMINO [149] is an IDS collaboration system that aims at monitoring Internet outbreaks at large scale. In DOMINO (Figure 3.3), heterogeneous IDSs located at diverse locations share their intrusion information with each other. There are typically three types of nodes: axis nodes, satellite nodes, and terrestrial contributors. Satellite nodes are organized hierarchically and are responsible for gathering intrusion data and sending it to parent nodes in the hierarchy. Parent nodes aggregate intrusion data and further forward data up the hierarchy until they reach axis nodes. Axis nodes analyze intrusion data, generate digested summary data, and then multicast them to other axis nodes. Network-based IDSs and active sink nodes (such as Honeypot [50]) are integrated into axis nodes to monitor unused IP addresses for incoming worms. Terrestrial contributors do not follow DOMINO protocols but can contribute to the system through DOMINO access points. In DOMINO, heterogeneous nodes are involved in the cooperation overlay. Information from axis nodes, satellite nodes, and terrestrial contributors is distinguished by different trust levels. This feature enables DOMINO to handle inter-administration-zone cooperation. DOMINO is a decentralized system organized in a hierarchical structure for better scalability.

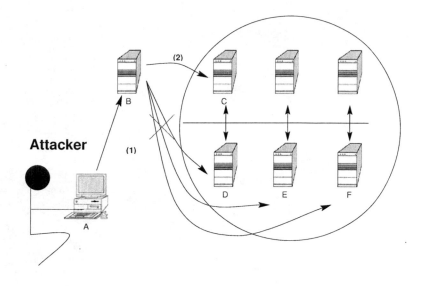

Figure 3.2: Indra architecture. (Adapted from [84].)

3.4.3 DShield

DShield [137] is a community-based firewall log correlation system. The central server receives firewall logs from worldwide volunteers and then analyzes attack trends based on the information collected. Similar systems include myNetWatchMan [17] and CAIDA [8]. DShield is used as a data collection engine behind the SANS Internet Storm Center (ISC) [23]. Analysis provided by DShield has been used in the early detection of several worms, such as "Code Red" and "SQL Snake." Due to the number of participants and the volume of data collected, DShield is a very attractive resource, and its data is used by researchers to analyze attack patterns. However, DShield is a centralized system and does not provide real-time analysis or rule generation. Also, due to privacy issues, payload information and some headers cannot be shared, which makes classification of attacks often impossible.

3.4.4 NetShield

NetShield [44] is an IDN that uses the Chord DHT [131] to reduce communication overhead. In this system, however, within the system architecture (Figure 3.4), IDSs contribute and retrieve information from the system through a P2P overlay (the Chord DHT). Each IDS maintains a local prevalence table to record the number of occurrences of each content block signature locally as well as its corresponding source address and destination address. An update will be triggered if the local prevalence of the content block exceeds a local threshold (for example, site A in Figure 3.4). If the global prevalence is higher than a given threshold, and the address dispersion ex-

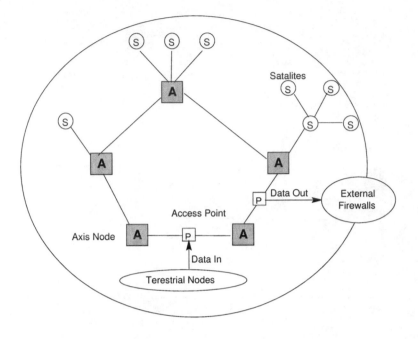

Figure 3.3: DOMINO architecture. (Adapted from [149].)

ceeds a certain threshold, then an alarm is raised regarding the corresponding content block. Netshield targets epidemic worm outbreaks or DoS attacks. However, using content blocks as attack identification is not effective against polymorphic worms. Also, NetShield assumes all IDN participants are honest, which makes it vulnerable to collusion attacks and malicious nodes.

3.4.5 CIDS

Another collaborative intrusion detection system (CIDS) proposed by Zhou et al. [157] also uses the Chord DHT system to organize IDSs into a peer-to-peer network. Each IDS shares its blacklist with others through a fully distributed P2P overlay. If a suspicious IP address is reported more than a threshold N, then all the IDSs that reported it will be notified. CIDS is considered scalable and robust because it is built on a P2P overlay. However, the limitation of this system is that it only identifies potential intruders by IP addresses. Thus, it is not effective against worms having a spreading degree of less than N. Also, the system can be vulnerable to colluding malicious nodes. Because this IDN utilizes blacklists sharing, it can be categorized into a knowledge-based IDN.

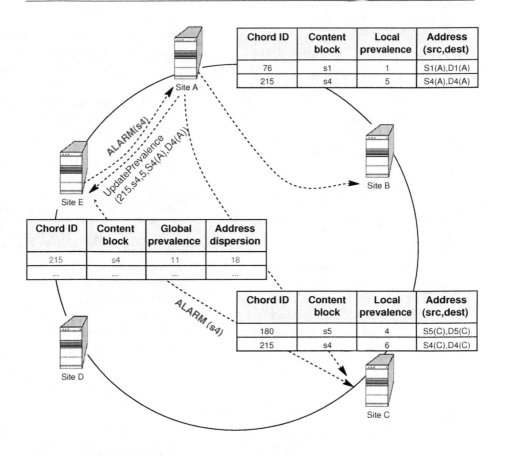

Figure 3.4: NetShield architecture. (Adapted from [44].)

3.4.6   Gossip

Denver et al. [52] proposed a gossip-based collaborative worm detection system (Gossip) for enterprise-level IDNs for host-based IDSs. A fully distributed model is adopted to avoid a single point of failure. In their system, host-based IDSs (local detectors) raise alerts only if the number of newly created connections per unit time exceeds a certain threshold. The alert will then be propagated to neighbors for aggregation. A Bayesian-network-based alert aggregation model is used for alert aggregation at global detectors. Their proposed system is aimed at detecting slow-propagating worms in a local area network. However, their system only uses the new connection rate as a sign of possible worm spread. This is not effective for worms that are spread in a connectionless manner, such as UDP worms.

3.4.7 Worminator

Worminator [97] was proposed to enable IDSs to share alert information with each other to detect worm propagation. Alert correlation is used to gain better detection accuracy. Different from most other systems, Worminator is concerned with the privacy of exchanging alerts, and uses a bloom filter to encode IP addresses and port numbers in the alerts in order to preserve the privacy of collaborators. The authors claimed that the system topology can be either centralized or decentralized, depending on the size of the network.

3.4.8 ABDIAS

Ghosh et al. proposed an agent-based distributed intrusion alert system (ABDIAS) [77]. In the architecture design (Figure 3.5), IDSs (agents) are grouped into communities (neighborhoods). Each agent collects information inside its neighborhood and uses a Bayesian network analysis model to diagnose possible threats. Inter-neighborhood communication only happens if a consensus cannot be reached within a neighborhood. This system supports early warnings for pre-attack activities in order to gain time for administrators to respond to potential attacks. This system also supports a simple majority-based voting system to detect compromised nodes.

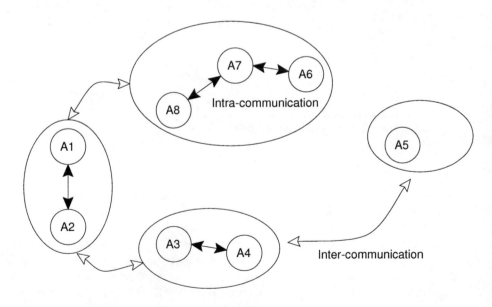

Figure 3.5: ABDIAS architecture. (Adapted from [77].)

3.4.9 CRIM

CRIM [49] is a cooperative IDS where alerts from individual IDSs are sent to a central analyzer for clustering and correlation. A set of correlation rules are generated offline by security administrators by analyzing attack descriptions. These correlation rules are then used to analyze alerts collected from IDSs in order to recognize global attack scenarios. CRIM is a semi-automatic alert correlation system, as it relies on human interactions to define attack descriptions. It is also a centralized system.

3.4.10 ALPACAS

ALPACAS [154] is a cooperative spam filtering system aimed at preserving the privacy of emails as well as maintaining the scalability of the system. The system is built on a peer-to-peer overlay to avoid the deficiency of a centralized system. Spam mails and Ham mails are distributed to agents based on the range of their feature signatures. An email is divided into feature trunks, and trunks are digested into feature fingerprints to preserve the content privacy of emails. The fingerprints of an email are then sent to corresponding agents to compare with stored spam emails and Ham emails by estimating the maximum signature overlap with spam (MOS) and the maximum signature overlap with Ham (MOH). An email is labeled as spam if the difference between MOS and MOH exceeds a certain threshold. ALPACAS is a fully distributed system.

3.4.11 CDDHT

The Cyber Disease Distributed Hash Table (CDDHT) [94] was proposed as a distributed data fusion center. In its architecture, each node is a local intrusion detection system that attempts to locally detect attacks and generate corresponding alerts. Each alert is assigned a disease key based on the related intrusions. The alert is then sent to a corresponding sensor fusion center (SFC) using a DHT-based P2P system. SFCs are selected among nodes based on their capacity and resources. The goal of this system is to avoid the bottleneck problem inherent to a centralized fusion center and to use alert categorization techniques for balancing the load among the SFCs. CDDHT is a decentralized system.

3.4.12 SmartScreen Filter

SmartScreen Filter [31] is a tool in Microsoft^{TM} Internet Explorer 8 that helps users avoid socially engineered malware phishing websites and online fraud when browsing the Web. A centralized mechanism is used to maintain a list of phishing sites and malicious websites URLs. Users browsing listed phishing sites or malicious websites will receive warnings to prevent them from being defrauded. Users are allowed to report suspicious websites to the central server through a secure channel. Users' feedback is analyzed together with input from the SmartScreen spam filter and input from other trusted sources to generate the URLs blacklist. Other similar phishing filters are provided by EarthLink and eBay.

3.4.13 CloudAV

CloudAV [114] was proposed by Oberheide et al. in 2008. It is a centralized collaborative malware scanning system, where antivirus software is organized into a cloud-based malware scanning service. In such a system, service consumers (for example, mobile phones) send suspicious files to the CloudAV system for scanning. A central service dispatches the files to all participating antivirus scanners and aggregates their scanning results using a simple threshold-based decision method. Then the central service replies to service requesters with the aggregated scanning results. CloudAV is able to provide a higher malware detection rate while maintaining a low false positive rate, compared to a single antivirus service. It is especially useful for end users with less powerful intrusion detection engines, such as mobile phones. CloudAV is a consultation-based IDN.

3.4.14 FFCIDN

Fast-flux service networks (FFSN) are one type of botnet that uses compromised nodes to form a robust phishing domain. To detect fast-flux networks and prevent them from causing further damage, Zhou et al. [155, 156], proposed a collaborative IDN to detect FFSNs. The work is based on an observation that the number of IP addresses returned after a DNS request is larger than usual. The collaboration system collects query results from nodes from different locations and correlates them to obtain the number of unique IP addresses and the number of unique fast-flux domains. The relationship between the number of DNS queries and the number of unique IP addresses and domains is traced. A corresponding DNS query threshold is derived to speed up FFSN detection. Zhou et al.'s results showed that detecting FFSNs using collaboration from nodes in different name domains is more efficient than detecting them from a single node. This system is a centralized system.

3.4.15 CMDA

Collaborative Malware detection on Android (CMDA) [122] was proposed by Schmidt et al., wherein Android phones assist each other when suspicious files are detected but the host device does not have enough confidence in malware decision. Then the host device sends the suspicious executable to its neighbors for diagnosis. Each neighbor evaluates the received executable based on its own knowledge and trained classifier and then sends the diagnosis results back to the host device. A final decision is made based on the aggregated feedback from all neighbor nodes. CMDA is a decentralized system and a consultation-based IDN.

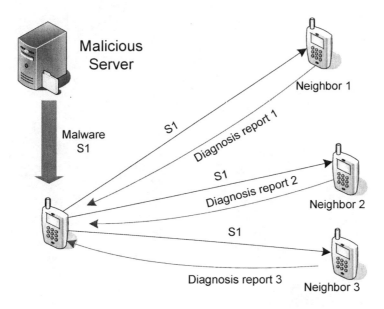

Figure 3.6: Topology design for collaborative malware detection on Android.

3.5 Summary

IDSs are important countermeasures to cyber attacks. However, a single IDS is vulnerable to attacks that are unknown to its security vendors of system administrators. Intrusion detection networks (IDNs) allow IDSs to exchange intrusion information and detection knowledge, hence improving the intrusion detection accuracy by using the collective knowledge from others. Several IDNs have been proposed in the literature. However, most of them focused on designing efficient and scalable network overlays for the exchange of intrusion information. Some IDNs investigated information aggregation, but only few have addressed the problems of malicious insiders and free-riders. Malicious insiders pose a significant challenge to IDNs because adversaries have high motivation to attack and compromise the IDSs in the network. Designing IDNs that are robust to malicious insiders is therefore of paramount importance. Free-riders also pose a significant challenge to collaboration in an IDN. They are self-interested, do not share their resources, and try to take advantage of the resources shared by others in the network. To address the free-rider problem, an incentive mechanism design should be in place to discourage selfish behaviors. It is therefore necessary to provide an IDN design that is not only scalable and efficient in intrusion detection, but is also robust against malicious insiders and discourages free-riding.

DESIGN OF AN INTRUSION DETECTION NETWORK

Chapter 4

Collaborative Intrusion Detection Networks Architecture Design

CONTENTS

4.1 Introduction

A intrusion detection network (IDN) is an overlay network that enables IDSs to exchange intrusion information and knowledge in order to improve the overall detection accuracy. IDSs in an IDN network can have a more global view of cyber intrusions by receiving alerts from other IDSs in the networks. IDSs can also send consultation requests to their collaborators when suspicious activities are detected but the local IDS does not have enough confidence to make a decision. For example, an IDS may receive a new file that can be flagged by the anomaly detection process. However, anomaly detection commonly results in a high false positive rate. The IDS can send the suspicious file to other IDSs for consultation. The collected feedback from other IDSs can be used to make a more confident intrusion decision.

In Chapter 3 we surveyed a number of existing IDNs where IDSs share information with others in order to detect intrusions that otherwise would not be detected by a single IDS. Most of them are *information-based IDNs*. However, information-based IDNs cause large communication overhead because they exchange observations and not all exchanged observations are useful to others in the network. In turn, consultation-based IDNs only exchange observations when the host IDS cannot make a confident decision, which leads to lower communication overhead. In addition, existing IDNs focus on the efficiency of information exchange and the aggregation of collected information to make intrusion decisions. Only few studies have addressed the problems of malicious insiders, free-riders, and how to select and maintain IDN participants.

In the remainder of this book, we focus on consultation-based IDNs and design solutions to address the problems of malicious insiders and free-riders. An IDN framework that is scalable, efficient, and robust to attacks is discussed in this chapter. We first describe a modular-based IDN architecture design consisting of seven components. We then briefly describe the functionality of each component addressing the solutions mentioned above.

4.2 Collaboration Framework

As discussed in the introduction, IDN scalability can be achieved through completely decentralized topology design and IDN efficiency through consultation-based IDN design. In this perspective, we focus here on IDN design where IDSs from different vendors or open-source providers are connected in a peer-to-peer overlay. We also focus on IDN design, where IDSs send consultation requests to collaborators to ask for a diagnosis when suspicious activities are detected but the host IDS does not have enough confidence to make a correct decision. For this purpose, each IDS maintains a list of "good" collaborators. For example, IDSs may choose to collaborate with other IDSs with which they had good experience in the past (e.g., have been helpful in identifying intrusions). We consider the case where the IDN participants have differing detection expertise levels and may act dishonestly or selfishly in collaboration. For collaboration to be sustainable and efficient, we identify the following IDN design requirements:

1. IDN nodes should have an effective trust evaluation capability to reduce the negative impact of dishonest and incompetent nodes.

2. Allocation of IDN node resources for collaboration should be incentive-compatible to discourage selfish behavior and encourage active collaboration.

3. IDN nodes should possess an efficient feedback aggregation capability to minimize the cost of false intrusion detections.

4. The IDN should be robust against insider attacks.

5. The IDN should be scalable in network size.

To satisfy the above requirements, we describe a collaborative intrusion detection network (CIDN) architecture design similar to a social network. The IDN topology, as shown in Figure 4.1, consists of IDSs (nodes), which may be network-based IDSs (NIDSs) or host-based IDSs (HIDSs). IDN nodes are connected if they have a collaborative relationship. Each node maintains a list of other nodes that it currently collaborates with. We call such nodes *acquaintances*. Each node in the IDN has the

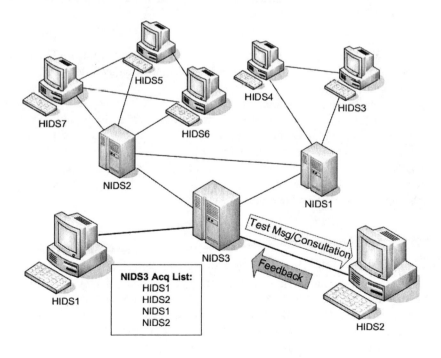

Figure 4.1: Topology of a consultation-based collaborative intrusion detection network.

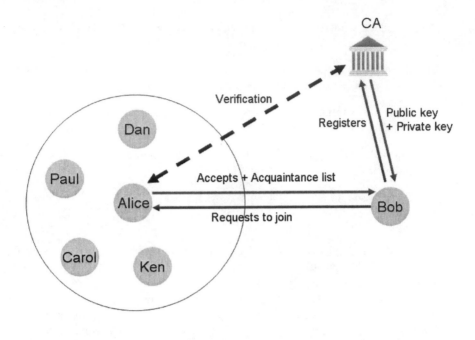

Figure 4.2: Communication protocol design for IDN.

freedom to choose its acquaintances based on their trustworthiness. The communication between collaborating nodes consists of intrusion evaluation requests and corresponding feedback. There are two types of requests: *intrusion consultation requests* and *test messages*. The architecture of the IDN is shown in Figure 4.3. It is composed of seven components, namely the intrusion detection system, communication overlay, trust management, acquaintance management, resource management, feedback aggregation, and mediator. In the following subsections we first describe the IDN network join process for each user and then introduce the consultation and test messages initiated after the join process. Finally we describe the functionality of each component in the architecture.

4.2.1 Network Join Process

To join the IDN, a user needs to register to a trusted digital *certificate authority* (Figure 4.2) and get a public and private key pair that uniquely identifies the machine. Note that we identify the (machine, user) tuple. This is because a different machine means a different IDS instance. However, the network allows only one user on the same machine in the IDN at a time, for the purpose of preventing attackers from influencing the IDN operation using a large number of pseudonym nodes (Sybil attack). However, multiple users can be registered on the same machine becuse a different user of the same machine may have a different configuration of its IDS. After a node

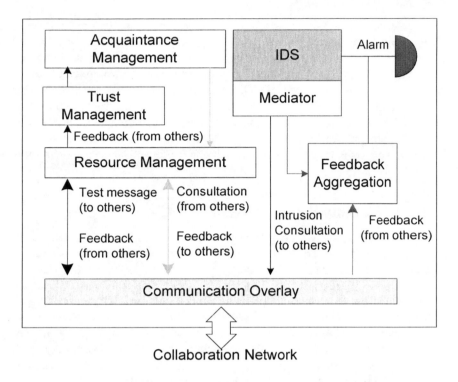

Figure 4.3: Architecture design of an IDN.

joins the IDN, it is provided with a preliminary *acquaintance list*. This list is customizable and contains identities (or public keys) of other nodes within the network along with their *trust values* and serves as the contact list for collaboration.

4.2.2   Consultation Requests

After joining in the IDS network, when an IDS detects a suspicious activity but is unable to make a decision as to whether or not it should raise an alarm, it sends *consultation requests* to its acquaintances for diagnosis. Feedback from acquaintances is aggregated and a final intrusion detection decision is made based on the aggregated results. The amount of information in the consultation request depends on the trust level of each acquaintance. For example, a node may want to share all alert information, including data payload, with the nodes inside its local area network, and digest or even remove some some alert information when sent to acquaintances in the broader Internet.

4.2.3 Test Messages

In order for the nodes in the IDN to gain experience with each other, IDSs use *test messages* to evaluate the trustworthiness of others. Test messages are "bogus" consultation requests that are sent to measure the trustworthiness of another node in the acquaintance list. They are sent out in a way that makes them difficult to distinguish from a real consultation request. The testing node knows the true diagnosis result of the test message and uses the received feedback to derive a trust value for the tested node. This technique can discover inexperienced and/or malicious nodes within the collaborative network. A test message can be a previous consultation message with which the ground truth has been verified, or a random pick taken from its knowledge base.

4.2.4 Communication Overlay

The *communication overlay* is the component that handles all the communications with other peers in the collaborative network. The messages passing through the communication overlay include test messages from the host node to its acquaintances, intrusion consultations from the host node to its acquaintances, feedback from acquaintances; consultation requests from acquaintances, and feedback to acquaintances. The communication overlay dispatches incoming requests and messages to corresponding components in the system and routes outgoing requests and messages to their destinations. For example, when the communication overlay component receives a consultation request, it calls the local IDS component for diagnosis and returns the received feedback (diagnosis result) back to the sender.

4.2.5 Mediator

The *mediator* is the component that helps heterogeneous IDSs communicate with each other. It translates consultation requests and consultation feedback into a common protocol (such as IDMEF [15]) and data format understood by different IDSs.

4.2.6 Trust Management

The *trust management* component allows IDSs in the IDN to evaluate the trustworthiness of others based on previous experience with them. The host node can use test messages to gain experience quickly. Indeed, the verified consultation results can also be used as experience. In our IDN design, we have used a Dirichlet-based trust management model (Chapter 5) to evaluate the trustworthiness of IDSs. In this trust model, IDSs evaluate the trustworthiness of others based on the quality of their feedback. The confidence of trust estimation is modeled using Bayesian statistics, and the results show that the frequency of test messages is proportional to the confidence level of trust estimation. The trust management model is closely connected to the resource management and acquaintance management models, as the trust values of the collaborators are essential inputs for the latter models.

4.2.7   Acquaintance Management

It is intuitive that when an IDS consults more acquaintances, it achieves higher accuracy and confidence in intrusion detection. However, more acquaintances results in a higher maintenance cost, because the IDS needs to allocate resources for each acquaintance as sending and receiving test messages to those acquaintances is a necessary resource expenditure, and it is needed to maintain the confidence of trust evaluation and to maintain the collaboration connection. *Acquaintance management* is responsible for selecting and maintaining collaborators for each participant. In addition to the acquaintances list, our system also maintains a consultation list. The nodes on the consultation list are randomly selected from the acquaintances that have passed the probation period. Test messages are sent to all acquaintances, while consultation requests are only sent to the nodes in the consultation list. The acquaintance list is updated on a regular basis to recruit new nodes or remove unwanted ones. A dynamic acquaintance management system (Chapter 8) can be used to recruit higher-quality peers and remove less-helpful peers based on their trustworthiness and expertise in intrusion detection.

4.2.8   Resource Management

In an IDN, malicious or compromised peers can launch a denial-of-service attack by sending a large number of consultation messages to overwhelm the targeted IDSs. Some peers may also free-ride the system by only receiving help from others without contributing to the collaboration network. To address the above problems, a *resource management* system is required to decide whether the host should allocate resources to respond to a given consultation request. An incentive-compatible resource management can assist IDSs to allocate resources to their acquaintances so that other IDSs are fairly treated based on their past assistance to the host IDS. Therefore, an IDS that abusively uses the collaboration resource will be penalized by receiving fewer responses from others. The resource allocation system also decides how often the host should send test messages to its acquaintances, protecting the system from being overloaded. An incentive-compatible resource allocation system is described in Chapter 7 leveraging a multi-player noncooperative game design for IDSs in the IDN.

4.2.9   Feedback Aggregation

When the IDS of the host node cannot make a confident intrusion diagnosis for a suspicious event, the host node may consult the other IDSs in the collaboration network for opinions/diagnosis. The received feedback is then used to make a decision as to whether or not the host IDS should raise an alarm to its administrator. The *feedback aggregation* component is responsible for making a decision based on the feedback. It decides not only on which criteria to use to measure the quality of decisions, but also on how to reach a decision in an efficient way. This component is one of the most important, because it has a direct impact on the accuracy of the collaborative intrusion detection. If an alarm is raised, the suspicious intrusion flow will be suspended and the system administrator investigates the intrusion immediately. On one hand, false alarms may waste human resources. On the other hand, undetected intrusions may cause damage. To leverage the false positive and false negative rate, a Bayesian approach (Chapter 6) can be used to measure the rate of false alarms, that is, false positive (FP) rate, and the rate of missing intrusions, that is, false negative (FN) rate, of participating IDSs based on collected experience with them in the past. The cost of collaborative decision-making can be modeled using false positive cost and false negative cost. A hypothesis testing model is used to find a decision that leads to minimum overall cost.

In the following chapters we focus on four major components of the IDN architecture: trust management, acquaintance management, resource management, and feedback aggregation. For each component, we provide the underlying model and algorithms, and evaluate their efficiency against several metrics, including robustness, scalability, efficiency, fairness, and incentive compatibility.

4.3 Discussion

In the previous sections we discussed the topology, communication protocol, and architecture design of an efficient, robust, and scalable intrusion detection network. In this section we discuss how privacy issues and malicious insiders problems are handled in the IDN.

4.3.1 Privacy Issues

One concern for collaboration networks is privacy issues. When an IDS chooses to send a consultation request to its collaborators for opinions, the request may contain some private information of the sender. For example, when an IDS receives a file scanning request from its collaborator, some information about the collaborator, such as which file it has downloaded recently or whether someone is using the computer at the moment, may be observed by the request receiver. We call this a *receiver speculation attack*. In addition, a *man-in-the-middle attack* may also occur, where an adversary can eavesdrop and interpret the messages exchanged between IDSs.

To prevent a *man-in-the-middle attack*, the exchanged information among IDSs is encrypted. To prevent a receiver speculation attack, the use of test messages can effectively cloak the consultation messages so it is hard for the receiver to distinguish consultation messages from test messages. Therefore, the message receiver cannot speculate if the files received are the new files downloaded by the sender or they are only test messages.

4.3.2 Insider Attacks

Insider attacks can be a serious problem to an intrusion detection network because adversaries may be able to disguise as a legitimate IDS and join the IDN. We show a few common attacks against IDNs and how the IDN design can defend against those insider attacks.

Sybil attacks occur when a malicious peer in the system creates a large amount of pseudonyms (fake identities) [58]. Such a malicious peer uses fake identities to gain larger influence in the network and use it in false ranking of alerts. Our defense against sybil attacks relies on the authentication mechanism in place and our acquaintance management system. Authentication makes registering fake identities difficult. Our model can use a certificate issuing authority that only allows one identity per (user, machine) tuple. In addition, our trust management model requires IDSs to first build up their trust before they can affect the decision of others, which is costly to do with many fake identities. This way, our security and trust mechanisms protect our collaborative network from sybil attacks.

Identity cloning attacks occur when a malicious node steals some node's identity and tries to communicate with others on its behalf. Our communication model is based on asymmetric cryptography, where each node has a pair of public and private keys. The certificate authority certifies the ownership of key pairs and in this way protects the authenticity of node identities.

Dishonest insiders attacks occurs when dishonest nodes join the IDN and behave dishonestly about the consultations. For example, the dishonest nodes may send random results or even false consultation results in order to save resources or degrade the IDN. Our system design incorporates a trust management component that can distinguish dishonest insiders from others. Our detailed design of trust component is described in Chapter 5.

Insider flooding attacks occur when insider nodes send excessive consultation requests/test messages to other nodes in the network for the purpose of benefiting themselves or overwhelming the other nodes in the network. Our IDN design can effectively prevent this attack by using fair, incentive-compatible resource allocation mechanism 7 and automatic acquaintance management 8. The amount of requests a node sends to others needs to be negotiated beforehand. Nodes sending excessive consultation messages will be identified as malicious and therefore be removed from the acquaintance list of others.

4.4 Summary

In this chapter we introduced the topology design and architecture design of a consultation-based intrusion detection network. The system consists of several components and each has its distinct functionalities to contribute to the structure of an efficient, scalable, robust, and incentive-compatible intrusion detection network. We also discussed some potential challenges and attacks that may occur in an intrusion detection network. In the next a few chapters, we particularly focus on the detailed design of a few essential components, namely trust management, collaborative decision making, resource allocation, and acquaintance management.

Chapter 5

Trust Management

CONTENTS

5.1 Introduction

In the previous chapter we presented the architecture design of a peer-to-peer-based intrusion detection network. In this chapter we focus on the trust component design. Trust management is critical because it is used to distinguish malicious peers from honest ones and improve intrusion detection accuracy. It is a central component in the IDN architecture because most other components, including resource management, acquaintance management, and collaborative intrusion components, rely on its input. In an IDN, a malicious (or malfunctioning) IDS can send false intrusion assessments or useless information to degrade the performance of other IDSs in the collaboration network. If some nodes are controlled by the same adversaries, they can easily collude and send false intrusion assessments. Moreover, IDSs may have different levels of expertise in intrusion assessment so that the quality of their information varies. To protect an IDN from malicious attacks as well as find expert IDSs to consult for intrusion assessment, it is important to evaluate the trustworthiness of participating IDSs. Because the trust model itself may also be the target of malicious attacks, robustness is a desired feature of the trust management scheme in collaborative intrusion detection networks.

In this chapter we discuss the design of a Bayesian trust management model that is robust, scalable, and suitable for distributed IDS collaboration. The *Dirichlet family* of probability density functions is adopted in this trust management model for estimating the likely future behavior of an IDS based on its past history. We show in this chapter that this model cannot only compute trust values of IDSs efficiently, but can also track the uncertainty in estimating the trustworthiness of the IDS. The trust model can be used to deploy a secure and scalable IDN where effective collaboration can be established between IDSs.

To demonstrate the effectiveness of the trust management design, it is important to evaluate the effectiveness of the model. In Section 5.6 we use a simulated collaborative IDS network to evaluate the trust model. In the simulated IDN, IDSs are distributed and may have different expertise levels in detecting intrusions. An IDS may also turn malicious due to runtime bugs, having been compromised, having been updated with a faulty new configuration, or having been deliberately made malicious. Several potential threats are also simulated; for example, betrayal attacks where malicious IDSs masquerade as honest ones to gain trust, and then suddenly act dishonestly. The experimental results demonstrate that the trust management model yields a significant improvement in detecting intrusions, is robust against various attacks, and improves the scalability of the system, as compared to existing collaborative IDS systems.

The remainder of this chapter is organized as follows. In Section 5.2 we overview existing trust models in intrusion detection networks and other related areas. In Section 5.3 we present the Dirichlet trust management model design. A dynamic test message mechanism is presented in Section 5.4 to improve the scalability of the trust system, where the test message rate is adaptive to the test levels of the collaborator. To demonstrate robustness of the trust model, several insider attack models against the trust model are presented, and corresponding defence mechanisms are discussed in Section 5.5. The evaluation of the trust model is presented in Section 5.6. Finally, Section 5.7 concludes the chapter and identifies directions for future research.

5.2 Background

Most of the existing work on distributed collaborative intrusion detection relies on the assumption that all IDSs are trustworthy and faithfully report intrusion events. The Indra system [84] distributes among peers information about attack attempts on different machines so as to proactively react and increase the chance of detecting an attack. This system also allows peer neighbors to share information about intrusion attempts in order to enhance the overall system security. Another example is the distributed intrusion alert fusion system called Cyber Disease Distributed Hash Table (CDDHT) [95]. The CDDHT system provides several load-balancing schemes to evenly distribute intrusion alarms among the sensor fusion centers in order to increase the scalability, fault-tolerance, and robustness of the system. However, the systems mentioned above are all vulnerable to malicious IDS attacks. False information about intrusion events sent by malicious IDSs may heavily degrade the performance of these IDNs.

To protect an IDN, it is important to evaluate the trustworthiness of participating IDSs. ABDIAS [77] is a community-based IDN where IDSs are organized into groups and exchange intrusion information to gain better intrusion detection accuracy. A simple majority-based voting system was proposed to detect compromised nodes. However, such a system is vulnerable to colluded voting. Duma et al. [59] propose to address possibly malicious IDSs (peers) by introducing a trust-aware collaboration engine for correlating intrusion alerts. Their trust management scheme uses each peer's past experience to predict others' trustworthiness. However, their trust model is simplistic and does not address security issues within the collaborative network. For instance, in their system, the peer's past experience has the same impact on the final trust values of others, and therefore is vulnerable to betrayal attacks where compromised peers suddenly change their behavior. In our model, we use a forgetting factor when calculating trust in order to rely more on the peer's recent experience and be robust to the changes of other peers' behavior. Our previous work [72] proposed a robust trust management model that uses test messages to gain personal experience and a forgetting factor to emphasize most recent experiences. However, this model needs to repeatedly aggregate all past experience with a peer when updating its trust, which makes it not scalable over time. It uses a linear model to calculate the average satisfaction levels of past interactions and lacks a theoretical foundation. Also, this approach does not capture trust modeling uncertainties or provide statistical confidence information on intrusion decisions. Our new model uses Dirichlet distributions to model peer trustworthiness. It makes use of dynamic test message rates in order to allow for better scalability. Also, our new model further improves robustness over our previous one through the use of flexible test message rates.

Researchers in multi-agent systems have also been developing trust models to evaluate the trustworthiness of buying and selling agents in e-marketplaces [152]. One of the earliest trust models developed by Marsh [101] computes the trustworthiness of selling agents by taking into account direct interactions between buying and selling agents. The trust-oriented learning strategy proposed by Tran and Cohen [134] uses reinforcement learning to determine the trustworthiness of selling agents, after the true value of delivered goods is evaluated and compared to the buying agent's expected value for the goods. Selling agents can be classified as untrustworthy if their trust values fall below a certain threshold, and buying agents try to select the trustworthy selling agent with the highest expected value for the goods. The Beta Reputation System (BRS) of Whitby et al. [144] and the TRAVOS model of Teacy et al. [133] estimate the trustworthiness of a selling agent by employing a Beta probability density function representing a probability distribution of a continuous variable. The work of Zhang and Cohen [152] focuses on coping with inaccurate reputation information about selling agents shared by malicious buying agents in e-marketplaces. The REGRET model of Sabater et al. [121] offers a multi-dimensional view of trust that includes a social dimension taking into consideration the social relationships among agents. However, it is difficult to clearly determine social relationships among IDSs in IDNs.

The Dirichlet trust model we present in this chapter is different from the above trust models in several aspects. First, the Dirichlet model is focused on long-term collaboration trust. Repetitive direct interactions between two agents are common in an IDN environment. Second, the cost of experience in IDN is much lower than in e-commerce and it allows IDSs to send test messages to better establish trust relationships with others. Third, the Dirichlet model uses fine-grained experience quality rather than a binary measurement such as "good" or "bad." Instead, it is categorized into multiple levels. Finally, this model uses direct trust modeling rather than reputation models. It is because the reputation model may suffer from collusion attacks where a group of malicious IDSs cooperate together by providing false reputation information about some IDSs to bad-mouth these targets, for example.

Different reputation models were proposed in distributed systems [86, 132]. These reputation models allow peers to get advice when evaluating the trustworthiness of other peers. For example, [86] uses global reputation management to evaluate distributed trust by aggregating votes from all peers in the network. Sun et al. [132] propose for the communication in distributed networks an entropy-based model and a probability-based one. The models are used to calculate indirect trust, propagation trust, and multi-path trust. They, however, involve a lot of overhead, which limits their scalability. Another important concern is that IDSs can be easily compromised and become deceptive when reporting the trustworthiness of others. The reputation models for peer-to-peer networks, such as PowerTrust [116], TrustGuard [130], Malicious detector [103], and Fine-Grained reputation [153] are capable of detecting malicious peers. However, they are purposed to detect deceiving nodes in a P2P network and cannot be directly used in IDNs to improve the intrusion detection accuracy. A trust model in IDN should not only detect malicious nodes, but also improve the overall intrusion detection accuracy and offer robustness and scalability.

5.3 Trust Management Model

In this section we describe a robust and scalable trust model that uses a Bayesian approach to evaluate the trustworthiness between each pair of IDSs. Specifically, we use a Dirichlet family of probability density functions to estimate the likely future behavior of an IDS based on its past history. A weighted majority method is used to aggregate feedback to make intrusion decisions.

5.3.1 Satisfaction Mapping

In this model, an IDS sends requests to its peers and evaluates the *satisfaction level* of received feedback. Note that the request can be a test message or a real request. The true answer of a test message is known beforehand, while that of a real request is verified by administrators after some delay through the observed impact of the corresponding alert.

IDSs may have different metrics to rank alerts. Snort [24], for example, uses three levels (low, medium, high), while Bro [7] allows up to 100 different levels. We assume the existence of a function H, which maps an IDS alert ranking onto the [0,1] interval, where 0 denotes benign traffic and 1 highly dangerous intrusions. H preserves the "more severe than" partial order relationship. That is, if alert a_j is more severe than alert a_i, then H preserves that relationship by having $H(a_j) > H(a_i)$.

The satisfaction level of feedback is determined by three factors: the expected answer ($r \in [0,1]$), the received answer ($a \in [0,1]$), and the difficulty level of the test message ($d \in [0,1]$). The larger is d, the more difficult it is to correctly answer the request. Note that the difficulty of the test message can be roughly estimated by the age of the corresponding signatures or knowledge. For example, the difficulty level is low for test messages generated from old signatures; medium difficulty is for test messages generated from new signatures; high difficulty for malicious traffic taken from honeypots and no local signature is able to detect it.

To quantitively measure the quality of feedback, we use a function $Sat(r,a,d)$ ($\in [0,1]$) to represent the level of satisfaction of the received answer based on its distance to the expected answer and the difficulty of the test message, as follows:

$$Sat(r,a,d) = \begin{cases} 1 - \left(\frac{a-r}{\max(c_1 r, 1-r)}\right)^{d/c_2} & a > r \\[3mm] 1 - \left(\frac{c_1(r-a)}{\max(c_1 r, 1-r)}\right)^{d/c_2} & a \leq r \end{cases} \tag{5.1}$$

where c_1 controls the extent of penalty for wrong estimates. It is set > 1 to reflect that estimates lower than the exact answer get stronger penalty than those that are higher. Parameter $c_2 \in R^+$ controls satisfaction sensitivity, with larger values reflecting more sensitivity to the distance between the correct and received answers. The equation also ensures that low difficulty level tests are more severe in their penalty to incorrect answers. The shape of the satisfaction function is depicted in Figure 5.1.

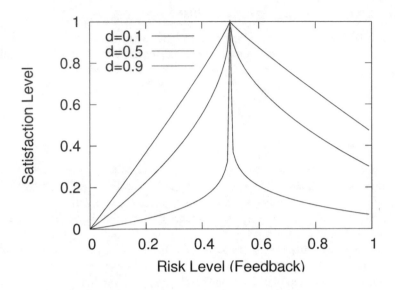

Figure 5.1: Satisfaction level for feedback ($r = 0.5$, $c_1 = 2$, $c_2 = 1$).

5.3.2 Dirichlet-Based Model

Bayesian statistics provide a theoretical foundation for measuring the uncertainty in a decision that is based on a collection of observations. We demonstrate the distribution of satisfaction levels of the answers from each peer IDS and, particularly, use this information to estimate the satisfaction level of future consultations. For the case of a binary satisfaction level {satisfied,¬satisfied}, a Beta distribution can be used as appeared in [152]. For multi-valued satisfaction levels, Dirichlet distributions are more appropriate.

A Dirichlet distribution [120] is based on initial beliefs about an unknown event represented by a prior distribution. The initial beliefs combined with collected sample data can be represented by a posterior distribution. The posterior distribution well suits our trust management model because the trust is updated based on the history of interactions.

Let X be the discrete random variable denoting the satisfaction level of the feedback from a peer IDS. X takes values in the set $\mathcal{X} = \{x_1, x_2, ..., x_k\}$ ($x_i \in [0,1]$, $x_{i+1} > x_i$) of the supported levels of satisfaction. Let $\vec{p} = \{p_1, p_2, ..., p_k\}$ ($\sum_{i=1}^{k} p_i = 1$) be the probability distribution vector of X, that is, $P\{X = x_i\} = p_i$. Also, let $\vec{\gamma} = \{\gamma_1, \gamma_2, ..., \gamma_k\}$ denote the vector of cumulative observations and initial beliefs of X. Then we can model $\vec{p}$ using a posterior Dirichlet distribution as follows:

$$f(\vec{p}|\xi) = Dir(\vec{p}|\vec{\gamma}) = \frac{\Gamma(\sum_{i=1}^{k} \gamma_i)}{\prod_{i=1}^{k} \Gamma(\gamma_i)} \prod_{i=1}^{k} p_i^{\gamma_i - 1} \qquad (5.2)$$

where ξ denotes the background knowledge, which in here is summarized by $\vec{\gamma}$.

Let

$$\gamma_0 = \sum_{i=1}^{k} \gamma_i \tag{5.3}$$

The expected value of the probability of X to be x_i given the history of observations $\vec{\gamma}$ is given by:

$$E(p_i|\vec{\gamma}) = \frac{\gamma_i}{\gamma_0} \tag{5.4}$$

In order to give more weight to recent observations over old ones, we embed a *forgetting factor* λ in the Dirichlet background knowledge vector $\vec{\gamma}$ as follows:

$$\vec{\gamma}^{(n)} = \sum_{i=1}^{n} \lambda^{t_i} \times \vec{S^i} + c_0 \lambda^{t_0} \vec{S^0} \tag{5.5}$$

where n is the number of observations; $\vec{S^0}$ is the initial beliefs vector. If no additional information is available, all outcomes have an equal probability making $S_j^0 = 1/k$ for all $j \in \{1,..,k\}$. Parameter $c_0 > 0$ is a priori constant, which puts a weight on the initial beliefs. Vector $\vec{S^i}$ denotes the satisfaction level of the ith evidence, which is a tuple containing $k-1$ elements set to zero and only one element set to 1, corresponding to the selected satisfaction level for that evidence. Parameter $\lambda \in [0,1]$ is the forgetting factor. A small λ makes old observations quickly forgettable. Parameter t_i denotes the time elapsed (age) since the ith evidence $\vec{S^i}$ was observed. Let $\Delta t_i = t_i - t_{i+1}$. For the purpose of scalability, the $\vec{\gamma}^{(n)}$ in Equation (5.5) can be rewritten in terms of $\vec{\gamma}^{(n-1)}$, $\vec{S^n}$ and Δt_n as follows:

$$\vec{\gamma}^{(n)} = \begin{cases} c_0 \vec{S^0} & n = 0 \\ \lambda^{\Delta t_n} \times \vec{\gamma}^{(n-1)} + \vec{S^n} & n > 0 \end{cases} \tag{5.6}$$

5.3.3 Evaluating the Trustworthiness of a Peer

After a peer receives the feedback for an alert evaluation, it assigns a satisfaction value to the feedback according to Equation (5.1). This satisfaction value is assigned with one of the satisfaction levels in the set $\mathcal{X} = \{x_1, x_2, ..., x_k\}$ that has the closest value. Each satisfaction level x_i also has a weight w_i.

Let p_i^{uv} denote the probability that peer v provides answers to the requests sent by peer u with satisfaction level x_i. Let $\vec{p}^{uv} = (p_i^{uv})_{i=1...k} \,|\, \sum_{i=1}^{k} p_i^{uv} = 1$. We model $\vec{p}^{uv}$ using Equation (5.2). Let Y^{uv} be the random variable denoting the weighted average of the probability of each satisfaction level in $\vec{p}^{uv}$.

$$Y^{uv} = \sum_{i=1}^{k} p_i^{uv} w_i \tag{5.7}$$

The *trustworthiness* of peer v as noticed by peer u is then calculated as

$$T^{uv} = E[Y^{uv}] = \sum_{i=1}^{k} w_i E[p_i^{uv}] = \frac{1}{\gamma_0^{uv}} \sum_{i=1}^{k} w_i \gamma_i^{uv} \tag{5.8}$$

where γ_i^{uv} is the cumulated evidence that v has replied to u with satisfaction level x_i. The variance of Y^{uv} is equal to (superscript uv is omitted for clarity)

$$\sigma^2[Y] = \sum_{i=1}^{k} \sum_{j=1}^{k} w_i w_j cov[p_i, p_j] \tag{5.9}$$

Knowing that the covariance of p_i and p_j $(i \neq j)$ is given by

$$cov(p_i, p_j) = \frac{-\gamma_i \gamma_j}{\gamma_0^2 (\gamma_0 + 1)} \tag{5.10}$$

We get

$$\sigma^2[Y] = \sum_{i=1}^{k} w_i^2 \sigma^2[p_i] + 2 \sum_{i=1}^{k} \sum_{j=i+1}^{k} w_i w_j cov[p_i, p_j]$$

$$= \sum_{i=1}^{k} w_i^2 \frac{\gamma_i (\gamma_0 - \gamma_i)}{\gamma_0^2 (\gamma_0 + 1)} + 2 \sum_{i=1}^{k} \sum_{j=i+1}^{k} w_i w_j \frac{-\gamma_i \gamma_j}{\gamma_0^2 (\gamma_0 + 1)}$$

$$= \frac{1}{\gamma_0^3 + \gamma_0^2} \sum_{i=1}^{k} w_i \gamma_i \left(w_i (\gamma_0 - \gamma_i) - 2 \sum_{j=i+1}^{k} w_j \gamma_j \right) \tag{5.11}$$

Let $C^{uv} \in (-1, 1]$ be the confidence level for the value of T^{uv}, and we describe it as

$$C^{uv} = 1 - 4\sigma[Y^{uv}] \tag{5.12}$$

where $4\sigma[Y^{uv}]$ is roughly the 95% confidence interval.

Lemma 5.1
The confidence level C^{uv} formulated by Equation (5.12) lies in bound $(-1, 1]$.

Proof 5.1
From Equation (5.12) and Equation (5.11), we have

$$C^{uv} = 1 - \frac{4}{\sqrt{1 + \gamma_0}} \sqrt{\sum_{i=1}^{k} w_i^2 \frac{\gamma_i}{\gamma_0} - (\sum_{i=1}^{k} w_i \frac{\gamma_i}{\gamma_0})^2} \tag{5.13}$$

where $w_i \in [0, 1], \forall i$ is the weight of the satisfaction level i, and $\gamma_0 = \sum_{i=1}^{k} \gamma_i >$

0. To prove the boundary of C^{uv}, we construct a discrete random variable $Z \in \{w_1, w_2, ..., w_k\}$, where $w_1 \leq w_2 \leq ... \leq w_k$ and $\mathbb{P}[Z = w_i] = \frac{\gamma_i}{\gamma_0}, \forall i$. Then we have

$$\sigma^2[Z] = \mathbb{E}(Z^2) - \mathbb{E}^2(Z) = \sum_{i=1}^{k} w_i^2 \frac{\gamma_i}{\gamma_0} - (\sum_{i=1}^{k} w_i \frac{\gamma_i}{\gamma_0})^2 \qquad (5.14)$$

We can see that the variation of Z is the major component of C^{uv}. It is not difficult to see that $\sigma^2[Z]$ reaches its maximum when $\mathbb{P}[Z = w_1] = \mathbb{P}[Z = w_k] = 0.5$ and $\mathbb{P}[Z = w_j] = 0, \forall j (1 < j < k)$. Therefore, we have $0 \leq \sigma^2[Z] \leq \frac{1}{4}$. After replacing Equation (5.14) back into Equation (5.13), we have $-1 < C^{uv} \leq 1$.

5.4 Test Message Exchange Rate and Scalability of Our System

Each IDS u in our system maintains an acquaintance list and a probation list with maximum length l_{max}^u. This length can be fixed according to the resource capacity of node u or slightly updated with the changes in IDN size. However, it is always set to a value small enough to account for scalability. Equation (5.6) ensures that the process of updating the trustworthiness of a peer after the reception of a response is performed with only three operations, making it linear with respect to the number of answers.

There is a trade-off to be resolved in order to account for scalability in the number of messages exchanged in the IDN. On one hand, the forgetting factor in Equation (5.6) decays the importance given to existing highly trusted peers. This implies that their corresponding test message rates need to be above a certain minimal value. On the other hand, sending too many requests to other peers may compromise scalability. To solve this issue, we adapt the rate of test messages to a given peer according to its estimated trustworthiness. The adaptation policy is provided in Table 5.1, where acquaintances are categorized into highly trustworthy, trustworthy, untrustworthy, and highly untrustworthy. There are three levels of test message rates: $R_l < R_m < R_h$. We can see in Table 5.1 that the test message rate to highly trustworthy or highly untrustworthy peers is low. This is because we are confident about our decision of including or not their feedback into the aggregation. A higher test message rate is assigned to trustworthy or untrustworthy peers because their trust values are close to the threshold and hence need to be kept under close surveillance.

Each peer in the system needs to actively respond to others' requests in order to keep up its trustworthiness and be able to receive prompt help when needed. However, actively responding to every other peer may cause bandwidth and/or CPU overloading. Therefore, as a consultant to others, a peer would like to limit the rate of answers it provides. In this regard, each peer in our system would respond to requests with a priority proportional to the amount of trust it places on the source of the request [163]. It will give higher priority to highly trusted friends. This obeys the

Table 5.1: Acquaintance Categorization

Peer Category	Criterion	Rate
Highly Trustworthy	$0 <th \leq T_l$	R_l
Trustworthy	$T_l <th \leq T$	R_h
Untrustworthy	$T <th \leq T_h$	R_m
Highly Untrustworthy	$T_h <th \leq 1$	R_l

social norm: "Be nice to others who are nice to you", and also provides incentives for encouraging peers to act honestly in order to receive prompt help in times of need.

5.5 Robustness against Common Threats

Trust management can effectively improve network collaboration and detect malicious peers. However, the trust management system itself may become the target of attacks and be compromised. In this section we describe common attacks and provide defense mechanisms against them.

5.5.1 Newcomer Attacks

Newcomer attacks occur when a malicious peer can easily register as a new user [118]. Such a malicious peer creates a new ID for the purpose of erasing its bad history with other peers in the network and create immediate damage. Our model handles this type of attack by assigning low trust values to all newcomers and enforcing the probation period for each new node. In this way, their feedback on the alerts is simply not considered by other peers during the aggregation process. Newcomers may gain more trust over time and eventually move to acquaintance list if they behave consistently well.

5.5.2 Betrayal Attacks

Betrayal attacks occur when a trusted peer suddenly turns into a malicious one and starts sending false feedbacks. A trust management system can be degraded dramatically because of this type of attack. We employ a mechanism which is inspired by the social norm: "It takes a long-time interaction and consistent good behavior to build up a high trust, while only a few bad actions to ruin it." When a trustworthy peer acts dishonestly, the forgetting factor (Equation (5.6)) causes its trust value to drop down quickly, hence making it difficult for this peer to deceive others or gain back its previous trust within a short time.

5.5.3 Collusion Attacks

Collusion attacks happen when a group of malicious peers cooperate together by providing false alert rankings in order to compromise the network. In our system, peers will not be adversely affected by collusion attacks. In our trust model, each peer relies on its own knowledge to detect dishonest peers. In addition, we use test messages to uncover malicious peers. Because the test messages are sent in a random manner, it will be difficult for malicious peers to distinguish them from actual requests.

5.5.4 Inconsistency Attacks

Inconsistency attacks happen when a malicious peer repeatedly changes its behavior from honest to dishonest in order to degrade the efficiency of the IDN. Inconsistency attacks are harder to succeed in the Dirichlet-based model because of the use of the forgetting factor and the dynamic test message rate, which make trust values easy to lose and hard to gain. This ensures that the trust values of peers with inconsistent behavior remain low and hence have little impact.

5.6 Simulations and Experimental Results

To demonstrate the effectiveness of the trust management design, it is important to evaluate the effectiveness of the model. In this section we present a set of experiments that are used to evaluate the efficiency, scalability and robustness of our trust management model in comparison with existing ones [59, 72]. The simulation program is written in Java programming language and it adopts discrete event simulation to simulate the communication between IDSs. Each experimental result presented in this section is derived from the average of a large number of replications with an overall negligible confidence interval.

5.6.1 Simulation Setting

In the simulation, an IDN environment is established with n IDS peers randomly distributed over an $s \times s$ grid region. The proximity distance is given by the minimum number of square steps between each two peers. The expertise level of a peer can be low (0.05), medium (0.5), or high (0.95). In the beginning, each peer receives an initial acquaintance list containing neighbor nodes based on proximity. The initial trust value of every peer in the acquaintance list is 0.5. To test the trustworthiness of acquaintances, each peer sends out test messages following a Poisson process with rates according to Table 5.1. The parameters we used are shown in Table 5.2.

Table 5.2: Simulation Parameters

Parameter	Value	Description
R_l	2/day	Low test message rate
R_m	10/day	Medium test message rate
R_h	20/day	High test message rate
λ	0.9	Forgetting factor
th	0.8	Trust threshold for aggregation
c_0	10	Priori constant
c_1	1.5	Cost rate of low estimate to high estimate
c_2	1	Satisfaction sensitivity factor
s	4	Size of grid region
k	10	Number of satisfaction levels

5.6.2 Modeling the Expertise Level of a Peer

To reflect the expertise level of each peer, a Beta distribution is used to simulate the decision model of answering requests. A Beta density function is given by

$$f(p|\alpha,\beta) = \frac{1}{B(\alpha,\beta)} p^{\alpha-1}(1-p)^{\beta-1}$$

$$B(\alpha,\beta) = \int_0^1 t^{\alpha-1}(1-t)^{\beta-1} dt \qquad (5.15)$$

where $f(p|\alpha,\beta)$ is the probability that a peer with expertise level l answers with a value of $p \in [0,1]$ to an alert of difficulty level $d \in [0,1]$. Higher values for d are associated to attacks that are difficult to detect, that is, many peers fail to identify them. Higher values of l imply a higher probability of producing correct alert rankings.

Let r be the expected ranking of an alert. We define α and β as follows:

$$\alpha = 1 + \frac{l(1-d)}{d(1-l)}\sqrt{\frac{r}{1-r}}\sqrt{\frac{2}{l}} - 1$$

$$\beta = 1 + \frac{l(1-d)}{d(1-l)}\sqrt{\frac{1-r}{r}}\sqrt{\frac{2}{l}} - 1 \qquad (5.16)$$

For a fixed difficulty level, the above model has the property of assigning higher probabilities of producing correct rankings to peers with higher levels of expertise. A peer with expertise level l has a lower probability of producing correct rankings for alerts of higher difficulty $(d > l)$. $l = 1$ or $d = 0$ represent the extreme cases where the peer can always accurately rank the alert. This is reflected in the Beta distribution by $\alpha, \beta \to \infty$. Figure 5.2 shows the feedback probability distribution for peers with different expertise levels, where we fix the expected risk level to 0.6 and the difficulty level of test messages to 0.5.

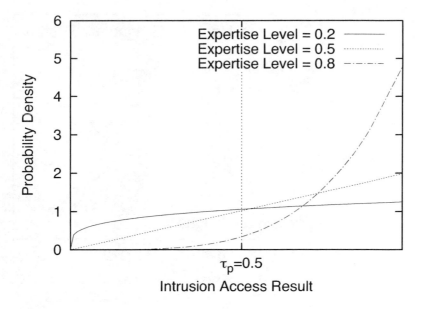

Figure 5.2: Decision density function for expertise levels.

5.6.3 Deception Models

A dishonest peer may adopt one of four deception models: *complementary, exaggerate positive, exaggerate negative,* or *maximal harm*. The first three deception models are described in [150], where an adversary may choose to send feedback about the risk level of an alert that is respectively opposite to, higher, or lower than the true risk level. In a maximal harm model, an adversary always chooses to report false feedback with the intention to bring the most negative impact to the request sender. Figure 5.3 shows the feedback curve for the different deception strategies. For instance, when a deceptive peer using the maximal harm strategy receives a ranking request and detects that the risk level of the request is "medium," it sends feedback "no risk" because this feedback can maximally deviate the aggregated result at the sender side.

5.6.4 Trust Values and Confidence Levels for Honest Peers

We first evaluate the effectiveness of the collaboration and the importance of our trust management. In this experiment, all peers are honest. We simulate the scenario where each peer u has a fixed size N^u of its acquaintance list. The peers are divided into three equally sized groups of *low, medium,* and *high* expertise levels, respectively. The first phase of the simulation is a learning period (50 days), during which peers learn about each other's expertise levels by sending out test messages. Figure 5.4 shows the resulting average trust values of the 30 acquaintances of peer u. The trust

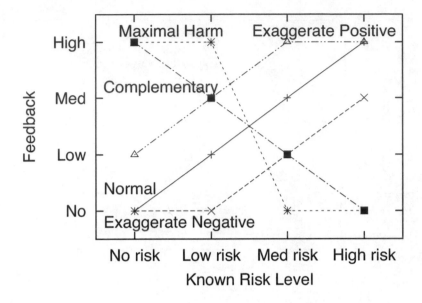

Figure 5.3: Feedback curves for different deception strategies.

values converge after 30 days of simulation and the actual expertise levels of the peers are able to be effectively identified by our trust model.

To study the impact of different test message rates on the confidence level of trust estimation (Equation (5.12)), we conduct a second experiment to let u use a fixed test message rate in every simulation round. The rate of sending test messages starts with one message per day and increases by five for every simulation round. We plot the confidence level of trust evaluation for each test message rate in Figure 5.5. We can observe that the confidence level increases with the increase of the test message rate. This confirms our argument that sending more test messages improves the confidence of trust estimation. We also observe that the confidence levels increase with the expertise levels. This is because peers with higher expertise levels tend to perform more consistently.

5.6.5 Trust Values for Dishonest Peers

The purpose of this experiment is to study the impact of dishonest peers using the four different deception strategies described in Section 5.6.3. To study the maximum impact of these deception strategies, we only use peers with a *high* expertise level as deceptive adversaries because they are more likely to know the true answers and can perform the deception strategies more accurately.

In this experiment we let peer u have an acquaintance list of 40 dishonest peers divided into four groups. Each group uses one of the four deception models: complementary, exaggerate positive, exaggerate negative, and maximal harm. We use a

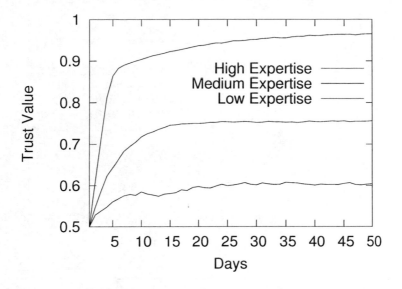

Figure 5.4: Convergence of trust values for different expertise levels.

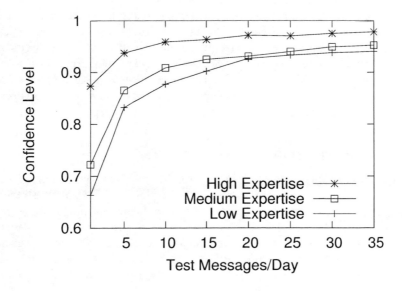

Figure 5.5: Confidence levels of estimation for different test message rates.

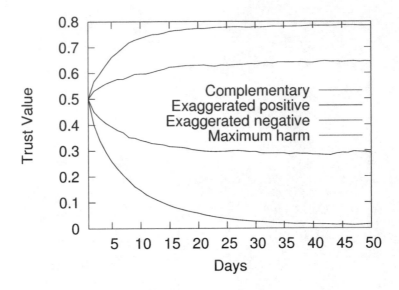

Figure 5.6: Trust values of deceptive peers with different deception strategies.

dynamic test message rate and observe the convergence curve of the average trust value for each group of deceptive peers. Results are plotted in Figure 5.6.

We notice that the trust values of all adversary peers converge to stable values after 30 days of the learning phase. It is not surprising that adversary peers using the maximal harm strategy have the lowest trust values, while adversary peers using the complementary strategy have the second lowest ones. The converged trust values of adversary peers using exaggerate positives are higher than those using exaggerate negatives. This is because we use an asymmetric penalization mechanism for inaccurate replies ($c_1 > 1$ in Equation (5.1)). We penalize more heavily peers that untruthfully report lower risks than those that untruthfully report higher risks.

5.6.6 Robustness of Our Trust Model

The goal of this experiment is to study the robustness of our trust model against various insider attacks. For the newcomer attack, malicious peers whitewash their bad history and re-register as new users to the system. If the trust value of a newcomer can increase quickly based on its short-term good behavior, the system is then vulnerable to newcomer attacks. However, a newcomer attack is difficult to succeed in our model. In our model, we use parameter c_0 in Equation (5.6) to control the trust value increasing rate. When c_0 is larger, it takes longer for a newcomer to gain a trust value above the trust threshold.

We compare our Dirichlet-based model with our previous model [72] and the model of Duma et al. [59] in Figure 5.7. We observe that in the Duma et al. model, the

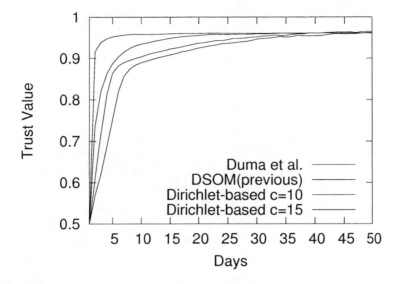

Figure 5.7: Trust values of newcomers under different trust models.

trust values of new users increase very fast and reach the aggregation trust threshold (0.8) on the first day, which reveals a high vulnerability to newcomer attacks. The reason for this is that their model does not have an initial trust to new peers and therefore their trust values change fast in the beginning. In the model we developed in [72], the trust values increase in a slower manner and reach the trust threshold after 3 days. However, that model is not flexible in that it does not offer control over the trust increase speed. In the Dirichlet-based model, the trust increase speed is controlled by the priori constant c_0. For $c_0 = 10$, it takes a newcomer 4 to 5 days of consistent good behavior to reach the same trust value. Larger values of c_0 make it even slower to reach high trust, hence offering robustness against newcomer attacks.

The second possible threat is the betrayal attack, where a malicious peer first gains a high trust value and then suddenly starts to act dishonestly. This scenario can happen, for example, when a peer is compromised. To demonstrate the robustness of our model against this attack type, we set up a scenario where u has seven peers in its acquaintance list, of which six are honest with an expertise level evenly divided between low, medium, and high. The malicious one has high expertise and behaves honestly in the first 50 days. After that, it launches a betrayal attack by adopting a maximal harm deceptive strategy. We observe the trust value of the betraying peer and the satisfaction levels of aggregated feedback in each day with respect to u.

Figure 5.8 shows the trust value of the betraying peer before and after the launching of the betrayal attack when respectively using Duma et al., our previous, and our current trust models. For the Duma et al. model, the trust value of the malicious peer slowly drops after the betrayal attack. This is because their model does not use a for-

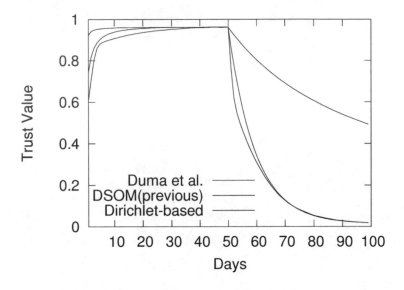

Figure 5.8: Trust of malicious peers under betrayal attack.

getting factor, hence providing the previous honest behavior of a malicious peer with a heavy impact on the trust calculation for a considerable amount of time. The trust value of the betraying peer drops much faster using our previous model, while the fastest rate is observed when using our Dirichlet-based model. This is because both models use a forgetting factor to pay more attention to the more recent behavior of peers.

We also notice that the Dirichlet-based model has a slight improvement over our previous model. The Dirichlet-based model adopts the dynamic test message rate and can react more swiftly. The rate of sending messages to malicious peers increases as soon as they start behaving dishonestly. Higher rates of test messages help in faster detection of dishonest behavior. However, in our previous model, the test message rate remains the same. This phenomenon can be further observed in Figure 5.10.

The results for the satisfaction levels of aggregated feedback with respect to u before and after the betrayal attack are shown in Figure 5.9. We notice that the satisfaction level of u for the aggregated feedback drops down drastically on the first day following the learning period and recovers after that in all three models. The recovery period is however much shorter for the Dirichlet-based and our previous models. This is again attributed to the use of the forgetting factor. The Dirichlet-based model has a slight improvement in the recovering speed over our previous model. This is because in the Dirichlet-based model, the trust values of betraying peers drop under the aggregation threshold faster than our previous model. Therefore, the impact of betraying peers is eliminated earlier than that in the previous model.

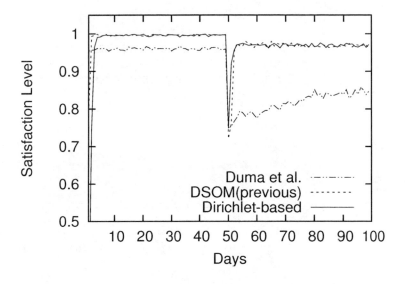

Figure 5.9: Impact on accuracy of betrayal attack.

5.6.7 Scalability of Our Trust Model

The result of test message rates under betrayal attack is shown in Figure 5.10. We notice that in our Dirichlet-based model, the average test message rates for highly trustworthy as well as highly untrustworthy peers are the lowest. The average test message sending rate to peers with the medium expertise level is higher but still below the medium rate (R_m). Compared to our previous model, the average message sending rate is much lower, which demonstrates the improved scalability of our Dirichlet-based model. Note that the spike from the betraying group on around day 50 is caused by the drastic increment of the test message rate. The sudden change of a highly trusted peer behavior will cause the trust confidence level to drop down quickly. The rate of sending messages to this peer then switches to R_h accordingly.

5.6.8 Efficiency of Our Trust Model

To demonstrate the efficiency of our Dirichlet-based trust model, we conduct another experiment to evaluate the intrusion detection accuracy. In this experiment, we let peer u have 15 acquaintances, which are evenly divided into low, medium, and high expertise groups. Among the expert peers, some are malicious and launch inconsistency attacks synchronously to degrade the efficiency of the IDN. More specifically, in each round of behavior changing, these malicious peers adopt the maximal harm deception strategy for 2 days, followed by 6 days of honest behavior.

In Figure 5.11 we vary the percentages of malicious peers from 0% to 80%. We inject daily intrusions to peer u with medium difficulty (0.5) and random risk levels.

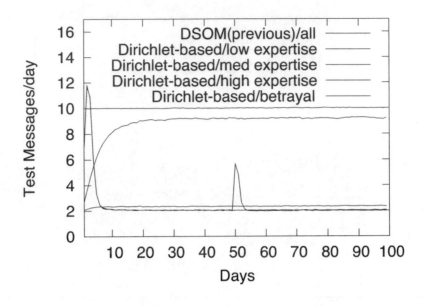

Figure 5.10: Comparison of average test message rates under different models.

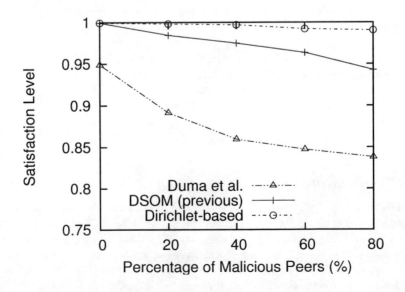

Figure 5.11: Aggregated feedback under inconsistency attack.

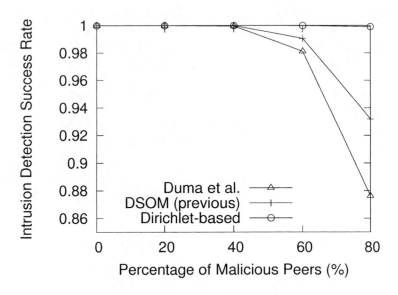

Figure 5.12: Intrusion detection success rate under inconsistency attack.

We then plot the average satisfaction level for the aggregated feedback. We observe that our Dirichlet-based model outperforms the others. This is because the dynamic test message rate in Dirichlet-based model causes the trust of malicious peers to drop faster and increase more slowly, hence minimizing the impact of dishonest behavior. Among the three models, Duma et al. has the least satisfaction level because of its slow response to sudden changes in peer behavior and its aggregation of all feedback from even untrustworthy peers.

Figure 5.12 shows the success rate of peer u in detecting intrusions. We notice that both our previous model and the Duma et al. model cannot effectively detect intrusions when the majority of peers are malicious. Our Dirichlet-based model shows excellent efficiency in intrusion detection even in the situation of a dishonest majority.

5.7 Conclusions and Future Work

In this chapter we described a trust management model for evaluating trustworthiness of intrusion detection systems in a collaborative intrusion detection network. The trust management uses Dirichlet density functions as its foundation, and is accordingly able to measure the uncertainty in estimating the likely future behavior of IDSs. The measured uncertainty allows the trust management to employ an adaptive message exchange rate, resulting in good scalability. Equipped with a forgetting factor, it is also robust against some common threats. The effectiveness, robustness, and scalability of our trust management have been further validated through experiments carried out in a simulated collaborative intrusion detection network. IDSs in the conducted experiments have different levels of expertise in detecting intrusions and adopt different deception strategies. The results show that the trust management is more effective compared to existing trust models. This is an important step forward because effective trust management is essential for the deployment of a secure IDN.

One possible direction for future work here is to incorporate a reputation model in our trust management. This will require addressing the important issues of inaccurate reputation information, scalability, and collusion attacks.

Chapter 6

Collaborative Decision

CONTENTS

6.1 Introduction

In the previous chapter we discussed the design of a robust, scalable, and efficient trust management for an IDN. An important function of trust evaluation is to find the expertise level of participant IDSs in order to improve the accuracy of collaborative intrusion detection. In this chapter we focus on the design of efficient and trustworthy *collaborative intrusion decision*, also referred to as feedback aggregation. Efficient and trustworthy feedback aggregation is a critical component in the design of IDNs because it has direct impact on the intrusion detection accuracy. In the IDN, each IDS evaluates its peer collaborators based on their false positive and false negative rates, which can be estimated from historical data and test messages. Accordingly assessments received from an incompetent or malicious insider will have less weight in the final decisions. This decision model is based on data analysis and hypothesis testing methods. Specifically, we design optimal decision rules that minimize Bayesian risks of IDSs in the network. In addition, for real-time applications, an IDS only needs to consult a subset of its acquaintances until desired levels of performance, such as probabilities of detection and false alarm, are achieved. In other words, this decision model provides a data-driven efficiently distributed sequential algorithm for IDSs to make decisions based on feedback from a subset of their collaborators. The goal is to reduce communication overhead and the computational resources needed to achieve a satisfactory feedback aggregation result when the number of acquaintances of an IDS is large.

In the model, we consider four possible outcomes of a decision: *false positive* (FP), *false negative* (FN), *true positive* (TP), and *true negative* (TN). Each outcome is associated with a cost. A sequential hypothesis testing-based collaborative decision model is used to improve the cost efficiency. Communication overhead is also improved because the IDS aggregates feedback until a predefined FP and TP goal is reached. An analytical model is used to estimate the number of acquaintances needed for an IDS to reach its predefined intrusion detection goal. Such a result is crucial to the design of an IDS acquaintance list in our IDN.

The highlight of this chapter can be summarized as follows: (1) a Beta distribution is used to model the false positive rate and true positive rate of each IDS; (2) a Bayesian approach to devise a decentralized feedback optimal-cost aggregation mechanism for each peer in the IDN; and (3) a sequential hypothesis model for each IDS to find the minimal number of collaborators to consult before a confident decision is made.

The remainder of this chapter is organized as follows. In Section 9.2 we survey some existing collaborative decision techniques for IDNs. The decision problem is formulated in Section 6.3, where we use hypothesis testing to minimize the cost of decisions, and sequential hypothesis testing to form consultation termination policy for predefined goals is described in Section 6.4. In Section 10.5 we use simulations to evaluate the effectiveness of the decision model and validate the analytical model. Section 6.6 concludes the chapter and identifies directions for future research.

6.2 Background

Recent studies on IDNs [72, 74, 77] have proposed the use of trust models to identify dishonest peers. Intrusion assessments from nodes with different trust values are assigned with different weights to improve intrusion detection accuracy. AB-DIAS [77] is a community-based IDN where IDSs are organized into groups and exchange intrusion information in order to gain better intrusion detection accuracy. A simple majority-based voting system is used to detect compromised nodes. However, this voting-based system is vulnerable to colluded voting. Another solution to detect compromised nodes is a trust management system where peers build trust with each other based on personal experience. Existing trust management models for IDN include the linear model [59, 72] and the Bayesian model [69, 74]. However, all these works used heuristic approaches to aggregate consultation results from other collaborators. In this chapter we present a Bayesian aggregation model that aims at finding optimal decisions based on collected information.

Bayesian approaches have been used in distributed detection in the past. Existing works, including [135] and [112], use Bayesian hypothesis testing methods to aggregate at a central data fusion center feedback from sensors distributed in a local area network. However, these methods require all participants to engage in every detection case, whereas in our context, IDSs may not be involved in all intrusion detections and the collected responses may come from different groups of IDSs each time.

The trustworthiness of IDNs has been ensured at various levels of the system architecture. In [162] and [163], a communication protocol with the property of reciprocal incentive compatibility has been used to provide IDS nodes incentives to send feedback to their peers, and hence to prevent malicious free-riders, denial-of-service attacks, and dishonest insiders. However, this approach only ensures the reliability and trustworthiness at the communication overlay of the IDN, and does not directly deal with the content of the feedback. In [161] and [68], a knowledge-sharing mechanism has been proposed to allow expert nodes to disseminate knowledge within the IDN to prevent zero-day attacks. The communication protocols in [161] are implemented at the higher application layers of the collaborative network.

6.3 Collaborative Decision Model

Consider a set of N nodes, $\mathcal{N} := \{1, 2, \cdots, N\}$, connected in a network, that can be represented by a graph $\mathcal{G} = (\mathcal{N}, \mathcal{E})$. The set $\mathcal{E}$ contains the undirected links between nodes, indicating the acquaintances of IDSs in the network. An IDS node $i \in \mathcal{N}$ has a set of n_i acquaintances, denoted by $\mathcal{N}_i \subseteq \mathcal{N}$, with $n_i = |\mathcal{N}_i|$. When node i observes suspicious activities and does not have enough experience to make an accurate evaluation of potential intrusions, it can send out its observed intrusion information to its acquaintances to ask for diagnosis. The feedback from its acquaintances can be used to make a final decision. The input to the IDS is the past history of each acquaintance

Table 6.1: Summary of Notations

Symbol	Meaning
$\mathcal{N}$	Set of IDSs in the collaborative network
$\mathcal{N}_i$	Set of acquaintances of IDS $i, i \in \mathcal{N}$
n_i	Number of acquaintances of IDS $i, i \in \mathcal{N}$
$Y_j^i,$	Reported decisions from IDS j to IDS i, $i \in \mathcal{N}, j \in \mathcal{N}_i$
$\mathbf{Y}^i$	Vector of complete feedback from IDS i's acquaintances
H_0	Hypothesis that there is no intrusion
H_1	Hypothesis that there is an intrusion
$r_{j,F,k}^i$	The diagnosis result at time k from acquaintance j to IDS i given that there is no intrusion
$r_{j,D,k}^i$	The diagnosis result at time k from acquaintance j to IDS j given that there is an intrusion
π_0^i, π_1^i	Prior probability of no-attack and under-attack
$\bar{\tau}^i$	Probability threshold for final decision
L^i	Likelihood ratio for IDS i's decision
L_n^i	Likelihood ratio for IDS i's sequential decision at stage n
R^i	Bayesian risk of IDS i
δ^i	Aggregation decision rule of IDS i
ϕ^i	Stopping decision rule of IDS i
$D_{KL}(p_1 \| p_2)$	Kullback-Leibler divergence between distributions p_1 and p_2
C_{10}^i, C_{01}^i	Cost of making false positive and false negative decisions for IDS i
C_{00}^i, C_{11}^i	Cost of making correct decisions for IDS i

regarding their detection accuracy, as well as their current feedbacks. The output is a decision on whether or not to raise an alarm.

Let $Y_j^i, j \in \mathcal{N}_i$, be a random variable denoting the decision of peer IDS $j, j \in \mathcal{N}_i$, on its acquaintance list $\mathcal{N}_i$ of node i. The random variable Y_j^i takes binary values in $\mathcal{Y} := \{0,1\}$ for all $j \in \mathcal{N}_i, i \in \mathcal{N}$. In the intrusion detection setting, $Y_j^i = 0$ means that IDS j decides and reports to IDS i that there is no intrusion, while $Y_j^i = 1$ means that IDS j raises an alarm of possible detection of intrusion to IDS i. Each IDS makes its decision based upon its own experience of the previous attacks and its own sophistication of detection. We let p_j^i as the probability mass function defined on $\mathcal{Y}$ such that $p_j^i(Y_j^i = 0)$ and $p_j^i(Y_j^i = 1)$ denotes the probability of reporting no intrusion and the probability of reporting intrusion from IDS j to IDS i, respectively.

We let $\mathbf{Y}^i := [Y_j^i]_{j \in \mathcal{N}_i} \in \mathcal{Y}^{n_i}$ be an observation vector of IDS i that contains feedbacks from its peers in the acquaintance list. Each IDS has two hypotheses H_0 and H_1. H_0 hypothesizes that no intrusion is detected, whereas H_1 forwards a hypothesis that intrusion is detected and alarm needs to be raised. Note that we intentionally drop the superscript i on H_0 and H_1 because we assume that each IDS attempts to make the same type of decisions. Denote by π_0^i, π_1^i the apriori probabilities on each hypothesis such that $\pi_0^i = \mathbb{P}[H_0], \pi_1^i = \mathbb{P}[H_1]$ and $\pi_0^i + \pi_1^i = 1$, for all $i \in \mathcal{N}$. Let p^i be the probability measure on $\mathcal{Y}^{n_i}$, for all $i \in \mathcal{N}$. The conditional probabilities $p^i(\mathbf{Y}^i = \mathbf{y}^i|H_l), l = 0, 1$, denotes the probabilities of a complete feedback being $\mathbf{y}^i \in \mathcal{Y}^{n_i}$ given the hypothesis H_0, H_1, respectively. Assuming that peers make decisions independently (this is reasonable if acquaintances are appropriately selected), we can rewrite the conditional probability as

$$p^i(\mathbf{Y}^i = \mathbf{y}^i|H_l) = \prod_{j \in \mathcal{N}_i} p_j^i(Y_j^i = y_j^i|H_l), \quad i \in \mathcal{N}, l = 0, 1 \qquad (6.1)$$

Our goal is to decide whether the system should raise an alarm to the system administrator based on the current received feedbacks. We need to point out that the decision model does not exclude the local diagnosis of the IDS itself. If an IDS is capable of making its own diagnosis, this one is aggregated with the feedbacks from its peers in the acquaintances. Table 10.1 summarizes the notations we use in this section.

In the following subsections we first model the past behavior of acquaintances and then model the decision problem using Bayesian risk function.

6.3.1 Modeling of Acquaintances

The conditional probabilities $p_j^i(Y_j^i|H_l), i \in \mathcal{N}, j \in \mathcal{N}_i, l \in \{0, 1\}$, are often unknown to IDS nodes and they need to be learned from previous data. In this section we use the Beta distribution and its Gaussian approximation to find these probabilities. We let $p_{j,M}^i := p_j^i(Y_j^i - 0|H_1)$ be the probability of miss of an IDS j's diagnosis to node i's request, also known as the false negative (FN) rate; and let $p_{j,F}^i := p_j^i(Y_j^i = 1|H_0)$ be the probability of false alarm or false positive (FP) rate. The probability of detection, or true positive (TP) rate, can be expressed as $p_{j,D}^i = 1 - p_{j,M}^i$.

Each IDS in the network maintains a history of data containing the diagnosis data from past consultations. The accuracy of peer diagnosis will be revealed after an intrusion happens. As mentioned in Section 4.2, test messages can also be used to assess the effectiveness of IDSs even though no intrusion history has been collected. IDS i can use these collected data from its peers to assess the distributions over its peer IDS j's probabilities of detection and false alarm using Beta functions, denoted by $p_{j,D}^i$ and $p_{j,F}^i$, respectively. The total reported diagnosis data from peer IDS $j, j \in \mathcal{N}_i$, to IDS i is denoted by the set $\mathcal{M}_j^i$, and they are classified into two groups: one is where the result is either false positive or true negative under no intrusion, denoted by the set $\mathcal{M}_{j,0}^i$; and the other is where the result is either false negative or true positive under intrusion, denoted by the set $\mathcal{M}_{j,1}^i$. Both sets are disjoint satisfying $\mathcal{M}_{j,0}^i \cup \mathcal{M}_{j,1}^i = \mathcal{M}_j^i$ and $\mathcal{M}_{j,0}^i \cap \mathcal{M}_{j,1}^i = \emptyset$.

We let the random variables $p_{j,F}^i$ and $p_{j,D}^i$ take the form of Beta distributions as follows:

$$p_{j,F}^i \sim \text{Beta}(x_j^i|\alpha_{j,F}^i,\beta_{j,F}^i) = \frac{\Gamma(\alpha_{j,F}^i+\beta_{j,F}^i)}{\Gamma(\alpha_{j,F}^i)\Gamma(\beta_{j,F}^i)}(x_j^i)^{\alpha_{j,F}^i-1}(1-x_j^i)^{\beta_{j,F}^i-1}, \qquad (6.2)$$

$$p_{j,D}^i \sim \text{Beta}(y_j^i|\alpha_{j,D}^i,\beta_{j,D}^i) = \frac{\Gamma(\alpha_{j,D}^i+\beta_{j,D}^i)}{\Gamma(\alpha_{j,D}^i)\Gamma(\beta_{j,D}^i)}(y_j^i)^{\alpha_{j,D}^i-1}(1-y_j^i)^{\beta_{j,D}^i-1}, \qquad (6.3)$$

where $\Gamma(\cdot)$ is the Gamma function; $x_j^i, y_j^i \in [0,1]$; $\alpha_{j,F}^i, \alpha_{j,D}^i$ and $\beta_{j,F}^i, \beta_{j,F}^i$ are Beta function parameters that are updated according to historical data as follows.

$$\alpha_{j,F}^i = \sum_{k\in\mathcal{M}_{j,0}^i}(\lambda_F^i)^{t_{j,k}^i}r_{j,F,k}^i, \quad \beta_{j,F}^i = \Sigma_{k\in\mathcal{M}_{j,0}^i}(\lambda_F^i)^{t_{j,k}^i}(1-r_{j,F,k}^i); \qquad (6.4)$$

$$\alpha_{j,D}^i = \sum_{k\in\mathcal{M}_{j,1}^i}(\lambda_D^i)^{t_{j,k}^i}r_{j,D,k}^i, \quad \beta_{j,D}^i = \Sigma_{k\in\mathcal{M}_{j,1}^i}(\lambda_D^i)^{t_{j,k}^i}(1-r_{j,D,k}^i). \qquad (6.5)$$

The introduction of the discount factors $\lambda_F^i, \lambda_D^i \in [0,1]$ above allows more weights on recent data from IDSs while less on the old ones. The discount factors on the data can be different for false negative and false positive rates. The parameter $t_{j,k}^i$ denotes the time when k-th diagnosis data generated by IDS $j, j \in \mathcal{N}_i$, to its peer IDS i. The parameter $r_{j,F,k}^i, r_{j,M,k}^i \in \{0,1\}$ are the revealed results of the k-th diagnosis data: $r_{j,F,k}^i = 1$ suggests that the k-th diagnosis data from peer j yields an undetected intrusion while $r_{j,F,k}^i = 0$ means otherwise; similarly, $r_{j,D,k}^i = 1$ indicates the data from the peer j results in a correct detection under intrusion, and $r_{j,D,k}^i = 0$ means otherwise.

The parameters $\alpha_{j,F}^i, \beta_{j,F}^i, \alpha_{j,D}^i, \beta_{j,D}^i$ in the distribution above also provide an empirical assessment of the trustworthiness of each peer of IDS i. They can be also seen as the trust values of the collaborators. A peer who is either malicious or incompetent will result in low values of $\alpha_{j,D}^i$ and higher values $\alpha_{j,D}^i$. To make the parametric updates scalable to data storage and memory, we can use the following recursive formulae to update these parameters as follows:

$$\alpha_{j,e,k}^i = (\lambda_e^i)^{t_{j,k}^i-t_{j,k-1}^i}\alpha_{j,e,k-1}^i+r_{j,e,k}^i, \quad k \geq 1, \qquad (6.6)$$

$$\beta_{j,e,k}^i = (\lambda_e^i)^{t_{j,k}^i-t_{j,k-1}^i}\beta_{j,e,k-1}^i+r_{j,e,k}^i, \quad k \geq 1, \qquad (6.7)$$

where $e \in \{F,D\}$; $\alpha_{j,D,k}^i, \beta_{j,D,k}^i$, are parameter values up to the k-th data point in their corresponding data set and $\mathcal{M}_{j,1}^i$; $\alpha_{j,F,k}^i, \beta_{j,F,k}^i$, are parameter values up to the k-th data point in their corresponding data set $\mathcal{M}_{j,0}^i$. We can see that when $\lambda_e^i = 0$, the system becomes memoryless; and when $\lambda_e^i = 1$, all past experiences are taken into account on an equal basis. The online iterative calculations also provide a method to assess the trust values with real-time data.

When parameters of the Beta functions α and β in Equation (6.2) are sufficiently large, that is, enough data are collected, the Beta distribution can be approximated by a Gaussian distribution as follows:

$$\text{Beta}(\alpha,\beta) \approx G\left(\frac{\alpha}{\alpha+\beta}, \sqrt{\frac{\alpha\beta}{(\alpha+\beta)^2(\alpha+\beta+1)}}\right), \qquad (6.8)$$

where the arguments of $G(\cdot,\cdot)$ are the mean value and the standard deviation, respectively. Note that we have dropped the superscripts and subscripts in Equation (6.8) for generality as it can be applied to all i and j in Equation (6.2). Hence, using the Gaussian approximation and Equation (6.4), the expected values for $p^i_{j,D}$ and $p^i_{j,M}$ are given by

$$\mathbb{E}[p^i_{j,F}] = \frac{\alpha^i_{j,F}}{\alpha^i_{j,F}+\beta^i_{j,F}}, \quad \mathbb{E}[p^i_{j,D}] = \frac{\alpha^i_{j,D}}{\alpha^i_{j,D}+\beta^i_{j,D}}. \qquad (6.9)$$

The mean values in Equation (6.9) under large data can be intuitively interpreted as the proportion of results of false alarm and detection in the set $\mathscr{M}^i_{j,0}$ and $\mathscr{M}^i_{j,1}$, respectively. They can thus be used in Equation (6.1) as the assessment of the conditional probabilities.

6.3.2 Collaborative Decision

The collaborative decision problem of IDS i can be seen as a hypothesis testing problem in which one finds a decision function $\delta^i(\mathbf{Y}^i) : \mathscr{Y}^{n_i} \to \{0,1\}$ to minimize the Bayes risk of IDS i

$$R^i(\delta^i) = R^i_0(\delta^i|H_0)\pi^i_0 + R^i_1(\delta^i|H_1)\pi^i_1, \qquad (6.10)$$

where $R^i(\delta^i|H_0)$ is the cost of false alarm and $R^i(\delta^i|H_1)$ is the cost of missed detection. An optimal decision function partitions the observation space $\mathscr{Y}^{n_i}$ into two disjoint sets $\mathscr{Y}^i_0$ and $\mathscr{Y}^i_1$, where $\mathscr{Y}^i_0 = \{\mathbf{y}^i : \delta^i(\mathbf{y}^i) = 0\}$ and $\mathscr{Y}^i_1 = \{\mathbf{y}^i : \delta^i(\mathbf{y}^i) = 1\}$.

To find an optimal decision function according to some criterion, we introduce the cost function $C^i_{ll'}, l, l' = 0, 1$, which represents IDS i's cost of deciding that H_l is true when $H_{l'}$ holds. More specifically, C^i_{01} is the cost associated with a missed intrusion or attack, and C^i_{10} refers to the cost of false alarm, while C^i_{00}, C^i_{11} are the incurred costs when the decision meets the true situation. Let

$$R^i_0(\delta^i|H_0) = C^i_{10}p^i[\delta^i = 1|H_0] + C^i_{00}p^i[\delta^i = 0|H_0], \qquad (6.11)$$

$$R^i_1(\delta^i|H_0) = C^i_{01}p^i[\delta^i = 0|H_1] + C^i_{11}p^i[\delta^i = 1|H_1]. \qquad (6.12)$$

It can be shown that decision functions can be picked as a function of the likelihood ratio given by $L^i(\mathbf{y}^i) = \frac{p^i(\mathbf{y}^i|H_1)}{p^i(\mathbf{y}^i|H_0)}$ (see [112, 135]).

A threshold Bayesian decision rule is expressed in terms of the likelihood ratio and is given by

$$\delta^i_B(\mathbf{y}^i) = \begin{cases} 1 & \text{if } L^i(\mathbf{y}^i) \geq \tau^i \\ 0 & \text{if } L^i(\mathbf{y}^i) < \tau^i \end{cases}, \qquad (6.13)$$

where the threshold τ^i is defined by

$$\tau^i = \frac{(C_{10}^i - C_{00}^i)\pi_0^i}{(C_{01}^i - C_{11}^i)\pi_1^i}. \tag{6.14}$$

If the costs are symmetric and the two hypothesis are equal likely, then the rule in Equation (6.13) reduces to the maximum likelihood (ML) decision rule

$$\delta_{ML}^i(\mathbf{y}) = \begin{cases} 1 & \text{if } p^i(\mathbf{y}^i|H_1) \geq p^i(\mathbf{y}^i|H_0) \\ 0 & \text{if } p^i(\mathbf{y}^i|H_1) < p^i(\mathbf{y}^i|H_0) \end{cases}, \tag{6.15}$$

Assume that $C_{00}^i, C_{11}^i = 0$. Using the results in Section 6.3.1, we can obtain the following decision rule for each IDS. The application of the optimal decision rules is summarized in Algorithm 6.1.

Proposition 6.3.1 *Let $\bar{\tau}^i := \frac{C_{10}^i}{C_{10}^i + C_{01}^i}$ and assume that historical data is relatively large. The optimal decision rule of IDS $i, i \in \mathcal{N}$, is*

$$\delta^i = \begin{cases} 1 \text{ (Alarm)} & \text{if } \bar{P}^i \geq \bar{\tau}^i, \\ \\ 0 \text{ (No alarm)} & \text{otherwise,} \end{cases} \tag{6.16}$$

where $\bar{P}^i$ can be obtained by Gaussian approximation as follows:

$$\bar{P}^i \approx \frac{1}{1 + \frac{\pi_0^i}{\pi_1^i} \prod_{j=1}^{n_i} \frac{\alpha_{j,D}^i + \beta_{j,D}^i}{\alpha_{j,F}^i + \beta_{j,F}^i} \left(\frac{\alpha_{j,F}^i}{\alpha_{j,D}^i}\right)^{y_j^i} \left(\frac{\beta_{j,F}^i}{\beta_{j,D}^i}\right)^{1-y_j^i}}.$$

The corresponding Bayes risk for the optimal decision is

$$R^i(\delta^i) = \begin{cases} C_{10}^i(1 - \bar{P}^i) & \text{if } \bar{P}^i \geq \bar{\tau}^i, \\ \\ C_{01}^i \bar{P}^i & \text{otherwise.} \end{cases} \tag{6.17}$$

Proof 6.1 The result follows directly from the applications of likelihood ratio test and the Gaussian approximations of Beta distributions under the assumption of large data sets.

6.4 Sequential Hypothesis Testing

The optimal decision rule in Section 6.3 requires each IDS to send requests to all the acquaintances. As the number of collaborators increases, it creates a lot of communication overhead and consumes a large amount of computational power to implement

---

Algorithm 6.1 Optimal Decision Rule for an IDS i

Step 1: Send out requests to all acquaintances of IDS i and collect their feedback results.

Step 2: Use Equation (6.16) to decide whether or not an intrusion occurs, and take corresponding actions.

Step 3: Update the data sets $\mathcal{M}_{j,0}^i$, $\mathcal{M}_{j,1}^i$, with the diagnosis results of each peer $j, j \in \mathcal{N}_i$ when the fact has been revealed a posteriori.

Step 4: Calculate Beta function parameters $\alpha_{j,F}^i, \alpha_{j,D}^i$ and $\beta_{j,F}^i, \beta_{j,F}^i$ using iterative schemes (6.6) and (6.7).

Step 5: Go to **Step 1** when new decisions needs to be made or the trustworthiness of new acquaintances needs to be evaluated using test messages.

Algorithm 6.1. Instead, it is desirable that IDSs can choose a sufficient number of acquaintances to guarantee a certain level of confidence in the final feedback aggregation. In this section we use sequential hypothesis testing to make decisions with a minimum number of feedbacks from peer IDSs [93, 142]. An IDS asks for feedback from its acquaintances until a sufficient number of answers are collected. Let Ω^i denote all possible collections of feedback from the acquaintance list of IDS i and $\omega^i \in \Omega^i$ denotes a particular collection of feedback. Let $N^i(\omega^i)$ be a random variable denoting the number of feedbacks used until a decision is made. A sequential decision rule is formed by a pair (ϕ, δ), where $\phi^i = \{\phi_n^i, n \in \mathbb{N}\}$ is a stopping rule and $\delta^i = \{\delta_n^i, n \in \mathbb{N}\}$ is the terminal decision rule. Introduce a stopping rule with n feedback, $\phi_n^i : \mathcal{Y}_n^i := \prod_{j \in \mathcal{N}_{i,n}} \mathcal{Y} \rightarrow \{0, 1\}$, where $\mathcal{N}_{i,n}$ is the set of nodes an IDS i asks up to time n. $\phi_n^i = 0$ indicates that IDS i needs to take more samples after n rounds whereas $\phi_n^i = 1$ means to stop asking for feedback and a decision can be made by the rule δ_n^i. The minimum number of feedbacks is given by

$$N^i(\omega^i) = \min\{n : \phi_n^i = 1, n \in \mathbb{N}\}. \qquad (6.18)$$

Note that $N^i(\omega^i)$ is the stopping time of the decision rule. The decision rule δ^i is not used until N. We assume that no cost has been incurred when a correct decision is made, while the cost of a missed intrusion is denoted by C_{01}^i and the cost of a false alarm is denoted by C_{10}^i. In addition, we assume each feedback incurs a cost D^i. We introduce an optimal sequential rule that minimizes Bayes risk given by

$$R^i(\phi^i, \delta^i) = R(\phi^i, \delta^i | H_0) \pi_0^i + R(\phi^i, \delta^i | H_1) \pi_1^i, \qquad (6.19)$$

where $R(\phi^i, \delta^i | H_l)$, $l = 0, 1$, are the Bayes risks under hypotheses H_0 and H_1, respectively:

$$R^i(\phi^i, \delta^i | H_0) = C_{10}^i p^i [\delta_N(Y_j^i, j \in \mathcal{N}_{i,N}) = 1 | H_0] + D^i \mathbb{E}[N | H_0],$$
$$R^i(\phi^i, \delta^i | H_1) = C_{01}^i p^i [\delta_N(Y_j^i, j \in \mathcal{N}_{i,N}) = 0 | H_1] + D^i \mathbb{E}[N | H_1].$$

Let $V^i(\pi_0^i) = \min_{\phi^i,\delta^i} R^i(\phi^i,\delta^i)$ be the optimal value function. It is clear that when no feedback is obtained from the peers, the Bayes risks reduce to

$$R^i(\phi_0^i = 1, \delta_0^i = 1) \quad = \quad C_{10}^i \pi_0^i, \tag{6.20}$$

$$R^i(\phi_0^i = 1, \delta_0^i = 0) \quad = \quad C_{01}^i \pi_1^i. \tag{6.21}$$

Hence, H_1 is chosen when $C_{10}^i \pi_0^i < C_{01}^i \pi_1^i$ or $\pi_0^i < \frac{C_{01}^i}{C_{10}^i + C_{01}^i}$, and H_0 is chosen otherwise. The minimum Bayes risk under no feedback is thus obtained as a function of π_0^i and is denoted by

$$T^i(\pi_0^i) = \begin{cases} C_{10}^i \pi_0^i & \text{if } \pi_0 < \frac{C_{01}^i}{C_{10}^i + C_{01}^i}, \\ C_{01}^i(1 - \pi_0^i) & \text{otherwise.} \end{cases} \tag{6.22}$$

The minimum cost function (6.22) is a piecewise linear function. For ϕ^i such that $\phi_0^i = 0$, that is, at least one feedback is obtained, let the minimum Bayes risk be denoted by $J^i(\pi_0^i) = \min_{\{(\phi^i,\delta^i):\phi_0^i=0\}} R^i(\phi^i,\delta^i)$. Hence, the optimal Bayes risk needs to satisfy

$$V^i(\pi_0^i) = \min\{T^i(\pi_0^i), J^i(\pi_0^i)\}. \tag{6.23}$$

Note that $J^i(\pi_0^i)$ must be greater than the cost of one sample D^i as a sample request incurs D^i and $J^i(\pi_0^i)$ is concave in π_0^i as a consequence of minimizing the linear Bayes risk (6.19). If the cost D^i is high enough so that $J^i(\pi_0^i) > T^i(\pi_0^i)$ for all π_0^i, then no feedback will be requested. In this case, $V^i(\pi_0^i) = T^i(\pi_0^i)$, and the terminal rule is described in Equation (6.22). For other values of $D^i > 0$, due to the piecewise linearity of $T^i(\pi_0^i)$ and concavity of $J^i(\pi_0^i)$, we can see that $J^i(\pi_0^i)$ and $T^i(\pi_0^i)$ have two intersection points π_L^i and π_H^i such that $\pi_L^i \leq \pi_H^i$. It can be shown that for some reasonably low cost D^i and π_0^i such that $\pi_L^i < \pi_0^i < \pi_H^i$, an IDS optimizes its risk by requesting another feedback; otherwise, an IDS should choose to raise an alarm when $\pi_0^i \leq \pi_L^i$ and report no intrusion when $\pi_0^i \leq \pi_L^i$.

Assuming that it takes the same cost D^i for IDS i to acquire a feedback, the problem has the same form after obtaining a feedback from a peer. IDS i can use the feedback to update its a priori probability. After n feedbacks are obtained, π_0^i can be updated as follows:

$$\pi_0^i(n) \quad = \quad \frac{\pi_0^i}{\pi_0^i + (1 - \pi_0^i)L_n^i}; \tag{6.24}$$

where $L_n^i := \prod_{j \in \mathcal{N}_{i,n}} \frac{p^i(y_j^i|H_1)}{p(y_j^i|H_0)}$. We can thus obtain the optimum Bayesian rule captured by Algorithm 1 below, known as the sequential probability ratio test (SPRT) for a reasonable cost D^i. The SPRT Algorithm 6.2 can be used to replace Step 2 in Algorithm 6.1. It is important to note that the choice between Algorithm 6.2 and Algorithm 6.1 depends on the number of acquaintances of an IDS and its computational and memory resources. For smaller scale IDS networks or new members of the IDN, Algorithm 6.2 is more desirable because it allows IDSs to collect more data and learn the level of expertise and trustworthiness of their peers. However, Algorithm 6.2 becomes more efficient when an IDS has a large number of collaborators and limited resources.

Algorithm 6.2 SPRT Rule for an IDS i

Step 1: Start with $n = 0$. Use Equation (6.25) as a stopping rule until $\phi_n^i = 1$ for some $n \geq 0$.

$$\phi_n^i = \begin{cases} 0 & \text{if } \pi_L^i < \pi_0^i(n) < \pi_H^i, \\ 1 & \text{otherwise.} \end{cases} \qquad (6.25)$$

or in terms of the likelihood ratio L_n^i, we can use

$$\phi_n^i = \begin{cases} 0 & \text{if } A^i < L_n^i < B^i \\ 1 & \text{otherwise} \end{cases},$$

where $A^i = \frac{\pi_0^i(1-\pi_H^i)}{(1-\pi_0^i)\pi_H^i}$ and $B^i = \frac{\pi_0^i(1-\pi_L^i)}{(1-\pi_0^i)\pi_L^i}$.

Step 2: Go to Step 3 if $\phi_n^i = 1$ or $n = |\mathcal{N}_i|$; otherwise, choose a new peer from the acquaintance list to request a diagnosis and go to Step 2 with $n = n + 1$.

Step 3: Apply the terminal decision rule as follows to determine whether or not there is an intrusion.

$$\delta_n^i = \begin{cases} 1 & \text{if } \pi_0^i(n) \leq \pi_L^i \\ 0 & \text{if } \pi_0^i(n) > \pi_H^i \end{cases} \quad \text{or} \quad \delta_n^i = \begin{cases} 1 & \text{if } L_n^i \leq A^i \\ 0 & \text{if } L_n^i > B^i \end{cases}$$

6.4.1 Threshold Approximation

In the likelihood sequential ratio test of Algorithm 6.2, the threshold values A and B need to be calculated by finding π_L^i and π_H^i from $J^i(\pi_0^i)$ and $T^i(\pi_0^i)$ in Equation (6.23). The search for these values can be quite involved using dynamic programming. However, in this subsection we introduce an approximation method to find the thresholds. The approximation is based on theoretical studies made in [142] and [93], where a random walk or martingale model is used to yield a relation between thresholds and false positive and false negative rates. Let P_D^i, P_F^i be the probability of detection and the probability of false alarm of an IDS i after applying the sequential hypothesis testing for feedback aggregation. We need to point out that these probabilities are different from the probabilities p_D^i, p_F^i discussed in the previous subsection, which are the raw detection probabilities without feedback in the collaborative network. Let $\bar{P}_D^i$ and $\bar{P}_F^i$ be reasonable desired performance bounds such that $P_F^i \leq \bar{P}_F^i$, $P_D^i \geq \bar{P}_D^i$. Then, the thresholds can be chosen such that $A^i = \frac{1-\bar{P}_D^i}{1-\bar{P}_F^i}$, $B^i = \frac{\bar{P}_D^i}{\bar{P}_F^i}$.

The next proposition gives a result on the bound of the users that need to be on the acquaintance list to achieve the desired performances.

Proposition 6.4.1 *Assume that each IDS makes independent diagnosis on its peers' requests and each has the same distribution* $p_0^i = \bar{p}_0 := \bar{p}(\cdot|H_0), p_1^i = \bar{p}_1 := \bar{p}(\cdot|H_1),$ $\bar{p}_0(y_i = 0) = \theta_0, \bar{p}_1(y_i = 0) = \theta_1,$ *for all* $i \in \mathcal{N}.$

Let $D_{KL}(\bar{p}_0||\bar{p}_1)$ *be the Kullback-Leibler (KL) divergence defined as follows.*

$$D_{KL}(\bar{p}_0||\bar{p}_1) = \sum_{k=0}^{1} \bar{p}_0(k) \ln \frac{\bar{p}_0(k)}{\bar{p}_1(k)} \tag{6.26}$$

$$= \theta_0 \ln \frac{\theta_0}{\theta_1} + (1 - \theta_0) \ln \frac{1 - \theta_0}{1 - \theta_1}, \tag{6.27}$$

and likewise introduce the K-L divergence $D_{KL}(\bar{p}_1||\bar{p}_0)$. *Then, on average, an IDS needs* N_i *acquaintances such that*

$$N_i \geq \max \left(\left\lceil -\frac{D_M^i}{D_{KL}(\bar{p}_0||\bar{p}_1)} \right\rceil, \left\lceil \frac{D_F^i}{D_{KL}(\bar{p}_1||\bar{p}_0)} \right\rceil \right), \tag{6.28}$$

where $D_M^i = P_F \ln \left(\frac{P_D^i}{P_F^i} \right) + P_D \ln \left(\frac{1 - P_D^i}{1 - P_F^i} \right)$ *and* $D_F^i = P_F^i \ln \left(\frac{1 - P_D^i}{1 - P_F^i} \right) + P_D^i \ln \left(\frac{P_D^i}{P_F^i} \right)$. *If* $P_F^i \ll 1$ *and* $P_M^i \ll 1$, *we need approximately* N_i *acquaitances such that*

$$N_i \geq \max \left(\left\lceil \frac{P_D^i - 1}{D_{KL}(\bar{p}_0||\bar{p}_1)} \right\rceil, \left\lceil -\frac{P_F^i}{D_{KL}(\bar{p}_1||\bar{p}_0)} \right\rceil \right). \tag{6.29}$$

Proof 6.2 The conditional expected number of feedback needed to reach a decision on the hypothesis in SPRT can be expressed in terms of P_F and P_D, [93], [142].

$$\mathbb{E}[N|H_0] = \frac{1}{-D_{KL}(\bar{p}_0||\bar{p}_1)} \left[P_F^i \ln \left(\frac{P_D^i}{P_F^i} \right) + P_D^i \ln \left(\frac{1 - P_D^i}{1 - P_F^i} \right) \right],$$

$$\mathbb{E}[N|H_1] = \frac{1}{D_{KL}(\bar{p}_1||\bar{p}_0)} \left[P_F^i \ln \left(\frac{1 - P_D^i}{1 - P_F^i} \right) + P_D^i \ln \left(\frac{P_D^i}{P_F^i} \right) \right].$$

Hence, to reach a decision we need to have at least $\max\{\mathbb{E}[N|H_0], \mathbb{E}[N|H_1]\}$ independent acquaintances. Under the assumption that both P_F and P_M^i are much less than 1, we can further approximate

$$\mathbb{E}[N|H_0] \sim -\frac{1 - P_D^i}{D_{KL}(\bar{p}_0||\bar{p}_1)}, \mathbb{E}[N|H_1] \sim -\frac{P_F^i}{D_{KL}(\bar{p}_1||\bar{p}_0)}.$$

These lead us to inequalities (6.28) and (6.29).

6.5 Performance Evaluation

In this section we use a simulation approach to evaluate the efficiency of the collaborative decision scheme and compare it with other heuristic approaches, such as the

Table 6.2: Simulation Parameters

Parameter	Value	Meaning
τ_{SA}	0.5	Decision threshold of the simple average model
τ_{WA}	0.5	Decision threshold of the weighted average model
n	10	Number of IDSs in the network
d	0.5	Difficulty levels of intrusions and test messages
λ	0.9	Forgetting factor
π_0, π_1	0.5	Probability of no-attack and under-attack
C_{00}, C_{11}	0	Cost of correct decisions

simple average aggregation and the weighted average aggregation (to be explained in more detail in this section).

We conduct a set of experiments to evaluate the average cost of the collaborative detection using the collaborative decision model in comparison with the simple average and the weighted average models. We validate and confirm our theoretical results on the number of acquaintances needed for consultation. Each experimental result presented in this section is derived from the average of a large number of replications with an overall negligible confidence interval. The parameters we use are shown in Table 6.2.

6.5.1   Simulation Setting

The simulation environment uses an IDN of n peers. Each IDS is represented by two parameters: expertise level l and decision threshold τ_p. Expertise level l represents the ability of the IDS to catch suspicious traces from a given observation, and τ_p represents the sensitivity of the IDS (to be elaborated more in Section 6.5.2). At the beginning, each peer receives an initial acquaintance list containing all the other neighbor nodes. In the process of the collaborative intrusion detection, a node sends out intrusion information to its acquaintances to request an intrusion assessment. The feedbacks collected from others are used to make a final decision, that is, whether or not to raise an alarm. Different collaborative decision schemes can be used to make such decisions. We implement three different feedback mechanisms, namely simple average aggregation, weighted average aggregation, and our aggregation model. We compare their efficiency by the average cost of false decisions.

6.5.1.1   Simple Average Model

If the average of all feedbacks is larger than a threshold, then raise an alarm.

$$\delta_{SA} = \begin{cases} 1 \text{ (Alarm)} & \text{if } \frac{\sum_{k=1}^{n} y_k}{n} \geq \tau_{SA}, \\ \\ 0 \text{ (No alarm)} & \text{otherwise,} \end{cases} \tag{6.30}$$

where τ_{SA} is the decision threshold for the simple average algorithm. It is set to be 0.5 if no cost is considered for making false decisions.

6.5.1.2 Weighted Average Model

Weights are assigned to feedbacks from different acquaintances to distinguish their detection capability. For example, high-expertise IDSs are signed with larger weight compared to low-expertise IDSs. In [59], [72], and [74], the weights are the trust values of IDSs:

$$\delta_{WA} = \begin{cases} 1 \text{ (Alarm)} & \text{if } \frac{\sum_{k=1}^{n} w_k y_k}{\sum_{k=1}^{n} w_k} \geq \tau_{WA}, \\ \\ 0 \text{ (No alarm)} & \text{otherwise,} \end{cases} \tag{6.31}$$

where w_k is the weight of the feedback from acquaintance k, which is the trust value of acquaintance k in [59], [72], and [74]. τ_{WA} is the decision threshold for the weighted average algorithm. It is fixed at 0.5 because no cost is considered for FP and FN. In this simulation, we adopt trust values from [74] to be the weights of feedbacks.

6.5.1.3 Bayesian Decision Model

As described in section 6.3.2, our feedback aggregation models each IDS with two parameters (FP and TP) instead of a single trust value. It also considers the costs of false positive and false negative decisions. This decision model investigates the cost of all possible decisions and chooses a decision that leads to a minimal expected cost.

6.5.2 Modeling of a Single IDS

To reflect the intrusion detection capability of each peer, we use a Beta distribution to simulate the decision model of an IDS. A Beta density function is given by

$$f(\bar{p}|\bar{\alpha},\bar{\beta}) = \frac{1}{B(\bar{\alpha},\bar{\beta})} \bar{p}^{\bar{\alpha}-1}(1-\bar{p})^{\bar{\beta}-1},$$

$$B(\bar{\alpha},\bar{\beta}) = \int_0^1 t^{\bar{\alpha}-1}(1-t)^{\bar{\beta}-1}dt, \tag{6.32}$$

where $\bar{\alpha}$ and $\bar{\beta}$ are defined as follows:

$$\bar{\alpha} = 1 + \frac{l(1-d)}{d(1-l)}r,$$

$$\bar{\beta} = 1 + \frac{l(1-d)}{d(1-l)}(1-r). \tag{6.33}$$

where $\bar{p} \in [0,1]$ is the assessment result from the IDS about the probability of intrusion, and $f(\bar{p}|\bar{\alpha},\bar{\beta})$ is the distribution of assessment $\bar{p}$ from a peer with expertise level l to an intrusion with difficulty level $d \in [0,1]$. Higher values of d are associated with attacks that are difficult to detect, that is, many peers may fail to identify them. Higher values of l imply a higher probability of producing correct intrusion assessment. $r \in \{0,1\}$ is the expected result of detection. $r = 1$ indicates that there is an intrusion, and $r = 0$ indicates that there is no intrusion.

For a fixed difficulty level, the above model has the property of assigning higher probabilities of producing correct rankings to peers with higher levels of expertise. A peer with expertise level l has a lower probability of producing correct rankings for alerts of higher difficulty ($d > l$). $l = 1$ or $d = 0$ represent the extreme cases where the peer can always accurately rank the alert. This is reflected in the Beta distribution by $\alpha, \beta \to \infty$. Figure 6.1 shows the feedback probability distribution for peers with different expertise levels, where we fix $r = 1$ and the difficulty level of test messages at 0.5.

τ_p is the decision threshold of $\bar{p}$. If $\bar{p} > \tau_p$, a peer sends feedback 1 (i.e., under-attack); otherwise, feedback 0 (i.e., no-attack) is generated. τ_p indicates the sensitivity of an IDS detector, lower τ value implies a more sensitive detector. That is, the

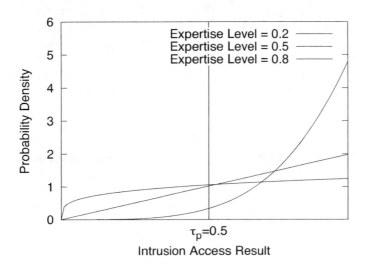

Figure 6.1: Expertise level and detection rate.

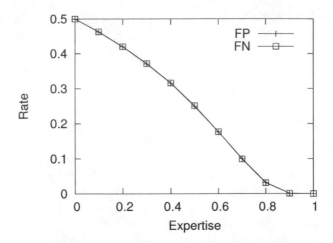

Figure 6.2: FP and FN versus expertise level l.

IDS is more likely to raise alert when suspicious trace is noticed. For a fixed difficulty level, the preceding model assigns higher probabilities of producing correct intrusion diagnosis to peers with a higher level of expertise. A peer with expertise level l has a lower probability of producing correct intrusion diagnosis for intrusions of higher detection difficulty ($d > l$). $l = 1$ and $d = 0$ represent extreme cases where the peer can always accurately detect the intrusion. This is reflected in the Beta distribution by $\bar{\alpha}, \bar{\beta} \to \infty$.

Figure 6.2 shows that both the FP and FN decrease when the expertise level of an IDS increases. We notice that the curves of FP and FN overlap. This is because the IDS detection density distributions are symmetric under $r = 0$ and $r = 1$. Figure 6.3 shows that the FP decreases with the decision threshold while the FN increases with the decision threshold. When the decision threshold is 0, all feedbacks are positive; when the decision threshold is 1, all feedbacks are negative.

6.5.3 Detection Accuracy and Cost

One of the most important metrics to evaluate the efficiency of a decision model is the average cost of incorrect decisions. We take into consideration the fact that the costs of FP decisions and FN decisions are different. In the following subsections we evaluate the cost efficiency of the aggregation algorithm compared with other models under homogeneous and heterogeneous network settings. Then we study the relation between decision cost and the consulted number of acquaintances.

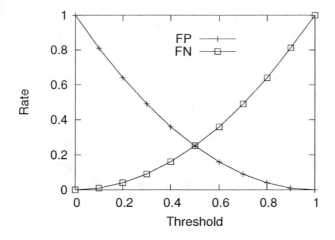

Figure 6.3: FP and FN versus threshold τ_p.

6.5.3.1 Cost under Homogeneous Environment

In this experiment we study the efficiency of the three aggregation models under a homogeneous network setting, that is, all acquaintances have the same parameters. We fix the expertise levels of all nodes at 0.5 (i.e., medium expertise) and set $C_{01} = C_{10} = 1$ for the fairness of comparison, because the simple average and the weighted average models do not account for the cost difference between FP and FN. We fix the decision threshold for each IDS (τ_p) to 0.1 for the first batch run and then increase it by 0.1 in each following batch run until it reaches 1.0. We measure the average cost of the three aggregation models. As shown in Figure 6.4, the average costs of false decisions yielded by our model remains the lowest among the three under all threshold settings. The costs of the weighted average aggregation and the simple average aggregation are close to each other. This is because under such a homogeneous environment, the weights of all IDSs are the same. Therefore, the difference between the weighted average and the simple average is not substantial. We also observe that changing the threshold has a big impact on the costs of the weighted average model and the simple average model, while the cost of the our model changes only slightly with the threshold. All costs reach a minimum when the threshold is 0.5 and increase when it deviates from 0.5.

6.5.3.2 Cost under Heterogeneous Environment

In this experiment we fix the expertise level of all peers at 0.5 and assign decision thresholds ranging from 0.1 to 0.9 to nodes 1 to 9, respectively, with an increment of 0.1. We set false positive cost $C_{10} = 1$ and false negative cost $C_{01} = 5$ to reflect the cost difference between FP and FN. We observe the detection accuracy in terms

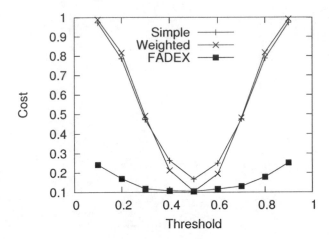

Figure 6.4: Average cost versus threshold τ_p.

of FP and FN rates and the average costs of false decisions at node 0 when three different collaborative decision models are used.

Figure 6.5 shows that the average costs of the three different models converge after a few days of the learning process. The cost of this model starts with a high value and drops drastically in the first 10 days, and finally converges to a stable value on day 30. We then plot in Figure 6.6 the steady-state FP, FN, and the cost. We observe that the weighted average model shows significant improvement in the FP and FN rates and cost compared to the simple average model. The decision model has a higher FP rate and a lower FN rate compared to the other two models. However, its cost is the lowest among the three. This is because the decision model trades some FP with FN to reduce the overall cost of false decisions.

6.5.3.3   Cost and the Number of Acquaintances

In this experiment we study the relation between average cost due to false decisions and the number of acquaintances that the IDS consults. We fix the expertise level of all IDSs in the network to $0.3, 0.5, 0.7, 0.8$, respectively, for different batch runs. Every IDS decision threshold is fixed at $\tau_p = 0.5$ in all cases. We observe in Figure 6.7 that, under all cases, the average cost decreases when more acquaintances are consulted. We also notice that for higher expertise acquaintances, fewer consultations are needed to reach the cost goal. For instance, in our experiments, the IDS only needs to consult 2 acquaintances, on average, to reach a cost of 0.1, under the case where all acquaintances are with high expertise level 0.8. Correspondingly, the number of acquaintances needed are 4 and 15, on average, when the acquaintance expertise levels are 0.7 and 0.5, respectively. In the case that all acquaintances are

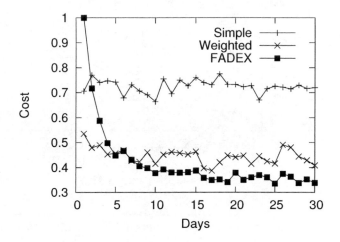

Figure 6.5: Average costs for three different aggregation models.

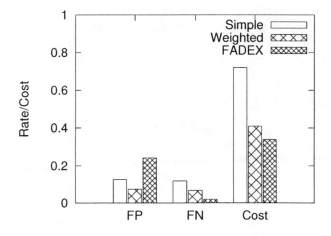

Figure 6.6: Comparison of three aggregation models.

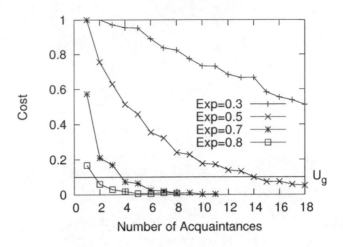

Figure 6.7: Average cost versus number of acquaintances consulted (U_g is the cost goal).

0.3 (i.e., of low expertise), the utility goal cannot be reached after consulting a small number (i.e., < 20) of acquaintances.

In the next experiment, the expertise levels of all nodes remain at 0.5 and their decision thresholds vary from 0.1 to 0.9. We set $C_{10} = C_{01} = 1$ in the first batch run and increase C_{01} by 1 in every subsequent batch run. We observe the costs under three different models. Figure 6.8 shows that the costs of the simple average model and the weighted average model increase linearly with C_{01}, while the cost of the hypothesis testing model grows the slowest among the three. This is because the hypothesis testing model has a flexible threshold to optimize its cost. The hypothesis testing model has superiority when the cost difference between FP and FN is large.

6.5.4 *Sequential Consultation*

In this experiment we study the number of acquaintances needed for consultation to reach a predefined goal. Suppose the TP lower-bound $\bar{P}_D = 0.95$ and FP upper-bound $\bar{P}_F = 0.1$. We observe the change of FP rate and TP rate with the number of acquaintances consulted (n). Figure 6.9 shows that the FP rate decreases and the TP rate increases with n. Consulting higher expertise nodes leads to a higher TP rate and a lower FP rate. In the next experiment we implement Algorithm 1 on each node and measure the average number of acquaintances needed to reach the predefined TP lower-bound and the FP upper-bound. Figure 6.10 compares the simulation results with the theoretical results (see Equation (6.29)), where the former confirms the latter. In both cases, the number of consultations decreases quickly with the expertise levels of acquaintances. For example, the IDS needs to consult around 50 acquaintances of expertise 0.2, while only 3 acquaintances of expertise 0.7 are needed for

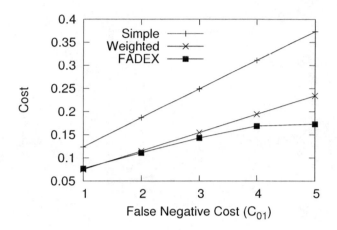

Figure 6.8: Cost versus C_{01} for the three models.

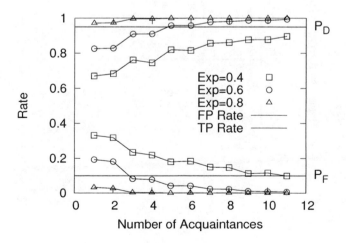

Figure 6.9: FP, TP versus number of acquaintances.

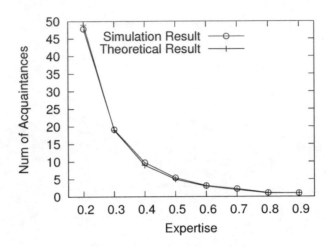

Figure 6.10: Number of acquaintances versus expertise.

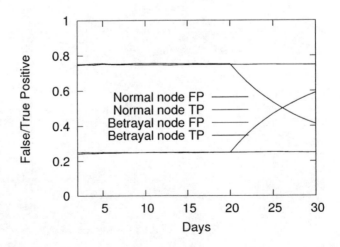

Figure 6.11: False positive and true positive of single IDS under betrayal attack.

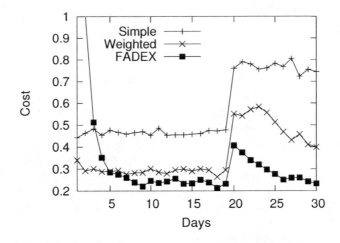

Figure 6.12: False decision cost under betrayal attack.

the same purpose. This is partly because low expertise nodes are more likely to make conflicting feedbacks and consequently increase the number of consultations. The analytical results can be useful for IDSs to design the size of their acquaintance lists.

6.5.5   Robustness and Scalability of the System

Robustness and scalability are two important features of an IDN. The collaborative decision model presented in this chapter is robust to malicious insiders because it has an inherent robust trust management model from [74] where malicious insiders can be quickly discovered and removed from the acquaintance list. To verify this, we simulate the scenario of a betrayal attack under a homogeneous environment. We fix all 10 IDSs with $l = 0.5$ and $\tau_p = 0.5$. We let one IDS turn malicious at day 20 and start to give opposite diagnosis. We observe the FP and TP rate of a malicious node and its impact on the decision of other nodes. From Figure 6.11 we can see that the FP rate and TP rate of the malicious node raise/drop quickly after day 20. Figure 6.12 shows that the cost of false decision of other normal nodes rises quickly at day 20 and drop back to normal after a few days. Compared with the other two aggregation models, the model receives the least impact from the malicious node.

This IDN is scalable because the number of acquaintances needed for consultation only depends on the expertise level of those acquaintances rather than the size of the network. Hence, the message rate from/to each IDS does not grow with the number of nodes in the network. Furthermore, the dynamic consultation algorithm reduces the number of consultation messages needed for collaborative intrusion detections.

6.6 Conclusion

In this chapter we presented a trustworthy and efficient collaborative decision model. We obtained optimal decision rules that minimize Bayes risks using hypothesis testing methods, and provided a data-driven mechanism for real-time efficient, distributed and sequential feedback aggregations. In this model, an IDS consults sequentially for peer diagnoses until it is capable of making an aggregated decision that meets Bayes optimality. The decision is made based on a threshold rule leveraging the likelihood ratio approximated by Beta distribution and thresholds by target rates. Our simulation results have shown that the decision model is superior to other models in the literature in terms of cost efficiency. Our simulation results have also corroborated our theoretical results on the average number of acquaintances needed to reach the predefined false positive upper-bound and true positive lower-bound. As future work, we want to investigate large-scale collaborative networks and their topological impact. Another possible research direction is to integrate our model with communication networks, and design defense mechanisms against different cyber attacks such as denial-of-service, man-in-the-middle, and insider attacks. Finally, our results can be extended to deal with the case of correlated feedbacks.

Chapter 7

Resource Management

CONTENTS

7.1 Introduction

As discussed in the previous chapters, collaborative intrusion detection networks can improve the intrusion detection accuracy of participating IDSs. However, malicious insiders in an IDN may compromise the system by providing false information/feedback or overloading the system with spam. Also, "free-riders" [88] can exploit the system by benefiting from others without contributing themselves. This can discourage IDN participants and eventually degrade the overall performance of the collaboration system. To solve the problems of malicious insiders and free-riders, trust management is necessary to distinguish dishonest or malicious insiders, and an incentive-compatible resource allocation mechanism can help participating IDSs contribute helping resources to collaborators in a fair manner (i.e., more active contributors should receive more helping resources). The resource allocation mechanism itself should be robust against various insider attacks.

In this chapter we present a resource allocation mechanism, based on reciprocal incentive design and trust management, where the amount of resources that each IDS allocates to assist its neighbors is proportional to the trustworthiness and the amount of resources allocated by its neighbors to help this IDS. The motivation for reciprocal incentive design is to encourage participants to contribute more in collaboration so as to keep their IDS knowledge up-to-date. This exchange of knowledge is particularly important in order for IDSs to protect the system from new or zero-day attacks. We formulate an N-person (or peer) noncooperative continuous-kernel game model to investigate incentive compatibility of the IDS collaboration system. In our design, each IDS finds an optimal resource allocation to maximize the aggregated satisfaction levels of its neighbors. We show that under certain controllable system conditions, there exists a unique Nash equilibrium. Our experimental results demonstrate that an iterative algorithm that we introduce converges geometrically to the Nash equilibrium, and that the amount of helping resources an IDS receives is proportional to its helpfulness to others. We also demonstrate security features of the system against free-riders, dishonest insiders, and DoS attacks.

The highlight of this chapter can be summarized as follows: (1) A mechanism for optimal resource allocation for each peer to maximize its social welfare with a convex utility function; (2) an N-person noncooperative game model and an iterative primal/dual algorithm to reach the Nash equilibrium; and (3) incentive compatibility and robustness that is derived from the resource allocation scheme to tackle the "free-riders," dishonest insiders, and DoS attacks.

The rest of the chapter is organized as follows: Section 7.2 presents a brief overview of related work of resource allocation and game theory from different areas. In Section 7.3, we describe our incentive-based resource allocation scheme for resource management in the IDN. In Section 7.4 we devise a primal/dual algorithm to compute the Nash equilibrium, and in Section 7.5 we evaluate the convergence and incentives of the resource allocation design. Finally, Section 7.6 concludes the chapter. A list of symbols and notations, as well as their information patterns, is given in Table 7.1 for readers' convenience.

7.2 Background

Many IDS collaboration systems have been proposed in the literature, such as [146], [149], and [157]. They all assume that IDSs cooperate honestly and unselfishly. The lack of a trust infrastructure leaves the systems vulnerable to malicious peers.

A few trust-based collaboration systems (e.g., [72] and [124]) and distributed trust management models (e.g., [59], [72], and [74]) have been proposed for effective IDS collaboration. However, none of these proposed models studied incentives for IDS collaboration. Our previous work proposed a trust management system where IDSs exchange test messages to build trust among themselves. The feedback from collaborators is evaluated and a numerical trust value is assigned to reflect the level of truthfulness of collaborators. [72] uses a simple weighted average model to predict the trust value while [74] uses a Bayesian statistics model to estimate the trust value as well as the confidence level of the trust estimation.

A variety of game-theoretic approaches have been applied to network resource allocation in traditional routing networks and peer-to-peer (P2P) networks. In traditional routing networks, noncooperative game models such as in [81] and [91] have been used in a dynamic resource allocation context; authors of these reference works have considered a network with a general topology where each source has a window-based end-to-end flow control. The available information for a user is the number of packets within the network not yet acknowledged. Each user aims to maximize his own throughput, with bounded delay, and hence faces a constrained optimization problem. The equilibrium obtained is decentralized because each user has only local information on his own unacknowledged packets. The focus has been on the maximal network performance with a given resource instead of incentive mechanisms. In peer-to-peer networks, Ma et al. [99] have used a game-theoretical approach to achieve differentiated services allocation based on the peer's contribution to the community. Yan et al. [148] have proposed an optimal resource allocation scheme for file providers. A max-min optimization problem has been constructed to find the optimal solution that achieves fairness in the resource allocation. Both works rely on an independent central reputation system. Reciprocity has not been incorporated. Also, the resilience and robustness of the system have not been their focus. Grothoff [79] has proposed a resource allocation economic model to deal with malicious nodes in peer-to-peer networks. It depends solely on the trust values of the peer nodes, and the resource allocation is priority based on the trust value of the request sender. Grothoff's model can effectively prevent malicious nodes from overusing the network resource because their requests will be dropped due to their low trust. It is also reciprocal-altruistic. However, this model may result in unfairness because nodes with the highest trust may take the entire resource. Our model differs from the above ones in that we have made use of the pair-wise nature of the network for designing scalable network algorithms, ensuring secure and resilient properties of the solution, and providing fairness and reciprocal incentive compatibility in resource allocation.

Recently, game-theoretical methods have been used for intrusion detection where in a two-player context, the attacker (intruder) is one player and the intrusion detection system (IDS) is the other player. In [158], and [161], noncooperative game frameworks have been used to address different aspects of intrusion detection. In [147], Liu et al. use a Bayesian game approach for intrusion detection in ad-hoc networks; a two-person non-zero-sum incomplete information game is formulated to provide a framework for an IDS to minimize its loss based on its own belief. Our previous work [163] provides a game-theoretical model for IDSs to allocate collaboration resources to achieve the goal of fairness and incentive compatibility. This

Table 7.1: Summary of Notations

Symbol	Meaning	Information Private to
T_v^u	Trust value of v perceived by u	u
p_{uv}	Frequency of help response from u to v	u, v
r_{vu}	Desired reply rate request of v to u	u, v
m_{vu}	Minimum reply rate request of v to u	u, v
C_u	Resource capacity of u	u
$S_{u,v}$	Satisfaction level of node u in response to v	u, v

chapter extends our previous work by integrating a complete IDN framework and a robustness evaluation.

7.3 Resource Management and Incentive Design

In this section we first mathematically model resource allocation in an IDN environment as individual optimization problems for its member peers. A game problem (GP) can then be introduced for each peer. We employ a Lagrangian approach to find the Nash equilibrium of the constrained game. Finally, we show that there exists a unique Nash equilibrium in the game and characterize the equilibrium solution in closed form.

7.3.1 Modeling of Resource Allocation

We consider a collaborative intrusion detection network (IDN) with N peers or nodes where all the nodes adopt the same resource allocation scheme. Each IDS user can distribute information to other IDS users in the form of messages (in bytes). We denote the set of nodes by $\mathcal{N} = \{1, 2, \cdots, N\}$. The set of neighbor nodes of peer u is denoted by $\mathcal{N}_u$. The communications between IDSs become constrained when the network size is large and the number of collaborators $|\mathcal{N}_u|$ grows. Note that information in the network is symmetric. If u is a neighbor of v, then v is also a neighbor of u. We can represent the topology of an IDN by a graph $\mathcal{G} := (\mathcal{N}, \mathcal{E})$, where $\mathcal{E}$ is the set of (u, v) pairs in the network. We use r_{vu} to denote the units of resource that node u should allocate in order to serve v with full satisfaction. The minimum acceptable resource from u to v is m_{vu}. Note that r_{vu}, m_{vu} are chosen by node v and informed to node u during negotiation. Let $p_{uv} \in \mathbb{R}_+$ be the resource that u allocates to v, for every $u, v \in \mathcal{N}$. The parameter p_{uv} is a decision variable of peer u and is private information between peer u and peer v. To satisfy neighbor v, node u should allocate resources to v over the interval $[m_{vu}, r_{vu}]$.

In this model we assume that each node has its own mechanism to evaluate the trust of its neighbors, and the trust values have already been determined. The trust evaluation mechanism has been discussed in Chapter 5. Let $T_v^u \in [0, 1]$ be the trust value of peer v assessed by peer u, representing how much peer u trusts peer v. The allocated resource p_{uv} from peer u to v is closely related to the trust value T_v^u perceived by u.

Each peer maximizes its effort to help its neighbor nodes under its capacity constraint C_u, which is dependent on its own resource capacity such as bandwidth, CPU, memory, etc. Then, resource allocation should satisfy the following capacity constraint:

$$\sum_{v \in \mathcal{N}_u} p_{uv} \leq C_u, \text{ for all } u \in \mathcal{N}. \tag{7.1}$$

Our system introduces a utility function for each peer to model the satisfaction level of its neighbors. The utility function S_{uv} is given by

$$S_{uv} = \frac{\ln\left(\alpha \frac{p_{uv} - m_{vu}}{r_{vu} - m_{vu}} + 1\right)}{\ln(\alpha + 1)}, \tag{7.2}$$

where $\alpha \in (0, \infty)$ is a system parameter that controls the satisfaction curve, and the term $\ln(\alpha + 1)$ in the denominator is the normalization factor. The function S_{uv} is a concave function on its domain under the condition $\alpha > 1$. The choice of logarithmic functions is motivated by the proportional fairness properties as in [106, 129] and has been used in the literature on power control, congestion control, and rate control in communication networks [129, 160, 164].

Let $U_u : \mathbb{R}_+^{L(u)} \to \mathbb{R}_+$ be the peer u's aggregated altruistic utility, where $L(u) = \text{card}(\mathcal{N}_u)$, the cardinality of the set $\mathcal{N}_u$. Let the payoff function, U_u, for u be given by

$$U_u = \sum_{v \in \mathcal{N}_u} w_{uv} S_{uv}, \quad w_{uv} = T_v^u p_{vu}, \tag{7.3}$$

where w_{uv} is the weight on peer v's satisfaction level S_{uv}, which is the product of peer v's trust value and the amount of helping resources allocated to u. A higher weight is applied on peer v's satisfaction level S_{uv} if peer v is better trusted and more generous to provide help to u. In this system, each peer $u \in \mathcal{N}$ in the IDN intends to maximize U_u within its resource capacity. A general optimization problem (OP) can then be formulated as follows:

$$\max_{\{p_{uv}, v \in \mathcal{N}_u\}} \quad \sum_{v \in \mathcal{N}_u} w_{uv} S_{uv} \tag{7.4}$$
$$\text{s.t.} \quad \sum_{v \in \mathcal{N}_u} p_{uv} \leq C_u$$
$$m_{vu} \leq p_{uv} \leq r_{vu}, \forall v \in \mathcal{N}_u,$$

where S_{uv} and w_{uv} are given by Equations (7.2) and (7.3), respectively. The upper and lower bounds on resources are imposed by the collaborators. The design of the utility function in OP is built upon the intuition behind how people form collaborations in social networks. With the freedom to choose and design collaborative schemes, we assume that all legitimate agents in the network start with an intent to form collaborations with each other.

Every peer in the network is faced with an optimization problem (OP) to solve. (OP) is a concave problem in which the objective function is a concave function in p_{uv} and the constraint set is an $L(u)$-dimensional simplex, where $L(u) = \text{card}(\mathcal{N}_u)$, the cardinality of the set $\mathcal{N}_u$. Under the assumptions that the size of the network is large and peers can only communicate locally within a distance d, we have N individual optimization problems in the form of (OP) for each node. Hence, we can introduce a corresponding game (GP) by the triplet $\langle \mathcal{N}, A_u, U_u \rangle$, where $\mathcal{N}$ is the set of players or peers, $A_u, u \in \mathcal{N}$, is the action set of each peer, and U_u is the payoff function of peer u, defined in Equation (7.3). An action of a peer here is a decision on the resource allocated to a neighbor peer. The action set of each peer A_u is given by $A_u = A_u^1 \cap A_u^2$, where $A_u^1 = \{ \mathbf{p}_u \in \mathbb{R}_+^{L(u)} \mid \sum_{v \in \mathcal{N}_u} p_{uv} \leq C_u \}$ and $A_u^2 = \{ \mathbf{p}_u \in \mathbb{R}_+^{L(u)} \mid m_{vu} \leq p_{uv} \leq r_{vu}, v \in \mathcal{N}_u \}$. It is not difficult to prove that under the condition $C_u \geq \sum_{v \in \mathcal{N}_u} m_{vu}$, the action set is nonempty.

We note that the decision variable of each peer is a vector $\mathbf{p}_u$ and the action sets of players are not coupled. We thus can use Lagrangian relaxation to penalize the constraints to solve for the Nash equilibrium. Let $\mathscr{L}_u(\mathbf{p}_u, \sigma_u, \mu_u, \lambda_u)$ as follows denote the Lagrangian of peer u's optimization problem:

$$\mathscr{L}_u = \sum_{v \in \mathcal{N}_u} T_v^u p_{vu} S_{uv} - \sum_{v \in \mathcal{N}_u} \mu_{uv}(p_{uv} - r_{vu})$$

$$+ \sum_{v \in \mathcal{N}_u} \sigma_{uv}(p_{uv} - m_{vu}) - \lambda_u \left(\sum_{v \in \mathcal{N}_u} p_{uv} - C_u \right), \qquad (7.5)$$

where $\mu_{uv}, \sigma_{uv}, \lambda_u \in \mathbb{R}_+$ are the Lagrange multipliers. Using Lagrangian relaxation, we can transform the game problem to its relaxed counterpart (RGP), where the abbreviation "R" is short for "Relaxed." The triplet of RGP is given by $\langle \mathcal{N}, \bar{A}_u, \mathscr{L}_u \rangle$, where $\bar{A}_u$ is the action set described by the base constraint $p_{uv} \geq 0$, that is, $\bar{A}_u = \{ \mathbf{p}_u \mid p_{uv} \geq 0, v \in \mathcal{N}_u \}$; and the payoff function is replaced by the relaxed Lagrangian function $\mathscr{L}_u$. [1]

By formulating the collaborative problem as a game, we use a noncooperative approach to model altruistic behavior among peers. The noncooperativeness is appropriate here because there is no centralized control agent in the network, and communications between peers are local and symmetric. The aggregated utility comes from peers' general intention to help other peers. We assume that peers intend to be altruistic when they are introduced into the network. Free-riding peers are penalized via the weighting of the aggregation function. When one peer appears to refuse to help other peers, the other peers will correspondingly decline to assist in return, and as a result free-riding is avoided.

The framework described in this subsection can be potentially applied to a wide

---

[1] In the definition of the relaxed game (RGP), we have chosen to relax simultaneously the two sets of constraints: capacity constraint and range constraints. Instead, we could have relaxed only the capacity constraint. In that case, the action set $\bar{A}_u$ in the relaxed game would include a range constraint, that is, $\bar{A}_u = \{ \mathbf{p}_u \mid m_{vu} \leq p_{uv} \leq r_{vu}, v \in \mathcal{N}_u \}$.

range of collaborative networks where reciprocal altruism is desirable. However, many distinct features of IDS networks have been incorporated into the design. First, an attacker can compromise nodes in the network and then start to spread malware to degrade the level of protection provided by the collaborative network. The special structure of the utility function together with the trust values have been used in the model to mitigate malicious and dishonest behaviors of compromised nodes. Second, insider threats in IDS networks have been considered by imposing upper and lower bounds on p_{uv}, which can be used to prevent denial-of-service attacks from the insiders.

Remark 7.3.1 *The choice of using the term* collaborative networks *is to distinguish this approach from its cooperative counterpart. Cooperative networks often refer to a network of nodes that are able to act as a team and then split the team utility among the members. This will require global communications, coordination, and bargaining. This appears to be unrealistic for IDN systems. In collaborative networks, nodes behave strategically, not because they are selfish agents but because they are unable to coordinate or act as a team. Our work is essentially different from noncooperative network formation problems, where all agents act selfishly to achieve their individual goals, which can be misaligned with each other. In our IDN design, the players have their goals aligned in a certain way to achieve efficient exchange of knowledge with each other. This is similar to classical strategic games such as Battle of the Sexes and the Bach and Stravinsky game [125]. However, the goals become less aligned when agents have low trust values. This flexibility in the model essentially attributes to the reciprocal altruism.*

7.3.2 Characterization of Nash Equilibrium

In this subsection we solve the GP for its Nash equilibrium. Each peer u has a concave optimization problem as in Equation (7.4). Applying the first-order KKT condition as in [40] and [42] to each peer's concave problem in OP, $\frac{\partial \mathcal{L}_u}{\partial p_{uv}} = 0, \forall v \in \mathcal{N}_u, u \in \mathcal{N}$, we find

$$\frac{\delta_{uv} T_v^u p_{vu}}{1 + \alpha'_{uv} p_{uv} - \alpha'_{uv} m_{vu}} = \xi_{uv}, \forall v \in \mathcal{N}_u, u \in \mathcal{N}, \tag{7.6}$$

where $\delta_{uv} = \frac{\alpha'_{uv}}{\ln(1+\alpha)}$; $\xi_{uv} = -\sigma_{uv} + \mu_{uv} + \lambda_u$, and $\alpha'_{uv} = \frac{\alpha}{r_{vu} - m_{vu}}$. In addition, from the feasibility condition, it is required that an optimal solution satisfies the base constraints in $\bar{A}_u$ and the complimentary slackness conditions for every $u \in \mathcal{N}$:

$$\lambda_u \left(\sum_{v \in \mathcal{N}_u} p_{uv} - C_u \right) = 0. \tag{7.7}$$

$$\sigma_{uv}(p_{uv} - m_{vu}) = 0, \forall v \in \mathcal{N}_u, \tag{7.8}$$

$$\mu_{uv}(p_{uv} - r_{vu}) = 0, \forall v \in \mathcal{N}_u. \tag{7.9}$$

The variable ξ_{uv} is composed of three Lagrange multipliers. If $\xi_{uv} \neq 0$, we can further simplify the first-order condition to

$$p_{uv} - \frac{T_v^u p_{vu}}{\xi_{uv} \ln(1+\alpha)} = \left(1 + \frac{1}{\alpha}\right) m_{vu} - \frac{1}{\alpha} r_{vu}. \tag{7.10}$$

Definition 7.3.2 *(Başar and Olsder, [37]) A Nash equilibrium $p_{uv}^*, u, v \in \mathcal{N}$ for the game (GP) is a point that satisfies $\mathcal{L}_u(\mathbf{p}_u^*, \mathbf{p}_{-u}^*) \geq \mathcal{L}_u(\mathbf{p}_u, \mathbf{p}_{-u}^*)$, $\forall \mathbf{p}_u \in A_u, u \in \mathcal{N}$, and $p_{uv} = p_{vu} = 0$, for $v \in \mathcal{N}_u \setminus \mathcal{N}_u$ and $u \in \mathcal{N}$, where the vector $\mathbf{p}_{-u} = \{\mathbf{p}_i : i \neq u, i \in \mathcal{N}\}$ is comprised of decision vectors of other peers.*

Proposition 7.3.3 *The game (GP) admits a Nash equilibrium in pure strategies.*

Proof 7.1 The action set A_u is a closed and bounded simplex and U_u is continuous in p_{uv} for all $u \in \mathcal{N}, v \in \mathcal{N}_u$ and concave in $\mathbf{p}_u$. By Theorem 4.4 in [37], there exists a Nash equilibrium to (GP).

With the existence of a Nash equilibrium at hand, we can further investigate the solutions to the relaxed game by looking at a pair of nodes u and v. Node u has its decision vector $\mathbf{p}_u$ satisfying Equation (7.10) and similarly, node v has its decision vector $\mathbf{p}_v$ satisfying Equation (7.10) by interchanging indices u and v. Hence, we obtain a pair of equations involving p_{uv} and p_{vu} and they are described by

$$\begin{bmatrix} 1 & \frac{-T_v^u}{\xi_{uv}(\ln(1+\alpha))} \\ \frac{-T_u^v}{\xi_{vu}(\ln(1+\alpha))} & 1 \end{bmatrix} \begin{bmatrix} p_{uv} \\ p_{vu} \end{bmatrix} = \begin{bmatrix} \left(1 + \frac{1}{\alpha}\right) m_{vu} - \frac{r_{vu}}{\alpha} \\ \left(1 + \frac{1}{\alpha}\right) m_{uv} - \frac{r_{uv}}{\alpha} \end{bmatrix},$$

or in the matrix form, $\mathbf{M}_{uv}\mathbf{q}_{uv} = \mathbf{b}_{uv}$, where $\mathbf{q}_{uv} = [p_{uv}, p_{vu}]^T$, and $\mathbf{b}_{uv}$ is the right-hand side vector and $\mathbf{M}_{uv}$ is the incident matrix.

Definition 7.3.4 *(M-matrix, [39]) An N by N real matrix $\mathbf{A} = [A_{ij}]$ is called an M-matrix if it is of the form $\mathbf{A} = \theta\mathbf{I} - \mathbf{P}$, where $\mathbf{P}$ is entrywise nonnegative and θ is larger than the spectral radius of $\mathbf{P}$, that is, $\theta > \rho(\mathbf{P})$. An M-matrix A has two key features:*

(F1) the sign patterns $a_{ii} > 0$, $i = 1, ..., N$, and $a_{ij} \leq 0$, $i \neq j$,

(F2) the eigenvalues of $\mathbf{A}$ have all positive real parts.

Theorem 7.3.5 *(Berman and Plemmons, [39]) If $\mathbf{A}$ is an M-matrix, then $\mathbf{A}^{-1} > 0$, that is, all of its entries are positive.*

Using Theorem 7.3.5, we next state a result on the uniqueness of a Nash equilibrium for a sufficiently large system parameter α.

Theorem 7.3.6 *Suppose that only capacity constraints are active and $\alpha > \max_{u,v}\{e^{\frac{T_v^u}{\xi_{uv}}}, \frac{r_{vu}}{m_{vu}}\} - 1$. Then, the game admits a unique Nash equilibrium. For each pair of peers u and v, the equilibrium is given by $\mathbf{q}_{uv}^* = \mathbf{M}_{uv}^{-1}\mathbf{b}_{uv}, \forall u, v \in \mathcal{N}$.*

Proof 7.2 Under the condition that the capacity constraints are active, $\xi_{uv} = k_v \lambda_u > 0$, because the objective function is an increasing function. First, we show that provided that $\alpha > e^{\frac{T_v^u}{\xi_{uv}}} - 1$, we have the inequality $1 > \frac{T_v^u}{\xi_{uv} \ln(1+\alpha)}$. For each pair of nodes u and v, matrix $\mathbf{M}_{uv}$ is an M−matrix in Equation (7.10); hence, $\mathbf{M}_{uv}$ are strictly diagonally dominant and thus nonsingular; and by Theorem 7.3.5, the entries of the inverse matrix $\mathbf{M}_{uv}^{-1}$ are strictly positive.

Second, provided that $\alpha > \frac{r_{uv}}{m_{vu}} - 1$, the vector $\mathbf{b}_{uv}$ is positive, that is, $\left(1 + \frac{1}{\alpha}\right) m_{vu} > \frac{1}{\alpha} r_{uv}$. Thus, we arrive at a unique solution $\mathbf{q}_{uv}^*$, whose entries are all positive, residing in the base constraint action set $\bar{A}_u$ for all u. Because Equation (7.10) holds for any interactive pair, the game admits a unique Nash equilibrium under conditions in Theorem 7.3.6.

Note that Theorem 7.3.6 provides a condition to choose the system parameter α. Because the system can determine the value of α, the condition can be met easily.

Remark 7.3.7 *Under general conditions, to have $\xi_{uv} > 0$ requires multipliers μ_{uv}, λ_u, σ_{uv} to satisfy $\mu_{uv} + \lambda_u k_v > \sigma_{uv}$. Because the payoff function U_u is increasing in p_{uv}, $\lambda_u > 0$ and only μ_{uv} and σ_{uv} can be zero. To ensure $\xi_{uv} > 0$, we can separate into three cases for general discussion: (1) when $\sigma_{uv} = 0$, $\mu_{uv} \neq 0$, we require $\mu_{uv} + \lambda_u k_v > 0$; (2) when $\sigma_{uv} = 0$, $\mu_{uv} = 0$, we require $\lambda_u k_v > 0$; (3) when $\sigma_{uv} \neq 0$, $\mu_{uv} = 0$, we require $\lambda_u k_v > \sigma_{uv}$. With an assumption as in Theorem 7.3.6 that only capacity constraint is active, it simply leads to $\xi_{uv} > 0$ itself.*

7.3.3 Incentive Properties

We call a network design reciprocal incentive compatible when at the steady state, the helping resource p_{uv} from peer u to v increases as the helping resource p_{vu} from peer v to u also increases. In addition, it is also desirable to have p_{uv} be proportional to the trust value of v, that is, the more peer u trusts peer v, the more help u is willing to give. We can further study these properties of the solution obtained in Theorem 7.3.6.

Proposition 7.3.8 *Under the conditions of Theorem 7.3.6, the Nash equilibrium solution of the game (GP) is reciprocal incentive compatible, that is,*

1. *The helping resource p_{uv} from u to v increases with helping resource p_{vu} from v to u;*

2. *When the system parameter α increases, the marginal helping resource from u to v decreases for all u and v;*

3. *When peer u trusts v more, that is, T_v^u increases, the marginal helping resource from u to v increases.*

Proof 7.3   Using Equation (7.6), we take the derivative with respect to p_{vu} and let $\partial p_{uv}/\partial p_{vu}$ denote the marginal helping rate from u to v.

Because $T_v^u > 0$, $\xi_{uv} > 0$, under the conditions in Theorem 7.3.6, we have $\partial p_{uv}/\partial p_{vu} > 0$, and thus p_{uv} is increasing with p_{vu} at the Nash equilibrium. The incentive compatibility results follow.

In the following, we study the incentives of nodes that decide on the lower and upper bounds on desired reply rates. We assume that the lower bound on reply rates are uniformly determined by the system once they join the network, that is, $m_{vu} = \bar{m}$ for all $v \in \mathcal{N}, u \in \mathcal{N}_v$.

Lemma 7.3.9 *Nodes do not have incentives to overstate their upper bound on the reply rate $r_{vu}, v \in \mathcal{N}, u \in \mathcal{N}_v$.*

Proof 7.4   From Equation (7.6) we can observe that $\frac{\partial p_{uv}}{\partial r_{vu}} = -1/\alpha < 0$. Hence, a higher level of request results in a lower value of p_{uv}.

Lemma 7.3.9 admits an intuitive interpretation. When a request level is high, it becomes harder for a node to satisfy it and the node will allocate resources to satisfy other ones with lower request levels first. Hence, a higher level of request will result in lower reply rates.

In the following we study the effect of understating the upper bound. We first introduce the notion of ε-resilience and then derive a condition for achieving it.

Definition 7.3.10 *The Nash equilibrium p_{uv}^* under truthful r_{vu}^* is ε-resilient if a deviation r_{vu} from r_{vu}^* results in an equilibrium p_{uv} such that $\|p_{uv}^* - p_{uv}\| \le \varepsilon \|r_{vu}^* - r_{vu}\|$ for all pairs of $(u,v) \in \mathcal{E}$.*

Proposition 7.3.11 *Suppose $\bar{m}$ is sufficiently small and only capacity constraints are active. The Nash equilibrium, if it exists, is ε-resilient if $\alpha \ge \frac{1}{\varepsilon} \max_{(u,v) \in \mathcal{E}} \left| \frac{T_v^u p_{vu}}{\sum_{v \in \mathcal{N}_u} p_{vu} T_v^u} - 1 \right|$.*

Proof 7.5   Let r_{vu}^* be the true upper bound, under which the reply rates are $\hat{p}_{uv}^* = \min\{\max\{\bar{m}, p_{uv}^*\}, r_{vu}^*\} \le r_{vu}^*$, where

$$p_{uv}^* = \left(1 + \frac{1}{\alpha}\right)\bar{m} - \frac{1}{\alpha}r_{vu}^* + \frac{T_v^u p_{vu}}{\xi_{uv}^* \ln(1+\alpha)}.$$

For any other $r_{vu} < r_{vu}^*$, the allocated resource is $\hat{p}_{uv} = \min\{\max\{\bar{m}, p_{uv}\}, r_{vu}\} \le r_{uv} < r_{vu}^*$, where

$$p_{uv} = \left(1 + \frac{1}{\alpha}\right)\bar{m} - \frac{1}{\alpha}r_{vu} + \frac{T_v^u p_{vu}}{\xi_{uv} \ln(1+\alpha)}.$$

Suppose that $\bar{m}$ is sufficiently small. Due to the assumption that only capacity constraints are active, we only need to study the case where $p_{uv} \leq r_{vu}$. Then, from Lemma 7.3.9, we obtain $p_{uv} > p_{uv}^*$ because $r_{vu} < r_{vu}^*$, and hence $p_{uv}^* < p_{uv} \leq r_{vu} < r_{vu}^*$. Therefore, $\|\hat{p}_{uv} - \hat{p}_{uv}^*\| = \|p_{uv} - p_{uv}^*\|$ and we have

$$\|p_{uv} - p_{uv}^*\| \leq \left\| -\frac{1}{\alpha}(r_{vu} - r_{vu}^*) + \frac{T_v^u p_{vu}}{\ln(1+\alpha)}\left[\frac{1}{\xi_{uv}} - \frac{1}{\xi_{uv}^*}\right]\right\|.$$

Under the relaxed conditions, we can use the closed form expression of the Lagrangian multiplier (7.16), which is derived later in Section 7.4, to obtain $\frac{1}{\xi_{uv}} - \frac{1}{\xi_{uv}^*} = \frac{1}{\lambda_u} - \frac{1}{\lambda_u^*} = \frac{\ln(1+\alpha)}{\alpha P_T}(r_{vu} - r_{vu}^*)$. Hence, combining with the result above, we arrive at

$$\|p_{uv} - p_{uv}^*\| \leq \frac{1}{\alpha}\left\|\frac{T_v^u p_{vu}}{P_T} - 1\right\| \|r_{vu} - r_{vu}^*\|.$$

Therefore, to ensure ε-resiliency, we need $\frac{\|p_{uv} - p_{uv}^*\|}{\|r_{vu} - r_{vu}^*\|} \leq \frac{1}{\alpha}\left\|\frac{T_v^u p_{vu}}{P_T} - 1\right\| \leq \varepsilon$, which leads to the result.

7.4 Primal / Dual Iterative Algorithm

In this section we introduce a dynamic algorithm to compute the unique Nash equilibrium. Let $p_{uv}(t)$ be the resource from peer u to v at step t. Consider the algorithm

$$\begin{cases} p_{uv}(t+1) = s_{uv} + t_{uv} p_{vu}(t) \\ p_{vu}(t+1) = s_{vu} + t_{vu} p_{uv}(t) \end{cases}, \tag{7.11}$$

where $s_{uv} = \left(1 + \frac{1}{\alpha}\right) m_{vu} - \frac{1}{\alpha} r_{vu}$, $t_{uv} = \frac{T_v^u}{\xi_{uv}(\ln(1+\alpha))}$, and s_{vu}, t_{vu} are defined similarly by interchanging indices u and v, with initial conditions $p_{uv}(0) = \min\left\{\frac{C_u}{\mathcal{N}_u}, r_{uv}\right\}, \forall u, v \in \mathcal{N}$.

Proposition 7.4.1 *Suppose that capacity constraints are active, and r_{vu} and m_{uv} are chosen such that the associated constraints become inactive constraints, that is, $\sigma_{uv} = 0, \mu_{uv} = 0$ in Equations (7.8) and (7.9). Given a Lagrange multiplier $\lambda_u^* \neq 0$ and provided that $\alpha > e^{\frac{T_v^u}{\lambda_u}} - 1$, the algorithm in (7.11) converges to the unique Nash equilibrium in Theorem 7.3.6 at dual optimal λ_u^*.*

The algorithm described in (7.11) depends on the Lagrange multiplier λ_u. We can exploit duality to devise an iterative algorithm for the Lagrange multiplier. Let $D_u(\lambda_u)$ be the dual functional given by $D_u(\lambda_u) = \max_{\mathbf{p}_u} \mathcal{L}_u(\mathbf{p}_u, \lambda_u)$. The dual function $D_u(\lambda_u)$ is a convex function, and a dual optimal λ_u^* solves the dual optimization problem (DOP)[2]

$$\min_{\lambda_u > 0} D_u(\lambda_u). \tag{7.12}$$

Using the solution from Theorem 7.3.6, we can obtain $D_u(\lambda_u)$ as follows:

$$D_u = \lambda_u \left(C_u + \frac{K_R}{\alpha} + \left(1 + \frac{1}{\alpha}\right) K_M \right) + \frac{\overline{P_T} - P_T}{\ln(\alpha + 1)},$$

and its first-order derivative as follows:

$$D'_u = C_u - \frac{\sum_{v \in \mathcal{N}_u} p_{vu} T_v^u}{\lambda_u \ln(1 + \alpha)} + \frac{1}{\alpha} \sum_{v \in \mathcal{N}_u} r_{vu} - \frac{\alpha + 1}{\alpha} \sum_{v \in \mathcal{N}_u} m_{vu},$$

where $P_T = \sum_{v \in \mathcal{N}_u} p_{vu} T_v^u$ is the sum of the weights; $K_M = \sum_{v \in \mathcal{N}_u} m_{vu}$; $K_R = \sum_{v \in \mathcal{N}_u} r_{vu}$. K_M and K_R can be interpreted as the total request weighted by marginal costs; and

$$\overline{P_T} = \sum_{v \in \mathcal{N}_u} p_{vu} T_v^u \ln \left(\frac{\alpha}{\ln(\alpha + 1)} \frac{p_{vu} T_v^u}{\lambda_u (r_{vu} - m_{vu})} \right). \tag{7.13}$$

The gradient of the dual function is dependent on the local capacity of node u and the information sent by the neighbor node v of peer u such as the helping resource p_{vu}, and the maximum (minimum) requested resources r_{vu} (m_{vu}) from v. All the information is available to peer u to calculate the gradient locally at each λ_u.

By taking the second-order derivative of the dual function, we obtain

$$D''_u(\lambda_u) = \frac{\sum_{v \in \mathcal{N}_u} p_{vu} T_v^u}{\lambda_u^2 \ln(1 + \alpha)}. \tag{7.14}$$

The dual function in Equaton (7.12) is not only a convex function but also a strong convex function, whose Hessian is bounded uniformly as in $L_1 \leq \nabla^2 D_u(\lambda_u)$, for some L_1 [42]. In addition, provided that the sum of weights w_{uv} is bounded from above, that is,

$$\sum_{v \in \mathcal{N}_u} p_{vu} T_v^u \leq M, \tag{7.15}$$

for some $M \in \mathbb{R}_{++}$, then $\nabla^2 D_u(\lambda_u) \leq L_2$, for some constant L_2.

Proposition 7.4.2 *Suppose that the sum of weights is bounded as in (7.15). The dual function D_u is strongly convex and its Hessian is bounded from above and below uniformly.*

Proof 7.6   First, λ_u is bounded from above by some constant $\bar{\lambda}_u$ because the dual problem is feasible. Thus, $\varepsilon_1 \leq \lambda_u \leq \bar{\lambda}_u, \varepsilon_1 > 0$. In addition, $\sum_{v \in \mathcal{N}_u} w_{uv} \neq 0$;

---

[2]Peer u's dual function is expressed in terms of λ_u and $\mathbf{p}_{-u}$, and the decision variable for peer u changes from a multidimensional vector $\mathbf{p}_u$ to a scalar variable λ_u. Using the dual function, we can reduce the dimension of the game and turn a constrained game into an unconstrained one.

otherwise, the primal problem is trivial because $w_{uv} = 0$, for all v. Therefore, $\varepsilon_2 \leq \sum_{v \in \mathcal{N}_u} w_{uv} \leq M, \varepsilon_2 > 0$. Hence, the statement is true.

Strong duality ensures a unique optimal solution. The unique dual optimal λ_u^* can be found explicitly by applying the unconstrained optimality condition, that is, $D_u'(\lambda_u) = 0$. As a result, we obtain

$$\lambda_u^* = \frac{P_T}{(C_u - K_M + \frac{1}{\alpha}(K_R - K_M)) \ln(1 + \alpha)}. \tag{7.16}$$

To find the dual optimal, we can also devise a dynamic algorithm that can be used in conjunction with algorithm (7.11). An iterative algorithm based on gradient methods to find λ_u is given by

$$\lambda_u(t + 1) = \lambda_u(t) - \beta_u D_u'(\lambda_u(t)), \forall u \in \mathcal{N}, \tag{7.17}$$

where $\beta_u \in (0, 1)$ is the step size. The gradient algorithm in (7.17) is distributed over the network. Each peer needs to collect openly accessible information from its neighboring peers to evaluate K_M, K_R, and P_T. With the property of strong convexity, we can show in the following the fast convergence of the algorithm to (7.16).

Proposition 7.4.3 *Suppose that $D_u'(\lambda_u)$ is Lipschitz with Lipschitz constant L_3 and $D_u(\lambda_u)$ is strongly convex with $D_u''(\lambda_u) \geq L_1$. The dual algorithm (7.17) converges geometrically to dual optimal λ_u^* in (7.16) with step size $\beta_u < \frac{\min(2, L_1)}{L_3}$.*

Proof 7.7 We can use the technique in [42] to prove the proposition. Using the property of strong convexity and the Lipschitz property, we obtain

$$\begin{aligned}
&\|\lambda_u(t+1) - \lambda_u^*\|^2 \\
&= \|\lambda_u(t) - \lambda_u^*\|^2 - 2\beta_u D_u'(\lambda_u(t))(\lambda_u(t) - \lambda_u^*) \\
&\quad + \beta_u^2 \|D_u'(\lambda_u(t))\|^2 \\
&\leq \|\lambda_u(t) - \lambda_u^*\|^2 - 2\beta_u(D_u(\lambda_u(t)) - D_u(\lambda_u^*)) \\
&\quad + \beta_u^2 L_3 \|\lambda_u(t) - \lambda_u^*\|^2 \\
&\leq \|\lambda_u(t) - \lambda_u^*\|^2 - \beta_u L_1 \|\lambda_u(t) - \lambda_u^*\|^2 \\
&\quad + \beta_u^2 L_3 \|\lambda_u(t) - \lambda_u^*\|^2 \\
&= (1 - \beta_u L_1 + \beta_u^2 L_3) \|\lambda_u(t) - \lambda_u^*\|^2.
\end{aligned}$$

Hence, when $\beta_u < \frac{\min(2, L_1)}{L_3}$, we have a contraction. In addition, $\|\lambda_u(t+1) - \lambda_u^*\|^2 \leq (1 - \beta_u L_1 + \beta_u^2 L_3)^{t+1} \|\lambda_u(0) - \lambda_u^*\|^2$. Hence, the convergence rate is geometric.

Note that the condition of strong convexity can be easily satisfied from Equation (7.14) if we eliminate trivial cases that all trust values of neighbors or p_{vu} are zeros.

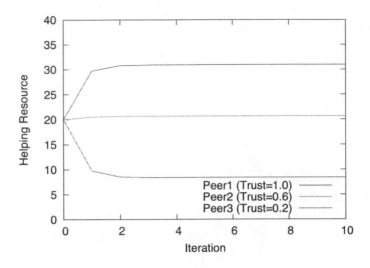

Figure 7.1: Helping resources versus time—first approach.

7.5 Experiments and Evaluation

In this section we perform numerical experiments and evaluate the trust and resource management capabilities of the resource allocation system as described in Sections 7.3 and 7.4. We follow two different approaches to evaluate the Nash equilibrium of the collaborative system. In the first experiment, we implement the dynamic algorithm in Section 7.4 to find the Nash equilibrium. We show that the algorithm yields the Nash equilibrium of the game at the steady state and the system is incentive compatible under the equilibrium. In the second experiment, we use a stochastic discrete-event-based simulation to model an IDS network. In the simulation, peers estimate the resources received from the other peers and adjust their allocations of resources to the others accordingly. We are interested in finding the Nash equilibrium and verifying the incentives in the collaborative system at the equilibrium.

7.5.1 Nash Equilibrium Computation

In this section we implement the dynamic algorithm described in Section 7.4 to calculate the Nash equilibrium centrally. We simulate a three-node network with initial trust values $0.2, 0.6, 1.0$, respectively. For ease of demonstration, we assume that the trust between peer nodes is homogeneous. that is, the trust value of node i is the same to all other nodes. We set the minimum demand of resource to 1 unit and the maximum to 20 units for all nodes. Every node has an equal capacity of 20 units and the system parameter $\alpha = 100$. We find that if all peers have the same trust values, then the resource is fairly and evenly distributed among all peers. When the trust values are different, peers with higher trust values receive more resources. Figure 7.1 shows

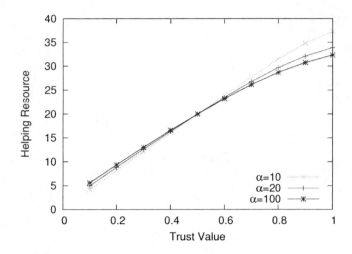

Figure 7.2: Helping resource received varies with trust value—first approach.

that the resources received by three peers with different trust values converge fast within two or three iterations. A peer with a higher trust value receives more help than a peer with a lower trust value.

Fixing the resource capacity of all peers to 20 units and the trust values of two of the nodes to 0.5, we vary the trust value of the third peer from 0.1 to 1.0. In Figure 7.2 we observe that the resource received by the third peer increases with its trust value under different α values. We also see that all curves cross at trust value 0.5 and resource 20 units. This is because all peers should receive an equal amount of resources when they are identically configured, regardless of the α value we choose. By fixing the trust values of all nodes to 1.0 and varying the resource capacity of the third peer from 3 to 30, we observe in Figure 7.3 that the amount of resources a peer receives is roughly linearly proportional to the resources it provides to the others. Similarly, all curves intersect at capacity 20 and resource 20. These results further confirm our theoretical analysis in Section 7.3. Figures 7.2 and 7.3 also reveal that a larger α value leads to a lower marginal helping resource. A smaller α value provides stronger incentive to the participants.

7.5.2 Nash Equilibrium Using Distributed Computation

In this experiment we use a stochastic discrete-event based simulation to model the IDN. Discrete-event simulation is commonly used to aid strategic decision making because it has the capability of emulating complex real-world problems. It concerns the modeling of a system as it evolves over time by representing the changes as separate events. It bridges over our model and a real-life IDS network. In this simulation, each node collaborates with others by sending out requests and waits for their

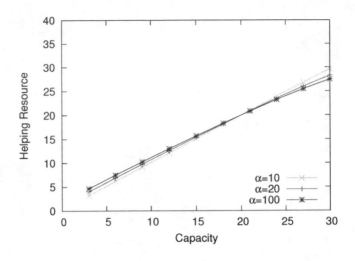

Figure 7.3: Helping resource received varies with resource contribution—first approach.

responses. At the beginning of each day, nodes send resource upper-bound/lower-bound to all their neighbors and wait for the resource quota from them. The resource quota allocation is determined by optimizing Equation (7.4). The consultation requests are generated randomly following a Poisson process with an average arrival rate equal to the resource quota they receive. Upon the arrival of a request at its destination queue, it will be replied by the corresponding peer on a first-come-first-serve basis. Each peer estimates the resource it receives from other peers by calculating the average number of consultation requests answered by each peer. In this experiment, all peers initialize with an unbiased allocation and then apply the resource allocation scheme.

For the purpose of comparing with the numerical experiment, we use the same experiment configuration as in Section 7.5.1, that is, we simulate a network of 3 nodes; we set the minimum resource requirement to 1 request/day and the maximum to 20 requests/day for all peers; each peer has a capacity of 20 requests; we set $\alpha = 100$ and the trust values of nodes to be 0.2, 0.6, and 1.0, respectively.

Figure 7.4 illustrates the received resources for all three nodes with respect to time. We note that the helping resource converges to the Nash equilibrium at steady state, and nodes with higher trust values obtain more resources. This confirms that our resource allocation scheme provides incentives in the collaborative network.

By fixing the resource capacity of all peers to 20, the trust values of two of the peers to 0.5, and varying the trust values of the third peer from 0.1 to 1.0, we obtain in Figure 7.5 that the received resource of the third peer increases with its trust value under different α values. Fixing the resource capacity of the first two peers to 20 requests/day and trust values to 1.0 for all peers, we vary the capacity of the third peer from 3 requests/day to 30 requests/day and observe that the resource received

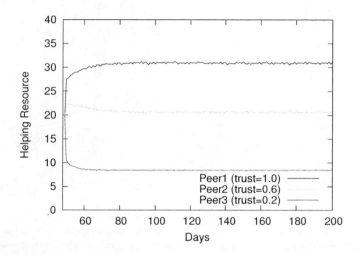

Figure 7.4: Helping resources versus time—second approach.

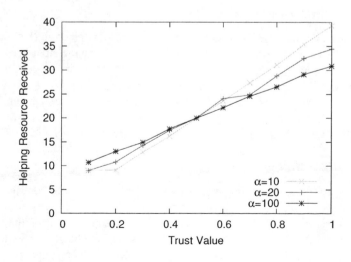

Figure 7.5: Helping resource received varies with trust value—second approach.

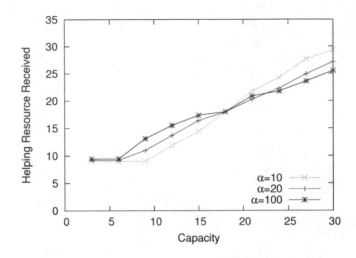

Figure 7.6: Helping resource received varies with resource contribution—second approach.

by the third node also increases with its resource capacity under different α values, as shown in Figure 7.6. The simulation results are consistent with the theoretical results obtained in Section 7.3 and the ones in Section 7.5.1.

7.5.3   Robustness Evaluation

Robustness is a required and important feature for the design of an IDN. In this subsection we discuss a few common insider threats against the incentive-based resource allocation mechanism, and we show how our design is robust to these attacks. Note that all participants in the IDN have to abide by the protocols with a given flexibility in parameter tuning. However, due to the reciprocity of the mechanism, IDSs with selfish or dishonest behaviors will be penalized and eventually removed from the network. This execution process is an integrated part of the IDN.

7.5.3.1   Free-Riding

Free-riders are nodes that enjoy resources from others while not contributing themselves [62, 78]. A free-rider in the IDN may collaborate with a large number of IDSs, aiming at receiving a good amount of accumulated resources $\bar{m}$ from the large number of collaborators. However, our IDN design is not beneficial to free-riders. First, the amount of help that a node receives is proportional to the resources it allocates to others. Second, the larger the number of collaborators a node has, the more demanding it is for the node to maintain the collaboration because each collaborator needs minimum resource $\bar{m}$ to be satisfied. Therefore, a node that does not contribute to the collaboration will end up receiving a bare minimum of helping resources from

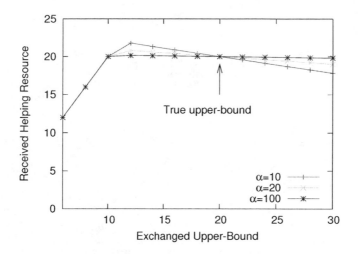

Figure 7.7: Resource received versus exchanged upper-bound.

others. We simulate a scenario where a free-rider with initial trust value 1.0 switches to a free riding mode at day 200 (Figure 7.8). We notice that the amount of helping resources received by the free-rider drops quickly and converges to a low level. This is because the collaborators of the free-rider can notice the drop of contributed resources from the free-rider and adjust their resource allocation according to Equation (7.4). The result corroborates that free-riding is not practical in the IDN with such a resource allocation design.

7.5.3.2 *Denial-of-Service (DoS) Attacks*

DoS attacks happen when malicious nodes send a large amount of information to overload the victim [107]. In our IDN, the amount of information exchanged between participant nodes is negotiated beforehand. A quota is calculated and sent to all nodes. If a node sends more data than the given quota, then it is considered malicious, and hence will be removed from the collaboration network.

7.5.3.3 *Dishonest Insiders*

In the IDN, dishonest nodes can report false information to gain advantages. For example, a dishonest node can misinform about its upper-bound and lower-bound requests for gaining more resources from its collaborators. We imposed a maximum lower-bound $\bar{m}$ for all nodes. In addition, experimental results in Figure 7.7 show that claiming a higher upper-bound than the true value lowers the received resource, while claiming a lower upper-bound may lead to a bounded gain that is controllable by system parameter α. A lower upper-bound will not lead to full satisfaction of the node when resource constraints are inactive.

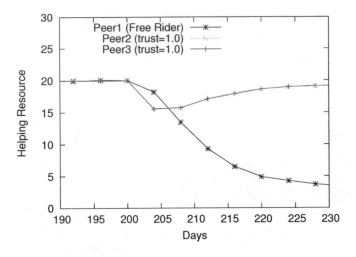

Figure 7.8: Resource received after free-riding attack.

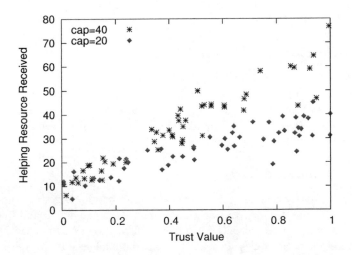

Figure 7.9: Resource received for peers with different trust values.

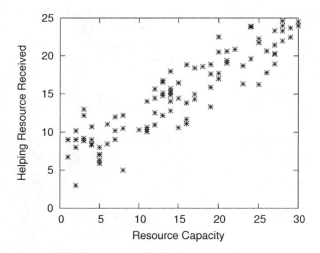

Figure 7.10: Resource received for peers with different resource capacities.

7.5.4 Large-Scale Simulation

Previous experiments were based on a small-scale network. In this subsection we design numerical experiments to study the resource allocation in a large-scale intrusion detection network. We set up a network of 100 nodes, which are randomly scattered in a 100×100 square. Each node shares its resources with the other nodes in the vicinity at a distance of 5. The trust values are generated according to a uniform distribution from 0 to 1.0. The lower-bound and the upper-bound on the requests are 1 and 20, respectively, for each node. We separate nodes into two groups: one group with a capacity of 20 units and the other with 40. In Figure 7.9 we can see that, in both groups, nodes with higher trust values tend to receive more assistance. The response to trust value appears to be more prominent for the group with capacity of 40 units. It can be explained by the fact that when the resource capacity is low, most of the resource is used to satisfy the lower-bound of all the neighbors and little is left to allocate based on incentives. In the second experiment, we fix trust values of all nodes to 1.0 and randomly choose the resource capacity of each node between 0 and 30. Figure 7.10 shows the resource received by nodes with different resource capacities. We note that, on the average, nodes with higher resource capacities receive more resources. This confirms the incentives under a large collaboration group.

7.6 Conclusion

In this chapter we presented incentive-based resource allocation mechanism based on trust management in the context of an IDN. By formulating an associated continuous-kernel noncooperative game, we have shown that a Nash equilibrium exists and is unique under certain system conditions. We have also shown that the unique Nash equilibrium possesses features that allow peers to communicate in a conducive environment in which peers endeavor to contribute knowledge and resources to assist neighbor nodes. Any selfish or free-riding behavior will receive a tit-for-tat response from the neighbors as a consequence. A dynamic algorithm is used to compute the Nash equilibrium. Experimental results showed that the algorithm converges to the Nash equilibrium at a geometric rate, further corroborating the theoretical results. We have also discussed the resistance of our IDN design to common insider attacks, such as free-riding, dishonest insiders, and DoS attacks. As future work, one can study other potential attacks to the IDN system, for example, the collusion attacks.

Chapter 8

Collaborators Selection and Management

CONTENTS

8.1 Introduction

As discussed in the precious chapters, malicious insiders in an IDN may send false information to mislead other IDSs into making incorrect intrusion decisions. This may render the collaboration system ineffective. Furthermore, IDSs in the collaboration network may have different intrusion detection expertise levels and capabilities. An effective trust management model should be capable of distinguishing honest participants from malicious ones, and low-expertise IDSs from high-expertise IDSs. Chapter 5 describes a Bayesian learning model for IDSs to evaluate the trustworthiness of their collaborators. However, a collaboration relationship is a mutual agreement between both participants, and it should only occur when both parties agree to collaborate with each other. As we discussed in Chapter 6, the expected cost of false decisions decreases when receiving feedback from more collaborators. However, it takes more computing resources to maintain a collaboration relationship; for example, sending test messages and responding to consultation requests from other collaborators requires CPU/memory and bandwidth to proceed. The extra cost of recruiting a new collaborator may exceed the benefit from that collaborator. How IDSs select collaborators to achieve optimal cost efficiency is an important problem to solve for an IDN. We define IDN *acquaintance management* as the process of identifying, selecting, and maintaining collaborators for each IDS. An effective acquaintance management model is crucial to the design of an IDN.

In this chapter we focus on the design of an effective acquaintance management mechanism with which IDSs can selectively recruit collaborators that can bring maximal benefit, taking into account both the false decision cost and maintenance cost. Acquaintance management can be divided into three parts: IDS identification, collaborator selection, and collaborator maintenance.

IDS identification is the process of learning the qualification of candidate collaborators based on past experience with them. A Bayesian learning model is used to help each IDS identify the quality and honesty of its candidate acquaintances, specifically the false positive (FP) rate and false negative (FN) rate of each collaborator. Dishonest collaborators can be identified and removed from the acquaintance list. We define *feedback aggregation* in IDNs as the decision-making process resulting in whether or not to raise an alarm based on the collected opinions (feedback) from collaborator IDSs. A Bayesian decision model is used for feedback aggregation, and Bayes theorem is used to estimate the conditional probability of intrusions based on feedback from collaborators. A false decision cost function is modeled to include both the false positive decision cost and the false negative decision cost. A decision as to whether or not to raise an alarm is made in order to achieve the minimum cost of false decisions.

For collaborator selection, an IDS may add all honest IDSs to its collaborator list to achieve maximal detection accuracy. However, including a large list of collaborators may result in a high maintenance cost because collaborating with them requires computer resource (e.g., CPU, memory, and network bandwidth) to process their consultation requests and to respond with consultation feedback. The overall cost includes both the false decision cost and the maintenance cost. We define the

acquaintance selection in IDNs as the process of finding the optimal list of collaborators to minimize the overall cost. Existing approaches for acquaintance management
often set a fixed number of collaborators [150] or a fixed accuracy threshold to filter
out less honest or low-expertise collaborators [69, 74, 152]. These static approaches
lack flexibility, and the fixed acquaintance length or accuracy threshold may not be
optimal when the context changes (e.g., some nodes leave the network and some
new nodes join the network). The acquaintance management mechanism presented
in this chapter can dynamically select collaborators in any context setting to obtain
high efficiency at minimum cost.

For collaborator maintenance, the IDSs in our system periodically update their
collaborator lists to guarantee an optimal cost. A probation list is used to explore
and allow sufficient time to learn the quality of new potential collaborators. New
collaborators stay on the probation list for a certain period (probation period) before
their feedback is considered for intrusion decision.

A simulated collaboration network using a Java-based discrete-event simulation
framework is used to evaluate the effectiveness of the acquaintance management
mechanism. The results show that this dynamic acquaintance management algorithm
outperforms the static approaches of setting a fixed acquaintance length or accuracy
threshold. Finally, this mechanism also achieves several desired properties for IDN,
such as efficiency, stability, robustness, and incentive compatibility.

The highlights of this chapter can be summarized as follows:

1. A dynamic acquaintance selection algorithm that automatically selects collaborators, leading to minimal overall cost, including false decision cost and
   maintenance cost;

2. A dynamic acquaintance management algorithm to integrate the concept of
   probation period and consensus negotiation.

The rest of the chapter is organized as follows. In Section 8.2 we discuss the
background of IDS identification, collaborative decision, and acquaintance management; Section 8.3 describes the formalization of our IDS learning model and feedback aggregation. Acquaintance selection and management algorithms are presented
in Section 8.4. We then present evaluation results demonstrating the effectiveness of
the acquaintance management and its desired properties in Section 8.5. We conclude
this chapter in Section 8.6.

8.2 Background

Various approaches have been proposed to evaluate the qualification of IDSs as input contributors to the feedback aggregation mechanism. However, all of them have
used a single trust value to decide whether an IDS will provide good feedback about
intrusions based on past experience with that IDS. For example, Duma et al. [59]
introduced a trust-aware collaboration engine for correlating intrusion alerts. Their

trust management scheme uses each peer's past experience to predict others' trustworthiness. In Chapter 5 we showed how a Dirichlet distribution can be used to model trust in peer IDSs based on past experience with them. The trust value is expressed using the trust value as well as confidence of estimation. However, these approaches do not reflect conditional detection accuracy such as false positives and false negatives. Conditional detection accuracy is necessary because the impacts of false positive decision and false negative decision may be different. Therefore, a single trust value may not be sufficient as an input to feedback aggregation. In this chapter we show how false positive (FP) and false negative (FN) rates can be determined using a Bayesian learning model and used simultaneously to represent the detection accuracy of an IDS. In this case both the FP and TP are used as inputs to the feedback aggregation process.

In terms of collaborative decision, the methods provided by Duma et al. [59] and Fung et al. [74, 69] are both simplistic and use a heuristic approach. They both use a weighted average approach to aggregate feedback, which does not capture the false decision cost. Another broadly accepted decision model in IDNs is the threshold-based decision method, which is adopted by CloudAV [114]. In this model, when the total number of antiviruses raising alarms exceeds a fixed threshold, an global alarm will be raised. However, this model not only lacks the awareness of false decision cost, but also does not consider the expertise difference of participating antiviruses. In this chapter we model the decision problem into a cost optimization problem and apply the well-established Bayes' theorem for feedback aggregation which achieves the least cost. This chapter focuses on the optimal collaboration decision and optimal acquaintance selection.

In terms of the acquaintance selection methods, most previous approaches set a fixed length on the acquaintance list, such as the model presented in [150]. Some others use a trust threshold to filter out less honest acquaintances [74, 152]. The advantage of the threshold based decision is its simplicity and ease of implementation. However, it is only effective in a static environment where participating nodes do not change, for example, the context that presented in [114]. In a dynamic environment, nodes join and leave the network and the acquaintance list changes over time. Therefore, finding an optimal threshold is a difficult task. Our Bayesian decision model is efficient and flexible. It can be used in both static and dynamic collaboration environments. Equipped with this Bayesian decision model, our acquaintance selection algorithm can find the smallest set of best acquaintances that can maximize the accuracy of intrusion detection. Based on this acquaintance selection algorithm, our acquaintance management method uses a probation list to explore potential candidates for acquaintances and balances the cost of exploration and the speed of updating the acquaintance list.

8.3   IDS Identification and Feedback Aggregation

Before aggregating the feedback from an acquaintance, an IDS should first learn the qualification of all candidate IDSs. In this section, a Bayesian learning model is used

Table 8.1: Summary of Notations

Symbol	Meaning
$X \in \{0,1\}$	Random variable denoting whether or not there is an attack
$Y \in \{0,1\}$	Random variable of positive or negative diagnosis from an IDS
$\mathbf{y}$	A feedback instance vector from acquaintances
$\mathbf{Y}$	Feedback vector from acquaintances
$\mathscr{C}$	Set of acquaintance candidates
$\mathscr{A}$	Set of acquaintances
l	The acquaintance list length
δ	The decision of raising alarm or not
$R(.)$	The risk cost of false alarms and miss intrusions
$M(.)$	The maintenance cost of acquaintances
C_{fp}, C_{fn}	Unit cost of false alarm and miss intrusion
C_a	Unit cost of maintaining each acquaintance
π_0, π_1	Priory probability of no-intrusion and with-intrusion
T_i, F_i	True positive rate and false positive rate of IDS i
λ	Forgetting factor of the past experience

to evaluate the detection accuracy including false positive (FP) rate and true positive (TP) rate of the candidates (IDS identification). A Bayesian decision model is then used to optimally aggregate feedback from acquaintances, which minimizes the cost of false decisions.

8.3.1 Detection Accuracy for a Single IDS

To better capture the qualification of an IDS, we use both *false positive* (FP) and *true positive* (TP) rates to represent the detection accuracy of an IDS. Let $\mathscr{A}$ denote the set of acquaintances and random variables F_k and T_k denote the FP and TP rates of acquaintance $k \in \mathscr{A}$, respectively. FP is the probability that the IDS gives a positive diagnosis (under-attack) under the condition of no-attack, and TP is the probability that the IDS gives a correct positive diagnosis under the condition of under-attack. Let random variable $X \in \{0,1\}$ represent the random event on whether or not there is an attack, and let random variable $Y \in \{0,1\}$ denote whether or not the IDS makes a positive diagnosis. Then FP and TP can be written as $\mathbb{P}[Y = 1 | X = 0]$ and $\mathbb{P}[Y = 1 | X = 1]$, respectively. The list of notations is summarized in Table 8.1.

Let $\mathscr{F}_k$ and $\mathscr{T}_k$ be the probability density functions of F_k and T_k whose support is $[0, 1]$. We use the notation $Z_0 : Y_k = 1 | X = 0$ and $Z_1 : Y_k = 1 | X = 1$ to represent the conditional variables that acquaintance k gives positive decision under the conditions where there is no attack and there is an attack, respectively. They can be seen as two independent random variables satisfying a Bernoulli distribution with successful rates F_k and T_k, respectively. The past experience with acquaintance k can be seen as the samples from the Bernoulli distributions. According to the Bayesian probability theory [76], the posterior distribution of $\mathcal{F}_k$ and $\mathcal{T}_k$ given a set of observed samples can be represented using a Beta function, written as follows:

$$\mathcal{F}_k \sim \text{Beta}(x_k | \alpha_k^0, \beta_k^0) = \frac{\Gamma(\alpha_k^0 + \beta_k^0)}{\Gamma(\alpha_k^0)\Gamma(\beta_i^0)} x_k^{\alpha_k^0 - 1} (1 - x_k)^{\beta_k^0 - 1}, \tag{8.1}$$

$$\mathcal{T}_k \sim \text{Beta}(y_k | \alpha_k^1, \beta_k^1) = \frac{\Gamma(\alpha_k^1 + \beta_k^1)}{\Gamma(\alpha_k^1)\Gamma(\beta_i^1)} y_k^{\alpha_k^1 - 1} (1 - y_k)^{\beta_k^1 - 1}, \tag{8.2}$$

where $\Gamma(\cdot)$ is the gamma function [87], and its parameters α_k^0, α_k^1 and β_k^0, β_k^1 are given by

$$\alpha_k^0 = \sum_{j=1}^{u} \lambda^{t_{k,j}^0} r_{k,j}^0 \qquad \beta_k^0 = \sum_{j=1}^{u} \lambda^{t_{k,j}^0} (1 - r_{k,j}^0);$$

$$\alpha_k^1 = \sum_{j=1}^{v} \lambda^{t_{k,j}^1} r_{k,j}^1 \qquad \beta_k^1 = \sum_{j=1}^{v} \lambda^{t_{k,j}^1} (1 - r_{k,j}^1), \tag{8.3}$$

where $\alpha_k^0, \beta_k^0, \alpha_k^1, \beta_k^1$ are the cumulated instances of false positive, true negative, true positive, and false negative, respectively, from acquaintance k. $r_{k,j}^0 \in \{0,1\}$ is the j-th diagnosis result from acquaintance k under no-attack. $r_{k,j}^0 = 1$ means the diagnosis from k is positive while there is actually no attack happening; $r_{k,j}^0 = 0$ means otherwise. Similarly, $r_{k,j}^1 \in \{0,1\}$ is the j-th diagnosis data from acquaintance k under attack, where $r_{k,0}^1 = 1$ means that the diagnosis from k is positive under attack, and $r_{k,0}^1 = 0$ means otherwise. Parameters $t_{k,j}^0$ and $t_{k,j}^1$ denote the time elapsed since the j-th feedback is received. $\lambda \in [0,1]$ is the forgetting factor on the past experience. A small λ makes old observations quickly forgettable. We use exponential moving average to accumulate past experience so that old experience takes less weight than new experience. u is the total number of no-attack cases among the past records and v is the total number of attack cases.

To make the parametric updates scalable to data storage and memory, we can use the following recursive formula to update α_k^0, α_k^1 and β_k^0, β_k^1:

$$\alpha_k^m(t_j) = \lambda^{(t_{k,j}^m - t_{k,j-1}^m)} \alpha_k^m(t_{k,j-1}^m) + r_{k,j}^m;$$

$$\beta_k^m(t_j) = \lambda^{(t_{k,j}^m - t_{k,j-1}^m)} \beta_k^m(t_{k,j-1}^m) + r_{k,j}^m, \tag{8.4}$$

where $l = 0, 1$ and $j - 1$ indexes the previous data point used for updating α_k^m or β_k^m. Through this way, only the previous state and the current state are required to be recorded, which is efficient in terms of storage compared to when all states are recorded in Equation (8.3).

8.3.2 Feedback Aggregation

When an IDS detects suspicious activities and is not confident about its decision, it sends out the description of the suspicious activities or the related executable files to its collaborators for consultation. The node receives diagnosis results from its collaborators, denoted by vector $\mathbf{y} = \{\mathbf{y}_1, \mathbf{y}_2, ..., \mathbf{y}_{|\mathscr{A}|}\}$, where $\mathbf{y}_i \in \{0, 1\}$, for $0 < i < |\mathscr{A}|$, is the feedback from acquaintance i. We use $X \in \{0, 1\}$ to denote the scenario of "no-attack" or "under-attack," and $\mathbf{Y} \in \{0, 1\}^{|\mathscr{A}|}$ to denote all possible feedback from acquaintances. The conditional probability of an IDS being "under-attack" given the diagnosis results from all acquaintances can be written as $\mathbb{P}[X = 1|\mathbf{Y} = \mathbf{y}]$. Using Bayes' Theorem [120] and assuming that the acquaintances provide diagnoses independently and their FP rate and TP rate are known, we have

$$
\begin{aligned}
&\mathbb{P}[X = 1|\mathbf{Y} = \mathbf{y}] \\
&= \frac{\mathbb{P}[\mathbf{Y} = \mathbf{y}|X = 1]\mathbb{P}[X = 1]}{\mathbb{P}[\mathbf{Y} = \mathbf{y}|X = 1]\mathbb{P}[X = 1] + \mathbb{P}[\mathbf{Y} = \mathbf{y}|X = 0]\mathbb{P}[X = 0]} \\
&= \frac{\pi_1 \prod_{k=1}^{|\mathscr{A}|} T_k^{\mathbf{y}_k}(1 - T_k)^{1-\mathbf{y}_k}}{\pi_1 \prod_{k=1}^{|\mathscr{A}|} T_k^{\mathbf{y}_k}(1 - T_k)^{1-\mathbf{y}_k} + \pi_0 \prod_{k=1}^{|\mathscr{A}|} F_k^{\mathbf{y}_k}(1 - F_k)^{1-\mathbf{y}_k}},
\end{aligned} \tag{8.5}
$$

where $\pi_0 = \mathbb{P}[X = 0]$ and $\pi_1 = \mathbb{P}[X = 1]$, such that $\pi_0 + \pi_1 = 1$, are the prior probabilities of the scenarios of "no-attack" and "under-attack," respectively. $\mathbf{y}_k \in \{0, 1\}$ is the k-th element of vector $\mathbf{y}$.

Becaue T_k and F_k are both random variables with distributions as in Equations (8.1) and (8.2), we can see that the conditional probability $\mathbb{P}[X = 1|\mathbf{Y} = \mathbf{y}]$ is also a random variable. We use a random variable P to denote $\mathbb{P}[X = 1|\mathbf{Y} = \mathbf{y}]$. Then P takes a continuous value over domain $[0, 1]$. We use $f_P(p)$ to denote the probability density function of P.

When α and β are sufficiently large, a Beta distribution can be approximated by Gaussian distribution according to $\text{Beta}(\alpha, \beta) \approx N\left(\frac{\alpha}{\alpha+\beta}, \sqrt{\frac{\alpha\beta}{(\alpha+\beta)^2(\alpha+\beta+1)}}\right)$. Then the density function of P can be also approximated using Gaussian distribution. By Gauss's approximation formula, we have

$$
\begin{aligned}
\mathbb{E}[P] &\approx \frac{1}{1 + \frac{\pi_0 \prod_{k=1}^{|\mathscr{A}|} \mathbb{E}[F_k]^{\mathbf{y}_k}(1 - \mathbb{E}[F_k])^{1-\mathbf{y}_k}}{\pi_1 \prod_{k=1}^{|\mathscr{A}|} \mathbb{E}[T_k]^{\mathbf{y}_k}(1 - \mathbb{E}[T_k])^{1-\mathbf{y}_k}}} \\
&= \frac{1}{1 + \frac{\pi_0}{\pi_1} \prod_{k=1}^{|\mathscr{A}|} \frac{\alpha_k^1 + \beta_k^1}{\alpha_k^0 + \beta_k^0} \left(\frac{\alpha_k^0}{\alpha_k^1}\right)^{\mathbf{y}_k} \left(\frac{\beta_k^0}{\beta_k^1}\right)^{1-\mathbf{y}_k}}.
\end{aligned} \tag{8.6}
$$

Let C_{fp} and C_{fn} denote the marginal cost of an FP decision and an FN decision. We assume there is no cost when a correct decision is made. We use marginal cost because the cost of an FP may change in time depending on the current state. C_{fn} largely depends on the potential damage level of the attack. For example, an intruder intending to track a user's browsing history may have lower C_{fn} than an intruder intending to modify a system file. We define a decision function $\delta(\mathbf{y}) \in \{0, 1\}$, where $\delta = 1$ means raising an alarm and $\delta = 0$ means no alarm. Then, the Bayes risk can be written as

$$
\begin{aligned}
R(\delta) &= \int_0^1 (C_{fp}(1-x)\delta + C_{fn}x(1-\delta))f_P(x)dx \\
&= \delta C_{fp}\int_0^1 (1-p)f_P(p)dp + (1-\delta)C_{fn}\int_0^1 pf_P(p)dp \\
&= \int_0^1 C_{fn}xf_P(x)dx + \delta\left(C_{fp} - (C_{fp}+C_{fn})\int_0^1 xf_P(x)dx\right) \\
&= C_{fn}\mathbb{E}[P] + \delta(C_{fp} - (C_{fp}+C_{fn})\mathbb{E}[P]),
\end{aligned}
\tag{8.7}
$$

where $f_P(p)$ is the density function of P. To minimize the risk $R(\delta)$, we need to minimize $\delta(C_{fp} - (C_{fp}+C_{fn})\mathbb{E}[P])$. Therefore, we raise an alarm (i.e., $\delta = 1$) if

$$
\mathbb{E}[P] \geq \frac{C_{fp}}{C_{fp}+C_{fn}}.
\tag{8.8}
$$

Let $\tau = \frac{C_{fp}}{C_{fp}+C_{fn}}$ be the threshold. If $\mathbb{E}[P] \geq \tau$, we raise an alarm; otherwise no alarm is raised. The corresponding Bayes risk for the optimal decision is

$$
R(\delta) = \begin{cases} C_{fp}(1-\mathbb{E}[P]) & \text{if } \mathbb{E}[P] \geq \tau, \\[2mm] C_{fn}\mathbb{E}[P] & \text{otherwise.} \end{cases}
\tag{8.9}
$$

An example of the Bayes risk for optimal decisions when $C_{fp} = 1$ and $C_{fn} = 5$ is illustrated in Figure 8.1.

8.4 Acquaintance Management

Intuitively when an IDS consults a larger number of acquaintances, it can achieve higher detection accuracy and lower risk of being compromised. However, having more acquaintances causes higher maintenance cost because the IDS needs to allocate resources for each node in its acquaintance list. When an IDS makes a decision about how many acquaintances to recruit, both the intrusion risk cost and the maintenance cost should be taken into account. When adding a node as an acquaintance does not lower the total cost, then the node shall not be added to the acquaintance list. However, how to select acquaintances and how many acquaintances to include are crucial to building an efficient IDN. In this section we first define the acquaintance selection problem, and then a corresponding solution is devised to find the optimal set of acquaintances. Finally, we use an acquaintance management algorithm for IDSs to learn, recruit, update, or remove their acquaintances dynamically.

8.4.1 Problem Statement

Let $\mathscr{A}_i$ denote the set of acquaintances of IDS i. Let $M_i(\mathscr{A}_i)$ be the cost for IDS i to maintain the acquaintance set $\mathscr{A}_i$. We use $R_i(\mathscr{A}_i)$ to denote the risk cost of missing

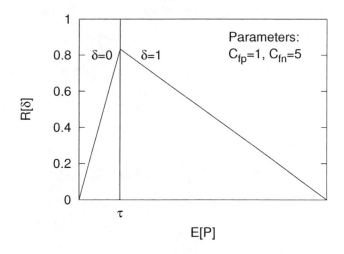

Figure 8.1: Bayes risk for optimal decisions when $C_{fp} = 1$ **and** $C_{fn} = 5$.

intrusions and/or false alarms for IDS i, given the feedback of acquaintance set $\mathscr{A}_i$. In the rest of this section, we drop subscript i from our notations for the convenience of presentation.

Our goal is to select a set of acquaintances from a list of candidates so that the overall cost $R(\mathscr{A}) + M(\mathscr{A})$ is minimized. We define the problem as follows:

Given a list of acquaintance candidates $\mathscr{C}$, we need to find a subset of acquaintances $\mathscr{A} \subseteq \mathscr{C}$, such that the overall cost $R(\mathscr{A}) + M(\mathscr{A})$ is minimized.

In practice, the maintenance cost of acquaintances may not be negligible because acquaintances send test messages/consultations periodically to ask for diagnosis. It takes resources (CPU and memory) for the IDS to receive, analyze the requests, and reply with corresponding answers. The selection of $M_i(.)$ can be user defined on each host. For example, a simple maximum acquaintance length restriction can be mapped to $M(\mathscr{A}) = C \max(|\mathscr{A}| - L, 0)$, where $L \in \mathscr{N}^+$ is the acquaintance length upper-bound and $C \in [0, \infty)$ is the penalty of exceeding the bound.

The risk cost can be expressed as

$$R(\mathscr{A}) = C_{fn} P[\delta = 0 | X = 1] P[X = 1]$$
$$+ C_{fp} P[\delta = 1 | X = 0] P[X = 0],$$

where C_{fn}, C_{fp} denote the marginal cost of missing an intrusion and raising a false alarm, respectively. $P[X = 1] = \pi_1, P[X = 0] = \pi_0$ are the prior probabilities of under-attack and no-attack, where $\pi_0 + \pi_1 = 1$. Note that in practice, π_1 can be learned from the history and be updated whenever a new threat is found. A moving average method can be used to update the estimated value.

The above equation can be further written as

$$R(\mathscr{A}) = C_{fn}\pi_1 \sum_{\forall \mathbf{y} \in \{0,1\}^{|\mathscr{A}|} | \delta(\mathbf{y})=0} P[\mathbf{Y} = \mathbf{y} | X = 1] \tag{8.10}$$

$$+ C_{fp}\pi_0 \sum_{\forall \mathbf{y} \in \{0,1\}^{|\mathscr{A}|} | \delta(\mathbf{y})=1} P[\mathbf{Y} = \mathbf{y} | X = 0]$$

$$= C_{fn}\pi_1 \sum_{\forall \mathbf{y} \in \{0,1\}^{|\mathscr{A}|} | \delta(\mathbf{y})=0} \prod_{i=1}^{|\mathscr{A}|} (T_i)^{y_i} (1 - T_i)^{1-y_i}$$

$$+ C_{fp}\pi_0 \sum_{\forall \mathbf{y} \in \{0,1\}^{|\mathscr{A}|} | \delta(\mathbf{y})=1} \prod_{i=1}^{|\mathscr{A}|} (F_i)^{y_i} (1 - F_i)^{1-y_i}$$

$$= C_{fn}\pi_1 \sum_{\forall \mathbf{y} \in \{0,1\}^{|\mathscr{A}|} | f(\mathbf{y})<1} \prod_{i=1}^{|\mathscr{A}|} (T_i)^{y_i} (1 - T_i)^{1-y_i}$$

$$+ C_{fp}\pi_0 \sum_{\forall \mathbf{y} \in \{0,1\}^{|\mathscr{A}|} | f(\mathbf{y})\geq 1} \prod_{i=1}^{|\mathscr{A}|} (F_i)^{y_i} (1 - F_i)^{1-y_i}$$

$$= \sum_{\mathbf{y} \in \{0,1\}^{|\mathscr{A}|}} min\{C_{fn}\pi_1 \prod_i T_i^{y_i} (1 - T_i)^{1-y_i},$$

$$C_{fp}\pi_0 \prod_i F_i^{y_i} (1 - F_i)^{1-y_i}\}$$

where T_i, F_i are the TP rate and FP rate of acquaintance i, respectively.

$$f(\mathbf{y}) = \frac{C_{fn}\pi_1 \prod_{i=1}^{|\mathscr{A}|} (T_i)^{y_i} (1 - T_i)^{1-y_i}}{C_{fp}\pi_0 \prod_{i=1}^{|\mathscr{A}|} (F_i)^{y_i} (1 - F_i)^{1-y_i}}.$$

$\forall \mathbf{y} \in \{0,1\}^l | \delta(\mathbf{y}) = 1$ refers to the combination of decisions that causes the system to raise an alarm, and vice versa.

8.4.2 Acquaintance Selection Algorithm

To solve such a subset optimization problem, the brute-force method is to examine all possible combinations of acquaintances and select the one that has the least overall cost. However, the computation complexity is $O(2^n)$. It is not hard to see that the order of selecting acquaintances does not affect the overall cost. We use an acquaintance selection algorithm based on a heuristic approach to find an acquaintance set that achieves satisfactory overall cost. In this algorithm, the system always selects the nodes that bring the lowest overall cost.

For ease of demonstration, we assume the maintenance cost can be written as follows:

$$M(\mathscr{A}) = C_a l = C_a |\mathscr{A}|, \tag{8.11}$$

where C_a is the unit maintenance cost of each acquaintance, which includes the cost of communication, detection assistance, and test messages. Note that any other form of maintenance cost can be easily included in the algorithm.

Algorithm 8.1 Acquaintance Selection ($\mathscr{C}, L_{min}, L_{max}$)

Require: A set of acquaintance candidates $\mathscr{C}$
Ensure: A set of selected acquaintances $\mathscr{A}$ with minimum length L_{min} and max length L_{max} that brings the minimum overall cost
1:   $Quit = false$ //quit the loop if $Quit = true$
2:   $\mathscr{A} \Leftarrow \emptyset$
3:   $U = min(\pi_0 C_{fp}, \pi_1 C_{fn})$ //initialize the overall cost while there is no acquaintance. $min(\pi_0 C_{fp}, \pi_1 C_{fn})$ is the cost when a node makes a decision without feedback from collaborators
4:   **while** $Quit = false$ **do**
5:      //select the node that reduces cost most in each iteration
6:      $D_{max} = -MAXNUM$ //initialize the maximum cost reduction to the lowest possible
7:      **for all** $e \in \mathscr{C}$ **do**
8:         $\mathscr{A} = \mathscr{A} \cup e$
9:         **if** $U - R(\mathscr{A}) - M(\mathscr{A}) > D_{max}$ //see Equation (8.10) and Equation (8.11) for $R(\mathscr{A})$ and $M(\mathscr{A})$ **then**
10:            $D_{max} = U - R(\mathscr{A}) - M(\mathscr{A})$
11:            $e_{max} = e$
12:         **end if**
13:         $\mathscr{A} = \mathscr{A} \setminus e$ //remove e from $\mathscr{A}$
14:      **end for**
15:      **if** $(D_{max} > 0$ and $|\mathscr{A}| < L_{max})$ or $|\mathscr{A}| < L_{min}$ **then**
16:         $\mathscr{A} = \mathscr{A} \cup e_{max}$
17:         $\mathscr{C} = \mathscr{C} \setminus e_{max}$ //remove e_{max} from $\mathscr{C}$
18:         $U = U - D_{max}$
19:      **else**
20:         $Quit = true$
21:      **end if**
22: **end while**

As shown in Algorithm 6.1, in the beginning, the acquaintance list is empty. The initial cost is the minimum cost of the decision based only on the prior information (line 3). For each loop, the system selects a node from the acquaintance candidate list that brings the lowest overall cost and stores it into e_{max} (lines 7–14), where $U - R(\mathscr{A}) - M(\mathscr{A})$ is the amount of cost reduced by adding a node to the acquaintance list. When such a node is found, it is then moved to the acquaintance list if the current acquaintance length is less than L_{min} or the cost is reduced by adding the new node and the acquaintance length does not exceed L_{max}. The loop stops when no node can be added into $\mathscr{A}$ any further.

8.4.3 Acquaintance Management Algorithm

In the previous section we devised an algorithm to select acquaintances from a list of candidates. However, collaboration is usually based on mutual consensus. If node A selects B as an acquaintance but B does not select A (nonsymmetric selection), then the collaboration is not established.

We employ a distributed approach for an IDS in the IDN to select and manage acquaintances and a consensus protocol to allow an IDS to deal with the nonsymmetric selection problem. To improve the stability of the acquaintance list, we use a probation period on each new IDS collaborator so that IDSs have time to learn about any new candidates before considering it as an acquaintance. For this purpose, each IDS maintains a *probation list*, where all new nodes remain during their probation periods. A node also communicates periodically with nodes in its probation list to evaluate their detection accuracy. The purpose of the probation list is thus to explore potential collaborators and keep introducing new qualified nodes to the acquaintance list.

Suppose that node i has two sets $\mathscr{A}_i$ and $\mathscr{P}_i$, which are the acquaintance list and the probation list, respectively. The corresponding false positive rate and true positive rate of both sets are $F_i^{\mathscr{A}}, T_i^{\mathscr{A}}$ and $F_i^{\mathscr{P}}, T_i^{\mathscr{P}}$. To keep learning the detection accuracy of the acquaintances, a node sends test messages to nodes periodically in both the acquaintance list and the probation list, and keeps updating their estimated false positive rates and true positive rates. Let l^{max} be the maximum number of IDSs in both the acquaintance and the probation list. We set this upper-bound because the amount of resources used for collaboration is proportional to the number of acquaintances it manages. l^{max} is determined by the resource capacity of each IDS. Let l^{min} be the minimum length of a probation list and q be the parameter that controls the length of the probation list l^p compared to the length of acquaintance list l^a, such that $l^{min} \leq l^p \leq q l^a$. The parameters l^{min} and q are used to tune the trade-off between the adaptability to the situation where nodes join or leave the network frequently ("high churn rate"), and the overhead of resources used for testing new nodes.

The acquaintance management procedure for each node is shown in Algorithm 6.2. The acquaintance list $\mathscr{A}$ is initially empty and the probation list $\mathscr{P}$ is filled by l^{ini} random nodes to utilize the resources in exploring new nodes. An acquaintance list updating event is triggered every t_u time units. $\mathscr{A}$ is updated by including new trusted nodes from $\mathscr{P}$. A node that stays at least t_p time units in probation is called a *mature node*. Only mature nodes are allowed to join the acquaintance list (lines 15–21). Mature nodes with bad qualification will be abandoned right away. After that, the acquaintance selection algorithm is used to find the optimal candidate list. Collaboration requests are sent out for nodes that are selected in the optimal list. If an acceptance is received before the expiration time, then the collaboration is confirmed; otherwise the node is abandoned (lines 22–26). Then $\mathscr{P}$ is refilled with new randomly chosen nodes (lines 28–31).

Algorithm 8.2 Managing Acquaintance and Probation Lists

 1: **Initialization** :
 2: $\mathscr{A} \Leftarrow \emptyset$ //Acquaintance list.
 3: $\mathscr{P} \Leftarrow \emptyset$ //Probation list.
 4: $l^p = l^{ini}$ //initial Probation length
 5: //Fill $\mathscr{P}$ with randomly selected nodes
 6: **while** $|\mathscr{P}| < l^p$ **do**
 7:    $e \Leftarrow$ select a random node
 8:    $\mathscr{P} \Leftarrow \mathscr{P} \cup e$
 9: **end while**
10: **set** new timer event(t_u, "**SpUpdate**")
11: **Periodic Maintenance:**
12: **at timer event** ev of type "**SpUpdate**" **do**
13: //Merge the first mature node into the acquaintance list.
14: $e \Leftarrow selectOldestNode(\mathscr{P})$
15: $\mathscr{C} \Leftarrow \mathscr{A}$ //$\mathscr{C}$ is the temporary candidate list
16: **if** $t_e > t_p$ //t_e is the age of node e in the probation list **then**
17:    $\mathscr{P} \Leftarrow \mathscr{P} \setminus e$
18:    **if** $T_e > T_{min}$ and $F_e < F_{max}$ //T_e and F_e are the true positive rate and false positive rates of the node e **then**
19:       $\mathscr{C} \Leftarrow \mathscr{C} \cup e$
20:    **end if**
21: **end if**
22: //Consensus protocol
23: $\mathscr{S} =$ Acquaintance Selection($\mathscr{C}, l^{min}, \max(l^{min}, \frac{q}{q+1} l^{max})$)
24: //Send requests for collaboration and receive responses
25: $S_{accp} \Leftarrow RequestandReceiveCollaboration(S, t_{timeout})$
26: $\mathscr{A} \Leftarrow S_{accp}$ //Only nodes that accept the collaboration invitations are moved into the acquaintance list
27: //Refill $\mathscr{P}$ with randomly selected nodes
28: **while** $|\mathscr{P}| < max(q|\mathscr{A}|, l^{min})$ **do**
29:    $e \Leftarrow$ Select a random node not in $\mathscr{A}$
30:    $\mathscr{P} \Leftarrow \mathscr{P} \cup e$
31: **end while**
32: **set** new timer event(t_u, "**SpUpdate**")
33: **end timer event**

Several properties are desirable for an effective acquaintance management algorithm, including convergence, stability, robustness, and incentive compatibility for collaboration. When our acquaintance management is in place, we are interested to know with whom the IDS nodes end up collaborating and how often they change their collaborators.

In Section 8.5 we evaluate our acquaintance management algorithm to determine whether or not it achieves the above properties.

8.5 Evaluation

In this section we describe the conducted simulation to demonstrate the desirable properties of our acquaintance management algorithm. We evaluate the cost efficiency of our Bayesian decision model, cost and time efficiency of the acquaintance selection algorithm, and several desired properties of the acquaintance management algorithm. Each simulation result presented in this section is derived from the average of a large number of replications with an overall negligible confidence interval.

8.5.1 Simulation Setting

We simulate an environment of n IDS peers collaborating together by adding each other as acquaintances. We adopt two parameters to model the detection accuracy of each IDS, namely false positive rate (FP) and false negative rate (FN). Notice that in reality most IDSs have low FP (< 0.1) and FN is normally in the range of $[0.1, 0.5]$ [114]. This is because false positives can severely damage the reputation of the product, so vendors strive to maintain their FP rate at a low level. In our experiment, we select parameters that reflect real-world properties. To test the detection accuracy of acquaintances, each peer sends test messages where their correct answers are known beforehand. Test messages are sent following a Poisson process with average arrival rate R. R will be determined in the next subsection. We use a simulation day as the time unit in our experiments. The diagnosis results given by an IDS are simulated following a Bernoulli random process. If a test message represents a benign activity, the IDS i raises an alarm with a probability of FP_i. Similarly, if the test message represents intrusions, an alarm will be raised with a probability of $1 - FN_i$. All parameter settings are summarized in Table 8.2.

8.5.2 Determining the Test Message Rate

The goal of our first experiment is to study the relationship between test message rates and FP, FN learning speed. We simulate two IDSs A and B. A sends B test messages to ask for diagnosis, and learns the FP and FN of B based on the quality of B's feedback. The learning procedure follows Equations (8.1), (8.2), and (8.3). We fix the FN of B to 0.1, 0.2, and 0.3 respectively. Under each case, we run the learning process under different test message rates, 2/day, 10/day, and 50/day, respectively.

Table 8.2: Simulation Parameters

Parameter	Value	Description
R	10/day	Test message rate
λ	0.95	Forgetting factor
C_{fp}/C_{fn}	20/100	Unit cost of false positive/negative decisions
C_a	0.01	Maintenance cost of one acquaintance
t_p	10 days	Probation period
t_u	1 day	Acquaintance list update interval
l^{ini}	10	Initial probation length
l^{max}	20	Maximum total number of acquaintances
l^{min}	2	Minimum probation list length
T^{min}	0.5	Minimum acceptable true positive rate
F^{max}	0.2	Maximum acceptable false positive rate
q	0.5	Length ratio of probation to acquaintance list
π_1	0.1	Prior probability of intrusions

We observe the change in estimated FN over time, plotted in Figure 8.2. We see that when R is 2/day, the estimated FN converges after around 30 days in the case of FN = 0.2. The converging time is slightly longer and shorter in the cases of FN = 0.3 and FN = 0.1, respectively. When R is increased to 10/day, the converging time decreases to around 10 days. In the case of R = 50/day, the corresponding converging time is the shortest (around 3 days) among the three cases. Increasing the test message

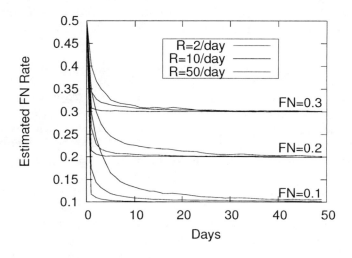

Figure 8.2: The convergence of learning speed and the test message rate.

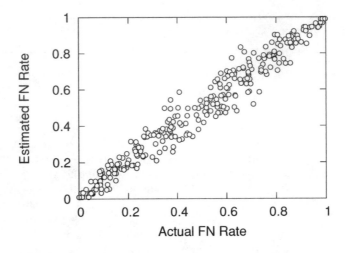

Figure 8.3: The distribution of estimated FN rate ($R = 10$/day).

rate R to 50/day does not reduce much learning process time. Based on the above observation, we choose $R = 10$/day and the probation period t_p to be 10 days as our system parameters. In this way, the test message rate is kept low and the learned FN and FP values converge after the probation period.

The second experiment is to study the efficiency of learning results after our chosen probation period. We fix $R = 10$/day, $t_p = 10$/day, and randomly choose FN of node B uniformly among [0, 1]. We repeat the experiments 100 times with different FNs. The FNs estimated using our learning process until the end of probation period are plotted in Figure 8.3. We can see that in all different settings of FNs, the estimated FN rates are close to the actual FN rates after the probation period.

8.5.3 Efficiency of Our Feedback Aggregation

In this experiment, we evaluate the effectiveness of our Bayesian decision based feedback aggregation by comparing it with a threshold based aggregation. We have described our Bayesian decision model in Section 8.3.2. In a simple threshold based feedback aggregation method, if the number of IDSs reporting intrusions is larger than a predefined threshold, then the system raises an alarm. The threshold-based decision is used in N-version cloud antivirus systems [114].

We set up eight IDSs $\{IDS_0, IDS_1, ..., IDS_7\}$ with their FP and FN rates randomly chosen from the range [0.1, 0.5]. IDS_0 sends consultations to all other IDSs, collects and aggregates feedback to make intrusion decisions. The costs of false positive and false negative decisions are $C_{fp}=20$ and $C_{fn}=100$ respectively. We compare the average false detection cost using the Bayesian decision model and the simple threshold-based approach. Figure 8.4 shows that the cost of threshold decision largely depends

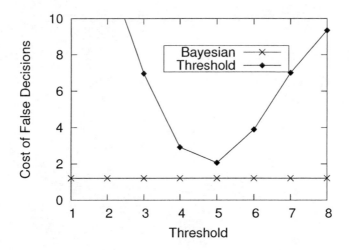

Figure 8.4: Comparison of cost using threshold decision and Bayesian decision.

on the chosen threshold value. An appropriate threshold can significantly decrease the cost of false decisions. In contrast, the Bayesian decision model does not depend on any threshold setting and prevails over the threshold decision under all threshold settings. This is because the threshold decision treats all participants equally, while the Bayesian decision method recognizes different detection capabilities of IDSs and takes them into account in the decision process. For example, if an IDS asserts that there is intrusion, our Bayesian model may raise an alarm if the IDS has a low FP rate and ignores the warning if the IDS has a high FP rate. However, the threshold-based decision model will either raise an alarm or not based on the total number of IDSs that raise warnings and compare it with a predefined threshold, irrespective of the individual that issued the warning.

8.5.4   Cost and the Number of Collaborators

We define *risk cost* to be the expected cost from false decisions such as raising false alarms (FP) and missing the detection of an intrusion (FN). We show that introducing more collaborators can decrease the risk cost. In this experiment we study the impact of the number of collaborators on the risk cost. We set up four groups with an equal number of IDSs. Nodes in all groups have the same FP rate of 0.03, but their FN rates vary from 0.1 to 0.4, depending on the group they are in. Inside each group, every node collaborates with every other node. We are interested in the risk cost as well as the maintenance cost. The *maintenance cost* is the cost associated with the amount of resource that is used to maintain the collaboration with other nodes, such as answering diagnosis requests from other IDSs. Because our purpose is to capture the concept of maintenance cost but not to study how much it is, we assume the

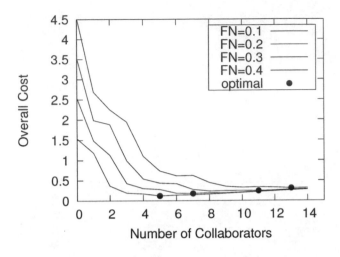

Figure 8.5: The average cost under different collaborator quality.

maintenance cost to be linearly proportional to the number of collaborators with a unit rate $C_a = 0.01$ (see Table 8.2).

We increase the size of all groups and observe the average cost of nodes in each group. From Figure 8.5 we can see that in all groups, the costs drop down fast in the beginning and slow down as the groups' sizes increase. After an optimal point (marked by large solid circles), the costs slowly increase. This is because when the number of collaborators is large enough, the cost saving by adding more collaborators becomes small, and the increment of maintenance cost becomes significant. We find that groups with higher detection accuracy have lower optimal costs. Also, they need a smaller number of collaborators to reach the optimal costs. For example, in the case of $FN = 0.4$, 13 collaborators are needed to reach the optimal cost, while the number of collaborators required is 5 in the case of $FN = 0.1$.

8.5.5 Efficiency of Acquaintance Selection Algorithms

We learned in the previous section that when the number of collaborators is large enough, adding more collaborators does not decrease the overall cost because of the associated maintenance cost. An acquaintance selection algorithm is described in Algorithm 3. In this section 10.2 we compare the efficiency of acquaintance selection using the brute-force algorithm and our acquaintance selection algorithm. We create 15 IDSs as candidate acquaintances with FP and FN rates randomly chosen from intervals $[0.01, 0.1]$ and $[0.1, 0.5]$, respectively. Both algorithms are implemented in Java and run on a PC with AMD Athlon dual core processor 2.61 GHz, and with 1.93

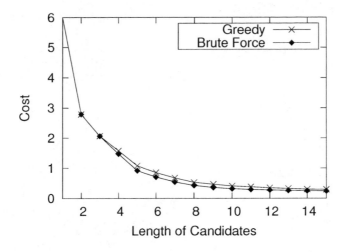

Figure 8.6: The cost using different acquaintance selection algorithms.

GB RAM. We start the candidate set size from 1 and gradually increase the size. We observe the cost efficiency and running time efficiency of both algorithms.

Figure 8.6 shows that the brute-force algorithm performs slightly better with respect to acquaintance list quality because the overall cost using its selected list is slightly lower. However, Figure 8.7 shows that the running time of the brute-force method increases significantly when the candidate set size exceeds 11, and continues to increase exponentially, while our algorithm shows much better running time efficiency. These experiments suggest to use the brute-force method only when the size of candidates list is small (≤ 11). When the candidates list is large, our greedy algorithm should be used to select acquaintances.

8.5.6 Evaluation of Acquaintance Management Algorithm

In this experiment we study the effectiveness of our acquaintance management algorithm (Algorithm 4). We set up a simulation environment of 100 nodes. For the convenience of observation, all nodes have a fixed FP rate of 0.1 and their FN rates are uniformly distributed in the range of $[0.1, 0.5]$. All nodes update their acquaintance list once a day ($t_u=1$). We observe several properties: convergence, stability, robustness, and incentive compatibility.

8.5.6.1 Convergence

Our first finding about our acquaintance management algorithm is that IDSs converge to collaborating with other IDSs with similar detection accuracy levels. We observed through experiments that IDSs collaborate with random other nodes in the network in the beginning (Figure 8.8). After a longer period of time (200 days), all IDSs col-

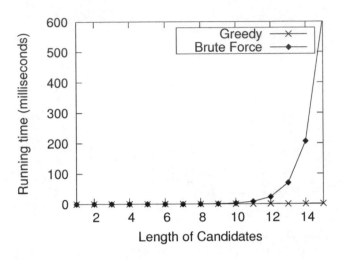

Figure 8.7: The running time using different acquaintance selection algorithms.

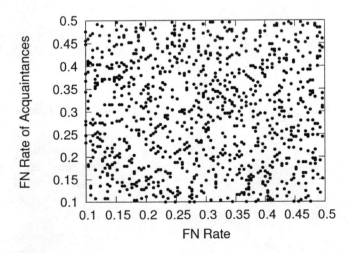

Figure 8.8: Acquaintances distribution on day 25.

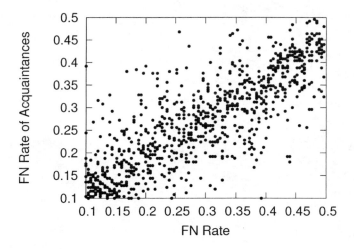

Figure 8.9: Acquaintances distribution on day 200.

laborate with others with similar detection accuracy, as shown in Figure 8.9. Our explanation is that the collaboration between pairs with high qualification discrepancy is relatively not stable because our collaboration algorithm is based on mutual consensus and consensus is hard to reach between those pairs.

Figure 8.10 plots the average overall cost in the first 365 days of collaboration for three nodes with FN values 0.1, 0.3, and 0.5, respectively. In the first 10 days, the costs for all nodes are high. This is because all collaborators are still in the probation period. After day 10, all cost values drop down significantly. This is because collaborators pass the probation period and start to contribute to intrusion decisions. The cost for high expertise nodes continues to drop while the cost for low expertise nodes increases partially after around day 20, and stabilizes after day 50. This is because the acquaintance management algorithm selects better collaborators to replace the initial random ones. We can see that the collaboration cost of nodes converges with time and becomes stable after the initial phase.

8.5.6.2 Stability

Collaboration stability is an important property because the collaboration between IDSs is expected to be long term. Frequently changing collaborators is costly because IDSs need to spend a considerable amount of time learning about new collaborators. In this experiment, we record the average time span of all acquaintances from the time they pass the probation period until they are replaced by other acquaintances. The result is shown in Figure 8.11, where the average collaboration time spans for three selected nodes are shown with different point shapes. We can see that collaboration among nodes with similar expertise levels is more stable than that between nodes with different expertise levels. For example, nodes with low $FN = 0.1$ form

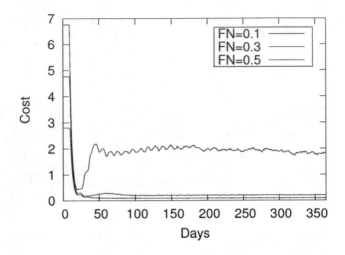

Figure 8.10: The average cost for collaboration.

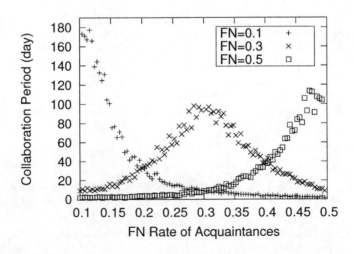

Figure 8.11: The collaboration time span.

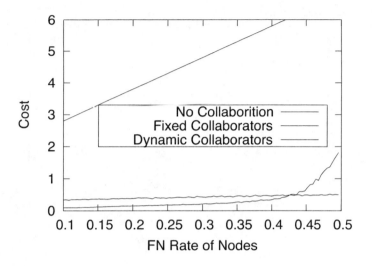

Figure 8.12: The converged cost distribution.

stable collaboration connections with other nodes with low FN (around 180 days in average), while the collaboration with IDSs with high FN is short (close to 0 day in average).

8.5.6.3   Incentive Compatibility

Collaboration among IDSs is expected to be a long-term relationship. Incentive is important for the long-term sustainability of collaborations because it provides motivation for peers to contribute [51, 61]. We compare the average overall cost of all nodes with different FN rates under three different conditions, namely no collaboration, fixed acquaintances collaboration (acquaintance length = 8), and dynamic acquaintance management collaboration. Figure 8.12 shows the distribution of the converged cost of all nodes. We can observe that the costs of all IDSs is much higher when no collaboration is performed in the network. On the other hand, collaborating with random fixed acquaintances can significantly reduce the cost of false decisions, however, the cost of high expertise nodes and low expertise nodes are very close. With our dynamic acquaintance management, high expertise nodes achieve much lower cost than nodes with low expertise, which reflects an incentive design of the collaboration system. Therefore, the system provides motivation for nodes to update their knowledge base and behave truthfully in cooperation.

8.5.6.4   Robustness

Robustness is a desired property of an IDN because malicious users may try to attack the collaboration mechanism to render it ineffective. We focus on the betrayal attack in this experiment. To study the impact from one malicious node, we set up

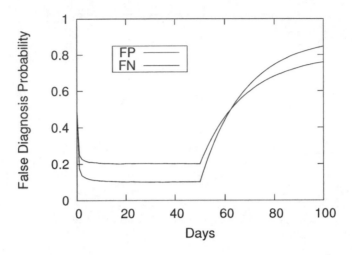

Figure 8.13: The FP and FN of betrayal node.

a collaboration scenario where IDS_0 is collaborating with a group of other IDSs with $FP = 0.1$ and $FN = 0.2$. Among the group, one IDS turns to be dishonest after day 50 and gives false diagnoses. We observe the FP rate and FN rates of this malicious node perceived by IDS_0, and the impact on the risk cost of IDS_0 under various collaborator group sizes. Figure 8.13 shows the perceived FP and FN rates of the malicious node during each simulation day. We can see that the perceived FP and FN increase rapidly after day 50. The malicious node is then removed from the acquaintance list of IDS_0 when its perceived FP and FN are higher than a predefined threshold. The cost of IDS_0 under a betrayal attack is depicted by Figure 8.14; we notice that the betrayal behavior introduces a spike of cost increment under all group sizes, but the magnitude of the increment decreases when the number of collaborators increases. However, the system can efficiently learn the malicious behavior and recover to normal by excluding malicious nodes from the acquaintance list.

8.6 Conclusion and Future Work

In this chapter we presented a statistical model to evaluate the trade-off between the maintenance cost and the intrusion cost, and an effective acquaintance management method to minimize the overall cost for each IDS in an IDN. Specifically, we adopted a Bayesian learning approach to evaluate the accuracy of each IDS in terms of its false positive and true positive rates in detecting intrusions. The Bayes' Theorem is applied for the aggregation of feedback provided by the collaborating IDSs. Our ac-

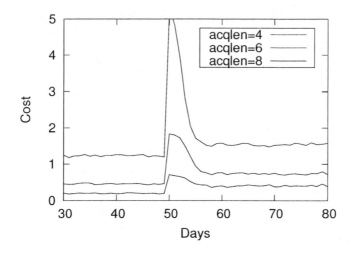

Figure 8.14: The cost of an IDS under a betrayal attack.

quaintance management explores a list of candidate IDSs and selects acquaintances using an acquaintance selection algorithm. This algorithm is based on a greedy approach to find the smallest number of best acquaintances and minimize the cost of false intrusion decisions and maintenance. The acquaintances list is updated periodically by introducing new candidates that pass the probation period.

Through a simulated IDN environment, we evaluated our Bayesian decision model against threshold-based decision models, and acquaintance selection algorithm against a brute-force approach. Compared to the threshold-based model, our Bayesian decision model performs better in terms of the cost of false decisions. Compared to the brute-force approach, our algorithm achieves similar performance but requires much less computation time. Our acquaintance management is also shown to achieve the desirable properties of convergence, stability, robustness, and incentive compatibility.

As future work, we plan to investigate other, more sophisticated attack models on the collaboration mechanism and integrate corresponding defense techniques. Robustness of the acquaintance management system is particularly critical if extended to support IDS peer recommendations. In this case, malicious IDSs may provide untruthful recommendations about other IDSs [104, 140, 152], or worse, collide to collaboratively bring down the system.

OTHER TYPES OF IDN DESIGN

Chapter 9

Knowledge-Based Intrusion Detection Networks and Knowledge Propagation

CONTENTS

9.1 Introduction

So far in this book we have focused on the design of consultation-based intrusion detection networks, where IDSs send consultation requests to collaborators when they observe suspicious activities. However, sending consultation requests may not be favorable to all users because the information about suspicious observations may contain confidential content that users do not want to share with others. Indeed, privacy breaches might be a concern for some users in a consultation-based IDN. In turn, knowledge-based IDNs do not have this problem and can be an alternative choice for IDS collaboration. A *knowledge-based IDN* can be defined as an overlay network that allows IDSs to share intrusion detection knowledge, such as blacklists, malware signatures, or intrusion detection rules, with others. However, how to propagate knowledge to the right recipients without excessive communication overhead is a challenging problem. Furthermore, an effective knowledge propagation mechanism should also be incentive compatible, which encourages participants to share knowledge actively and honestly, and robust to minimize the negative impact of malicious insiders. This chapter discusses an incentive-compatible knowledge-based intrusion detection networks, particularly emphasizing the propagation mechanism design.

How to protect computers and devices from cyber attacks has been an active research topic since the1980s. However, defencs against attackers has always been a challenging problem because a defender has to know all the possible attacks to ensure network security, whereas an attacker only needs to know a few attack techniques to succeed. Traditional IDSs work independently of each other and rely on downloading intrusion detection knowledge from their corresponding security vendors. However, one vendor often has incomplete knowledge of all attack techniques and consequently systems can be easily compromised by zero-day attacks unknown to their IDS vendors. A knowledge-based intrusion detection network allows IDSs to utilize collective knowledge from others for more effective intrusion detection.

The knowledge exchanged in IDNs can be from security vendors such as intrusion detection rules and malware signatures. It can also be generated at the edge of the network such as intrusion alerts, firewall logs, and blacklists. An effective knowledge exchange mechanism must propagate knowledge in such a way to improve intrusion detection efficiency overall. However, knowledge propagation itself can be the target of malicious attacks and can also be taken advantage of by free-riders. For example, compromised insiders can propagate a large amount of futile information to overwhelm a target IDS, or benefit from peers' intrusion knowledge without contributing to the collaboration network. Therefore, robustness to various attacks and incentive compatibility among peer IDSs are desirable properties of an effective IDN knowledge sharing network.

However, existing IDNs often assume that all nodes are honest and altruistic. Consequently, they are vulnerable to dishonest and opportunistic insiders. In this chapter we address this challenge and presents a robust and incentive-compatible IDN framework. The framework is based on a collaborative peer-to-peer network structure, where IDSs share knowledge about currently prevailing attacks with others in the network by means of pair-wise information exchange. We analyze the macroscopic propagation of intrusion detection knowledge in the network. A Bayesian learning model is used for each IDS to evaluate the helpfulness of other IDSs and identify spammers and malicious insiders. Each IDS determines the knowledge propagation rate to others following a two-level game model that provides incentive compatibility and fairness to all participants. We develop a distributed dynamic algorithms for each IDS to compute the optimal knowledge sharing rate, which converges to a Nash equilibrium. Our simulation results demonstrate that our knowledge sharing system has some desirable features for IDNs.

The highlights of this chapter are as follows: (1) A knowledge-based IDN and design an automatic knowledge sharing mechanism. The latter is based on a decentralized two-level optimization framework to determine information propagation rates among collaborators. An optimal knowledge sharing policy is used for each node and we show the existence of a prime Nash equilibrium in the model and study the knowledge propagation at the equilibrium. (2) Bayesian learning is employed for each node to estimate the trust values of others based on the empirical data collected by the node. A distributed dynamic algorithms is used to find the Nash equilibrium and perform comprehensive simulations to demonstrate the efficiency, robustness, incentive compatibility, fairness, and scalability of the knowledge sharing system.

The rest of the chapter is organized as follows. Section 9.2 provides an overview of collaborative intrusion detection systems and information sharing paradigms. Section 9.3 describes the knowledge sharing system framework. The system modeling and analysis are elaborated in Section 9.4. We discuss the Bayesian learning of trust values and the dynamic algorithms to find Nash equilibrium in Section 9.5. We evaluate the system using extensive simulations in Section 9.5. Finally, we conclude the chapter in Section 9.7.

9.2 Background

IDS collaboration networks utilize the collective intrusion information and knowledge from other IDSs to improve accuracy in intrusion detection. Existing IDNs can be categorized as knowledge-based and consultation-based. In a knowledge-based IDN, IDSs share intrusion knowledge such as intrusion alerts, intrusion detection rules, malware signatures, and blacklists with other nodes to improve overall intrusion detection efficiency for the whole network. Most works proposed in the past few years are knowledge-based IDNs, such as [36, 44, 137, 149, 157]. They are particularly effective in detecting epidemic worms and attacks, and new vulnerability exploitations. In a consultation-based IDN, suspicious data samples are sent to expert collaborators for diagnosis. Feedbacks from the collaborators are then aggregated to help the sender IDS detect intrusions. Examples of such IDNs include those described in [59, 72, 74], and [114]. Consultation-based IDNs are designed for collaboration among different security vendors and are effective in detecting some intrusion types such as malware and spam.

Information sharing among IDNs can be either centralized or decentralized. In centralized sharing, such as [137], nodes collect intrusion data and send them to a central node for analysis. In decentralized sharing, the workload of data analysis is distributed. Information routing in IDNs can follow a hierarchical structure [149] where data is passed up to parent nodes, a structured P2P network [44] where data is passed to a responsible node determined by hash mapping, or an unstructured P2P network [46, 72] where data is passed to neighboring nodes. Our system is designed based on an unstructured P2P network, where IDSs of similar interests and configurations collaborate with each other.

Information and knowledge propagation in a community can be realized through gossiping. Gossiping is a communication paradigm where information is propagated through multi-hop pair-wise communication. Gossiping has been used to exchange information in distributed collaborative intrusion detection, such as local gossiping [52], and global gossiping [151]. Sharing observations from distributed nodes is useful to detect and throttle fast-spreading computer worms. It is effective for communications in ad hoc or random networks, where a structured communication is difficult to establish. However, traditional gossiping relies on random pair-wise communication and information flooding. Therefore, it is not suitable when the network is large and the messages are only intended to be delivered to a small set of nodes. Mailing list broadcasting can be seen as a special type of gossiping where one node communicates with every other node in the network to deliver messages. Random walk [46] can also be used to propagate intrusion alerts within an IDN, where intrusion alerts start from a set of initial nodes and each node passes the information received to a randomly chosen neighbor unless the received information is a duplicate. However, random walk mechanisms are relatively slow in terms of propagation speed, and the source node has no control over the number of receivers.

Publish-subscribe systems can also be used for information delivery among IDSs, such as [44, 157]. Compared to gossiping, publish-subscribe systems allow customized information delivery. They can be either topic-based [117], or content-based, such as [44, 157]. In a topic-based system, publishers and subscribers are connected by predefined topics; content is published on well-advertised topics to which users can subscribe based on their interests. In a content-based system, users' interests are expressed through queries, and a content filtering technique is used to match the publishers' content to the subscriber. However, a simple publish-subscribe system does not take the quality of the information into consideration. It also does not provide incentives for IDSs to contribute to the collaboration network. Our system not only measures the trust of nodes, but also ensures incentive-compatible knowledge sharing.

9.3 Knowledge Sharing IDN Architecture

This section describes the architecture design of a knowledge-based IDN, including the IDN topology, network operation, and knowledge propagation protocol.

9.3.1 Network Topology

In our knowledge-based IDN, nodes are organized into a collaborative peer-to-peer network (Figure 9.1). Each node maintains a list of collaborators to communicate and exchange intrusion detection knowledge with. We call such a list an *acquaintance list*. The acquaintance list contains the collaborators' IDs, IP addresses, public keys, and trust values. Note that the acquaintance relationship is symmetric, that is, if node i is on node j's acquaintance list, then node j is on node i's acquaintance list. Intrusion detection knowledge is propagated from a node to its acquaintances in a pair-wise manner. The knowledge will be further propagated once it is proven to be effective on the receiver side, for example, resulting in high detection rates. Effective knowledge can be propagated to a large number of nodes through multi-hop peer-to-peer network communications.

To illustrate, we will focus in the remainder of this chapter on a collaborative IDN facilitating Snort rules sharing between Snort IDSs. Snort is an open-source network-based intrusion detection system (NIDS). An isolated Snort NIDS relies on downloading intrusion detection rules from a central server to keep its knowledge up to date. End users can also contribute Snort rules, such as rules against zero-day attacks, and update the new rules to the central server for verification. The central server verifies the new rules and pushes the useful ones to end users. However, in this centralized rule sharing system, the large number of end user contributed rules may be more than the central authority can handle and consequently cause a number of useful zero-day attack rules not being verified in time to benefit other users. The rest of this chapter discusses an architecture design of peer-to-peer (P2P) automatic Snort rule sharing systems and P2P rule propagation mechanism design.

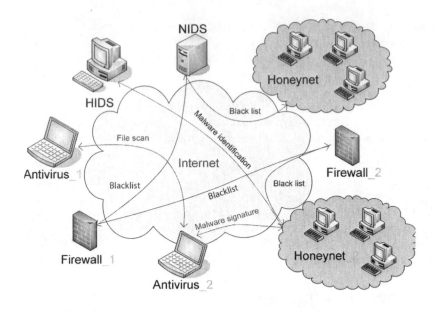

Figure 9.1: Topology of a knowledge-based intrusion detection network, where IDSs are connected to a peer-to-peer network and share intrusion detection knowledge with others.

9.3.2 Communication Framework

The communication framework is built on a Chord [131] peer-to-peer (P2P) communication overlay. Each node is assigned a key and maintains a finger table that contains a list of other nodes for key search (e.g., routing) in the Chord ring. Each node may have a long list of acquaintances and each acquaintance j has a certain probability $p_{ij} \in (0, 1]$ to be chosen to receive knowledge from the sender node i. A user on the receiver side evaluates knowledge (such as Snort rules) sent from its neighbors and may choose to "*accept*" or "*reject*" the rule. The decision is then recorded by a Bayesian learning algorithm to update the *compatibility ratio* of the sender. The *compatibility ratio* from i to j is the probability that the rules from the sender i are accepted by the receiver j. The higher a collaborator's compatibility, the more helpful it is in collaboration. The decision is also sent to a corresponding knowledge feedback collector. The feedback collector is a random node in the P2P network, determined by a key mapping function of the rule ID and the sender ID. The corresponding node holding the key will host the feedback of the rule. Inexperienced users can check feedback from others before they make their own decision whether or not to accept the rule. Users can also report false positives and true positives about the rule, so that the rule creator can collect feedback and make updates accordingly. More details about the feedback collector are provided in Section 9.3.5.

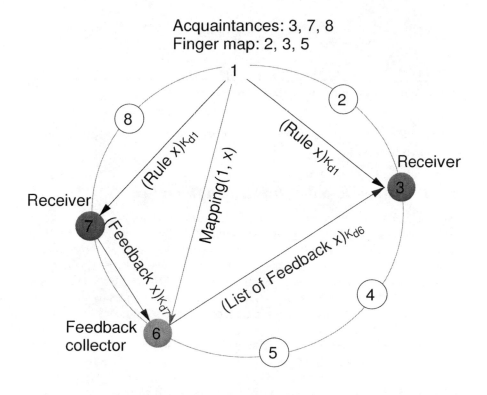

Figure 9.2: SMURFEN design of eight nodes on a Chord ring.

9.3.3 Snort Rules

Many intrusion detection systems, such as Snort, allow users to create and edit their own detection rules in their rule base. Snort rules are certified by the Vulnerability Research Team (Sourcefire), after being tested by security experts. Snort rules are vulnerability-based and written in plain text, hence can be easily interpreted and edited by users. Snort rules obtained from third parties can be adopted directly or indirectly with some changes. Snort rules can be independent or can be grouped together into rule units. The basic rule structure includes two logical sections: the header section and the option section. The rule header contains the rule's action, protocol, source and destination IP addresses and network masks, and the source and destination ports information. The rule option section contains alert messages and information on which parts of the packet should be inspected to determine whether the rule action should be taken [119]. Figure 9.3 illustrates a simple Snort rule. When a TCP packet with the destination IP and port number matching the specified pattern and data payload containing the specified binary content is detected, a "mounted access" alert is raised.

Sometimes the rules can be interdependent of each other; then the dependent rules shall be binded and shared as one unit. An example of interdependent rules is

```
alert tcp any any -> 192.168.1.0/24 111 \
    (content:"|00 01 86 a5|"; msg:"mountd access";)
```

Figure 9.3: An example Snort rule. (Adapted from [119].)

shown in Figure 9.4, where the second rule is triggered to record 50 packets after the first rule is triggered.

9.3.4 Authenticated Network Join Operation

We can assume that there exists a traditional *central authority* (CA) from which all nodes can obtain a public and private key pair. We enforce all knowledge exchanged in the network to be encrypted by the receiver's public key and signed by the sender's private key. Receivers can verify the sender of the knowledge by its signature.

When a new node attempts to join the network, it first contacts the CA to obtain an ID and public/private keys, as well as a list of bootstrap nodes to join the collaboration network. Then, the new node contacts the bootstrap nodes to obtain initial candidates for the acquaintance list.

When a node leaves the network temporarily, it can simply go offline. If a node leaves the network permanently, it can notify the CA and its collaborators to remove the node from their acquaintance lists. If a node goes offline or remains inactive for a long time, its entry in its collaborators' acquaintance lists may expire, and if so, it has to renew its membership by initiating a new operation to join the network.

9.3.5 Feedback Collector

When a user receives new rules from the community, she/he may evaluate the rules and determine whether or not to adopt the rule. A feedback collector is used to record the feedback on the rules from users. Less experienced users may check the feedback from others before making their decisions. As shown in Figure 9.5, rule author "A"

```
activate tcp !$HOME_NET any -> $HOME_NET 143 \
    (flags: PA; content: "|E8C0FFFFFF|/bin"; \
    activates: 1;msg: "IMAP buffer overflow!\";)
dynamic tcp !$HOME_NET any -> $HOME_NET 143 \
    (activated_by: 1; count: 50;)
```

Figure 9.4: An example of dependent Snort rules. The first rule triggers the alert and activates the second rule; The second rule records 50 packets after the first rule is triggered. (Adapted from [119].)

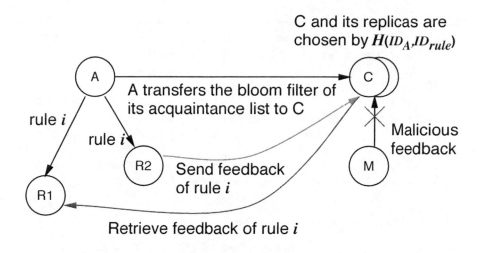

Figure 9.5: Feedback collection in SMURFEN. The malicious node M tries to leave fraudulent feedback but was blocked because it does not match the bloom filter on the feedback collector.

propagates a new rule i to its acquaintances R_1 and R_2. Both rule receivers can retrieve and send feedback from/to the feedback collector C, which is a random node in the P2P network determined by the key mapping of the creator and the rule ID. Replicas collectors can be used to improve the availability of the feedback collector service. All feedbacks are signed by their authors to prevent malicious tampering.

Moreover, to avoid feedback fraudulence, each feedback collector maintains a bloom filter [43] of the authorized nodes list. The rule author hashes all of its acquaintances into a bloom filter and passes it to the feedback collector. Only nodes with hashed IDs matching the bloom filter are allowed to leave feedback on the collector. The use of a bloom filter not only reduces the communication overhead to transfer long acquaintance lists, but also avoids unnecessary information leaking from the rule author.

9.3.6   *Trust Evaluation and Acquaintance Management*

Each node in the network shares its intrusion detection rules with their collaborators. However, trust evaluation is necessary to distinguish good/bad nodes in the network. For example, a malicious user may broadcast a large number of spam rules to others. To distinguish malicious collaborators, each IDS evaluates the trust values of others by rating the quality of the rules received from them. If a correct intrusion detection is made according to the received knowledge, it is labeled "*effective detection.*" If a false alarm is made, then it is labeled as "*false detection.*" If a knowledge results in no detection after a certain period, then it is labeled "*no detection.*" A Bayesian learning algorithm (Section 9.5) is then used to update the *trust value* of the sender based on the aggregated quality of the knowledge received. An effective detection will increase the trust value of the sender and a false alarm will penalize it. The *trust value* of node i perceived by node j can be seen as the level of helpfulness that node i provides to the receiver node j. The more helpful a collaborator is, the higher its trust value.

The collaboration relationship is based on mutual consent. Every new collaborator candidate is assigned a low trust value at the beginning and needs to pass a probation period before becoming a collaborator. During the probation period, the trust value of the new candidate will be evaluated by its peers. When the probation period expires, new candidates gaining high trust values will replace collaborators with low trust values in the acquaintance list. Collaborators with trust lower than a certain threshold will be removed and new ones will be recruited periodically.

9.3.7 Knowledge Propagation Control

Each IDS can share its intrusion detection rules with its collaborators. In our propagation system, nodes propagate rules to receivers directly, and the receivers rank the trust values of the senders based on the quality of the received knowledge. Knowledge that contributes to "effective detection" can be further propagated to the collaborators of the receiving node (see Figure 9.6). Otherwise, it will not be further propagated.

However, in such a network, free-riders may benefit from the collective knowledge without contributing to the network. In addition, malicious insiders may send excessive amounts of spam to others to downgrade the performance of a collaboration network. To cope with these problems, nodes in our system propagate knowledge to their collaborators at rates proportional to their trust values as well as their demanding rates (requested sending rate). Each node sets its demanding rate to collaborators based on its receiving capacity and the trust values of the collaborators. A decentralized two-level game framework is designed to optimize independently the node's

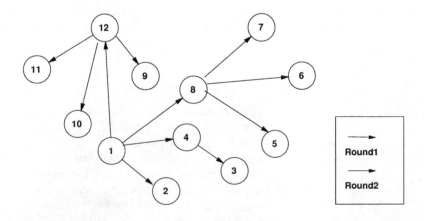

Figure 9.6: An example of knowledge propagation path.

public utilities and private utility (see Section 9.4 for a detailed description). This knowledge propagation scheme is incentive compatible and is robust to DoS attacks from insiders.

9.3.8 An Example

For a better understanding of the rule sharing framework, we illustrate the mechanism with an example (see Figure 9.2). Assume that user 1 (on node 1) detects a new software vulnerability and creates a new Snort rule x to protect the system before the official release from the VRT. User 1 is part of the rule sharing network. The new rule is automatically propagated to its acquaintances through a propagation process (described in Section 9.4). User 3 and user 7 receive rule x from user 1. The user 7 finds rule x to be useful to her/his network and can choose to *accept* or *reject* it. The decision is then notified to a feedback collector on node 6. If the rule is adopted and alerts are triggered by rule x, the decision of whether it is a true or false alarm is also forwarded to node 6. Users can reject a formally accepted rule any time when it causes large false positives or does not detect any attack after a certain amount of time. Rule x is also propagated to node 3. If user 3 finds that the rule covers vulnerabilities but does not have enough experience to judge the quality of the rule, then she/he chooses to inspect the feedback from other users about the rule from the feedback collector. The decision of acceptance or rejection can be delayed to allow enough time for observation.

9.4 Knowledge Sharing and Propagation Model

As previously mentioned, in a gossiping-based information propagation model, information is disseminated in a pair-wise and multi-hop fashion. However, existing gossip models are simplistic and either choose to propagate to all neighbors in turn or randomly choose nodes in the network to propagate to. They do not capture the quality of the information sender or the preference of the receiver. This section discusses the knowledge sharing control model used to decide how often an IDS should propagate snort rules to its acquaintances, based on the quality of the sender and the preference of the receiver, which are learned from previous interactions.

We model the rule sharing network into a set of n IDSs, denoted by $\mathcal{N}$. In the network, IDSs contribute and share intrusion detection knowledge with others. A node i propagates knowledge to its collaborators, denoted by $\mathcal{N}_i$, with a *knowledge propagation rate* $r_{ij}, j \in \mathcal{N}_i$, to achieve an optimal impact. We use a vector $\vec{r}_i$ to represent the knowledge propagation rate from node i to its collaborators. To avoid denial-of-service attacks from malicious collaborators, node j sets a maximum sending rate from each of its collaborators. We denote by $R_{ij}, i, j \in \mathcal{N}$, the *requested sending rate* from i to j. Note that R_{ij} is controlled by node j and informed to node i. We use $\vec{R}_j$ to denote the requested sending rates node j imposes on all its collaborators. Our system requires each node to control its sending rate under the requested sending rate, that is, $r_{ij} \le R_{ij}, \forall i, j \in \mathcal{N}$. To control the communication overhead, a node i sets the upper-bound $M_i \in \mathbb{R}_{++}$ on the total outbound knowledge propagation rate, that is, $\sum_{j \in \mathcal{N}_i} r_{ij} \le M_i$. We assume that each node contributes new detection knowledge and share it with its collaborators. Denote by $\bar{r}_i$ the *knowledge contribution rate* from node i. Note that the contributed knowledge can be created by the sender or effective knowledge received by the sender from others. The knowledge propagation rate from the sender node i to others shall not exceed the knowledge contribution rate of node i, as the maximum knowledge propagation rate is to propagate all the knowledge it has.

Not all propagated knowledge is useful to the recipients. To capture the metric of relationship on helpfulness, we use a matrix $\mathbf{T} = [T_{ij}]_{i,j \in \mathcal{N}}$ to denote the *trust value* of node i perceived by node j, where $T_{ij} \in [0,1], \forall i, j \in \mathcal{N}$, which represents the level of helpfulness of node i to node j. Note that the compatibility matrix can be asymmetric, that is, $T_{ij} \ne T_{ji}$.

Our goal is to devise a system-wide knowledge propagation protocol such that the knowledge contributed by all contributors is fairly distributed to other nodes to optimize their impact on the system. To achieve this goal, we model our system based on a two-level optimization problem formulation. At the lower level, an IDS i solves the optimization problem (PPi) where it chooses its propagation rate $\vec{r}_i$ to optimize its public utility function. At the upper level, an IDS i determines the request rate to all acquaintances $\vec{R}_i$ from a private optimization problem (Pi). The choice of R_{ji} at the upper level influences the decision-making at the lower public optimization level. We summarize the notations used in this section in Table 9.1.

Figure 9.7 is an illustration of the rule propagation protocol between IDS i and IDS j. Each IDS has a two-level decision process. IDS i optimizes the propagation rate r_{ij} based on an altruistic or public optimization (PPi) and uses a private optimization problem (Pi) to determine the requested sending rate R_{ji}, which will be passed to IDS j for its propagation decisions. It can be seen that the (PPj) decision of IDS j depends on the decision from (Pi) of IDS i. The interdependence of the agents leads to a Nash equilibrium.

Table 9.1: Summary of Notations

Symbol	Meaning
r_{ij}	The rule propagating rate from node i to node j
q_{ij}	Greed factor (the return ratio node j asks from node i)
R_{ij}	Requested sending rate from i to j (set by node j)
M_i	Sending resource capacity of node i
R_i	Receiving resource capacity of node i
T_{ij}	Compatibility from i to j
r_i	The rule generating rate from node i

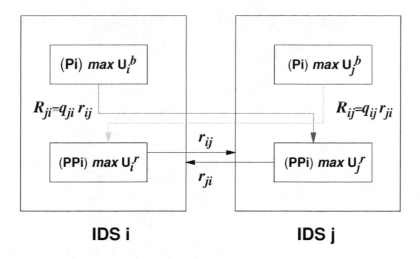

Figure 9.7: An illustration of the rule propagation protocol.

9.4.1 Lower Level – Public Utility Optimization

In this subsection we formulate an optimization framework for each node to decide on the propagation rate to all its collaborators to maximize its utility. The utility of each node U_i has two components: a public utility function U_i^p and a private utility function U_i^r. The utility U_i^p measures the aggregated satisfaction level experienced by node i's collaborators weighted by their trust values. It allows a node to provide more help to those with whom there was more helpful interaction in the past. On the other hand, U_i^r measures the satisfaction level of a node with respect to the amount of help it receives from its collaborators.

The basic argument for this algorithm is to tune the utility function so that we balance the weight of two purposes of rule propagation: send rules to whom need it most or to whom helped back most? In a need-based society where nodes put others' needs as the sole factor should result in a maximum utilization of rules created in the whole society, where the social warefare function is the total benefit of all members. However, this community creates no incentives for nodes to contribute to the collaboration as increasing their rule creation rate does not result in better payback. In a long run, the total warefare may decrease as a result of not enough contributors. The return-based warefare model sends rules to those who helped back most. This may result in a strong incentive for creating new rules to share with others because to return is proportional to the amount of contribution to others. However, under such a paradigm, nodes that create no rules will result in no help received.

The public optimization problem (PPi) seen by each node $i, i \in \mathcal{N}$, is given by

$$(\text{PP}i) \max_{\vec{r}_i \in \mathbb{R}^{n_i}} U_i^P(\vec{r}_i) \quad := \quad \sum_{j \in \mathcal{N}_i} T_{ji} S_{ij}(r_{ij}) \tag{9.1}$$

$$\sum_{j \in \mathcal{N}_i} r_{ij} \quad \leq \quad M_i, \tag{9.2}$$

$$r_{ij} \quad \leq \quad R_{ij}, \tag{9.3}$$

$$0 \leq r_{ij} \quad \leq \quad \bar{r}_i, \tag{9.4}$$

where $S_{ij} : \mathbb{R} \to \mathbb{R}$ is the satisfaction level of node j in response to the propagation rate r_{ij} of node i. We let S_{ij} take the following form:

$$S_{ij}(r_{ij}) := T_{ij} \log \left(1 + \frac{r_{ij}}{R_{ij}} \right). \tag{9.5}$$

The concavity and monotonicity of the satisfaction level indicate that a recipient becomes increasingly pleased when more knowledge is received but the marginal satisfaction decreases as the amount of knowledge increases. The parameter T_{ij} in (9.5) suggests that a node j is more content when the sender i is more trustable.

The objective function $U_i^P : \mathbb{R}^{n_i} \to \mathbb{R}$ in (9.1) aggregates the satisfaction level S_{ij} of node j by the compatibility factor T_{ji}. The utility U_i^P can be viewed as a public altruistic utility in that a node i seeks to satisfy its collaborators by choosing knowledge propagation rates $\vec{r}_i$. The problem (PPi) is constrained by (9.2) in that the total sending rate of a node i is upper bounded by its communication capacity. Constraint (9.3) says that the propagation rate from i to j shall not exceed the requested sending rate from the recipient j. The additional constraint (9.4) ensures that the propagation rate does not exceed its knowledge contribution rate $\bar{r}_i$. Note that the constraint (9.3) is imposed by its recipient j while constraint (9.4) is set by node i itself.

Because the utility function (9.1) is strictly convex in $\vec{r}_i$ and the feasible set is convex, the optimization problem (PPi) is in the form of convex programming and admits a unique solution.

It can be seen that when M_i is sufficiently large and (9.2) is an inactive constraint, the solution to (PPi) becomes trivial and $r_{ij} = \min(R_{ij}, \bar{r}_i)$ for all $j \in \mathcal{N}_i$. The situation becomes more interesting when (9.2) is an active constraint. Assuming that R_{ij} has been appropriately set by node j, we form the Lagrangian functional $\mathcal{L}^i : \mathbb{R}^{n_i} \times \mathbb{R} \times \mathbb{R}^{n_i} \to \mathbb{R}$

$$\mathcal{L}^i(\vec{r}_i, \mu_i, \delta_{ij}) := \sum_{j \in \mathcal{N}_i} T_{ji} T_{ij} \log \left(1 + \frac{r_{ij}}{R_{ij}} \right)$$

$$- \mu_i \left(\sum_{j \in \mathcal{N}_i} r_{ij} - M_i \right) - \sum_{j \in \mathcal{N}_i} \delta_{ij}(r_{ij} - \bar{r}_{ij}),$$

where $\mu_i, \delta_{ij} \in \mathbb{R}_+$ satisfy the complementarity conditions $\mu_i \left(\sum_{j \in \mathcal{N}_i} r_{ij} - M_i \right) = 0$, and $\delta_{ij}(r_{ij} - \bar{r}_{ij}) = 0, \forall j \in \mathcal{N}_i$, where $\bar{r}_{ij} := \min(R_{ij}, \bar{r}_i)$. We minimize the Lagrangian with respect to $\vec{r}_i \in \mathbb{R}_+^{n_i}$ and obtain the first-order Kuhn-Tucker condition: $\frac{T_{ij} T_{ji}}{r_{ij} + R_{ij}} =$

$\mu_i + \delta_{ij}$, $\forall j \in \mathcal{N}_i$. When (9.2) is active but (9.3) and (9.4) are inactive, we can find an explicit solution supplied with the equality condition

$$\sum_{j \in \mathcal{N}_i} r_{ij} = M_i, \tag{9.6}$$

and consequently, we obtain the optimal solution

$$r_{ij}^{\star} := \frac{T_{ij} T_{ji}}{\sum_{u \in \mathcal{N}_i} T_{iu} T_{ui}} \left(M_i + \sum_{v \in \mathcal{N}_i} R_{iv} \right) - R_{ij}. \tag{9.7}$$

When either one of the constraints (9.3) and (9.4) is active, the optimal solution is attained at the boundary. Because the log function has the fairness property, the optimal solution $r_{ij}^{\star}$ has non-zero entries when the resource budget $M_i > 0$. In addition, due to the monotonicity of the objective function, the optimal solution $r_{ij}^{\star}$ is attained when all resource budgets are allocated, that is, constraint (9.2) is active.

Remark 9.4.1 *We can interpret (9.7) as follows. The solution $r_{ij}^{\star}$ is composed of two components. The first part is a proportional division of the resource capacity M_i among $|\mathcal{N}_i|$ collaborators according to their compatibilities. The second part is a linear correction on the proportional division by balancing the requested sending rate R_{ij}. It is also important to notice that by differentiating $r_{ij}^{\star}$ with respect to R_{ij}, we obtain $\frac{\partial r_{ij}^{\star}}{\partial R_{ij}} = \left(\frac{T_{ij} T_{ji}}{\sum_{u \in \mathcal{N}_i} T_{iu} T_{ui}} - 1 \right) < 0$, suggesting that at the optimal solution, the propagation rate decreases as the recipient sets a higher requested sending rate. If a node wishes to receive a higher propagation rate from its collaborators, it has no incentive to overstate its level of request. Rather, a node j has the incentive to understate its request level to increase $r_{ij}^{\star}$. However, the optimal solution is upper bounded by $\min(\bar{r}_i, R_{ij})$. Hence, by understating its request R_{ij}, the optimal propagation rate is achieved at $\min(\bar{r}_i, R_{ij})$.*

9.4.2 Upper Level – Private Utility Optimization

An IDS i has another degree of freedom to choose its level of requested sending rate R_{ji} of its collaborators. R_{ji} states the maximum knowledge propagation rate from node j to i that node i can accept. In contrast to the public utility optimization, the optimization at this level is inherently nonaltruistic or private. The objective of an IDS i is to choose $\vec{R}_i$ so that its private utility $U_i^r : \mathbb{R}_+^{n_i} \to \mathbb{R}$ is maximized, that is,

$$(\text{P}i) \quad \max_{\vec{R}_i \in \mathbb{R}_+^{n_i}} U_i^r(\vec{R}_i), \tag{9.8}$$

subject to the following constraint from the total receiving capacity $\bar{R}_i$, that is,

$$\sum_{j \in \mathcal{N}_i} R_{ji} \leq \bar{R}_i. \tag{9.9}$$

Let U_i^r take the form of $U_i^r := \sum_{j \in \mathcal{N}_i} T_{ji} \log(1 + r_{ji}^* / \bar{R}_i)$, where r_{ji}^* is the optimal solution attained at (PPi). The log function indicates that an IDS intends to maximize its own level of satisfaction by choosing an appropriate level of request. The request capacity is imposed to prevent excessive incoming traffic as a result of a high level of requests. We assume that the capacity is sufficiently large so that the constraint is inactive. Therefore, the decision variable R_{ji} is uncoupled and the problem (Pi) can be equivalently separated into $|\mathcal{N}_i|$ optimization problems with respect to each j, that is, for every $j \in \mathcal{N}_i$,

$$(\text{P}ij) \quad \max_{R_{ji} \in \mathbb{R}_+} \log\left(1 + \frac{r_{ji}^*}{\bar{R}_i}\right). \tag{9.10}$$

As a recipient, node i needs to ensure that the receiving traffic does not exceed a level of R_i. Hence, the private utility optimization problem faced by node i is given by

$$(\text{P}i) \max_{q_{ij}} U_i^b \tag{9.11}$$

$$\sum_{j \in \mathcal{N}_i} r_{ji} \leq R_i \tag{9.12}$$

The properties of the solutions to (Pi) and (PPi) are illustrated in Figure 9.8 for an IDS i and its two neighboring peers. In this illustrative example, we look at the optimal propagation rule for node i to communicate with node 1 and 2. Node i solves (PPi) with constraints (1) $r_{i1} + r_{i2} \leq M_i$, (2) $r_{i1} \leq R_{i1}$, and (3) $r_{i2} \leq R_{i2}$. The shaded region is the feasible set of the optimization problem. The optimal allocation can be points on the face of $r_{i1} + r_{i2} = M_i$ of the feasible set. Given the request rates R_{i1} and R_{i2}, suppose the optimal allocation is found at the red point. At the higher level, nodes 1 and 2 need to solve the optimization problems (P1i) and (P2i), respectively. They have incentives to understate their requests. For example, node 1 can request a lower rate until it hits R_{i1}^* and the optimal allocation will increase until it reaches R_{i1}^*. This fact leads to the green point, which is the optimal solution to (PPi) found on the vertex of its feasible set given that $r_{i1} \leq R_{i1}^*$. Node 2 makes the same decision and results in R_{i2}^*.

9.4.3 Tuning Parameter R_{ij}

We have obtained Nash Equilibrium under the condition that the receiver does not have constraints of the total number of rules it receives per unit time, that is, $r_{ij} = \frac{T_{ij} T_{ji} M_i}{\sum_{u \in \mathcal{N}_i} T_{iu} T_{ui}}$. However, in practice, users prefer to set a limit on the number of rules it receives per day. The reasons are twofold: first, users can only investigate a limited number of rules per unit time due to their individual capabilities. Too many rules with average low quality can bring high false positives. Second, without setting a sending limit to senders, malicious nodes can flood with a large number of invalid rules (DoS) to slow down the efficiency of the intrusion detection on the receiver side.

Let parameter R_{ji} denote the sending limit node i set for node j so that node j

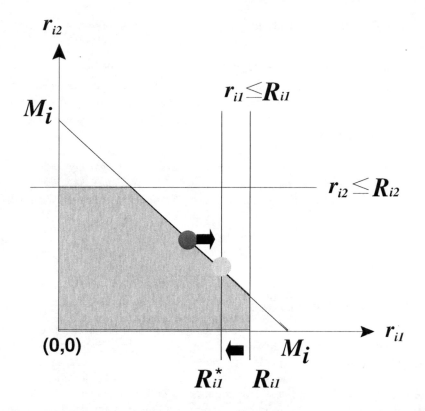

Figure 9.8: An illustrative example of a three-person system involving the set of nodes $\{i, 1, 2\}$. **Node** i **solves (PPi) while nodes 1 and 2 solve (P1i) and (P2i), respectively.**

shall not send rules to i with a rate higher than R_{ji}. We can prove that under the condition $\sum_{u \in \mathcal{N}_i} r_{ui} = \sum_{u \in \mathcal{N}_i} \frac{T_{iu}T_{ui}M_u}{\sum_{v \in \mathcal{N}_{iu}} C_{uv}C_{vu}} < R_i, \forall i$, the optimal solution is the unconstrained Nash solution. Under the condition that the sending resource is higher than receiving resource, the constraint of sending limit can be relaxed. Then we have $r_{ij} = \frac{T_{ij}R_j}{\sum_{i \in \mathcal{N}_j} T_{ij}}$

Theorem 9.1
Removing constraint (9.3) does not change the solutions to the optimization problem (9.1)

Proof 9.1
Suppose the optimal solution set is $\vec{r}_u{}^*$. Among the solution set, at least one value exceeds the upper-bound constraint, say $r_{ij}^* > R_{ij}$. Then we can find a corresponding

solution $r'_{ij} = 2R_{ij} - r^*_{ij}$. The new solution is $r'_{ij} < r^*_{ij}$, but it provides the same level of satisfaction to v, that is, $S(r'_{ij}) = S(r^*_{ij})$ (from (9.5)).

Now if we replace r^*_{ij} into r'_{ij} in the solution set $\vec{r_u}^*$, then we have some spare resource $r^*_{ij} - r'_{ij}$. We use the spare resource on R_{ji} and we can achieve improved utility U_p and therefore improved total utility (9.1). This contradicts the assumption that $\vec{r_u^*}$ is an optimal solution. Therefore, all optimal solutions should satisfy the upper-bound constraint.

Remark 9.4.2 *From Remark 9.4.1, we know the optimal strategy for node i is to understate R_{ji} until r^*_{ji} hits the boundary $\min(\bar{r}_j, R_{ji})$. We define the optimal response R^*_{ji} to be the lowest possible R_{ji} that achieves the highest r^*_{ji}. From (9.7) we have*

$$R^\star_{ji} = r^\star_{ji} = \frac{1}{2} \frac{T_{ij}T_{ji}}{\sum_{u \in \mathcal{N}_j} T_{ju}T_{uj}} \left(M_j + \sum_{v \in \mathcal{N}_j} R_{jv} \right). \tag{9.13}$$

9.4.4 Nash Equilibrium

In a collaboration network, each node responds to other nodes by choosing optimal propagation rates and requested sending rates. The two-level optimization problem leads to two game structures of interest. Let $\mathbf{G1} := \langle \mathcal{N}, \{\bar{r}_i\}_{i \in \mathcal{N}}, \{U_i^p\}_{i \in \mathcal{N}} \rangle$ be the game that corresponds to optimization problem (PPi) in which each node chooses its propagation rates given requested sending rates from its collaborators. Hence, the utilities of the users in (9.5) reduce to mere functions of r_{ij}. Denote by $\mathbf{G2} := \langle \mathcal{N}, \{\bar{r}_i, \bar{R}_i\}_{i \in \mathcal{N}}, \{U_i^p, U_i^r\}_{i \in \mathcal{N}} \rangle$ the game that corresponds to the two-level optimization problem (PPi) together with (Pi). In $\mathbf{G2}$, each node i chooses its propagation rates as well as its request rates. We study the existence and uniqueness properties of the Nash equilibrium (NE) of these two games as follows. The proofs can be found in the Appendix B.

Proposition 9.4.3 *Each of the games for $\mathbf{G1}$ and $\mathbf{G2}$ admits a Nash equilibrium (NE).*

Theorem 9.2
In $\mathbf{G2}$, there exists an NE such that $r_{ij} = R_{ij}$, $\forall i, j \in \mathcal{N}$.

The equilibrium that satisfies the conditions described in Theorem 9.2 is called a *prime* NE. In the following, we provide two results on the uniqueness of NE in $\mathbf{G1}$ and $\mathbf{G2}$.

Proposition 9.4.4 *Assume that only (9.2) is an active constraint in the optimization problem (Pi) of each node i in $\mathbf{G1}$. Let $\lambda_{ij} = \frac{T_{ij}T_{ji}}{\sum_{u \in \mathcal{N}_i} T_{iu}T_{ui}}$. Let $q_{ij} = \frac{R_{ij}}{r_{ji}}$ be the greed factor of i over j. Then there exists a unique NE for $\mathbf{G1}$ if $q_{ij}q_{ji} \neq \frac{1}{(1-\lambda_{ij})(1-\lambda_{ji})}$ for each pair of neighbor nodes i, j.*

Proposition 9.4.5 *Assume that $\bar{r}_i$ is sufficiently large. Let $n_i = |\mathcal{N}_i|$. Then there exists a unique NE for* **G2** *if $n_i \lambda_{ij} < 2$ for every pair of neighbor nodes i and j.*

The following proposition characterizes the optimal solution of **G2** under special conditions.

Proposition 9.4.6 *Assume that $\bar{r}_i$ and $\bar{R}_i$ are sufficiently large so that the constraints (9.4) and (9.9) are inactive. Then, the unique NE solution of* **G2** *is given by*

$$r_{ij}^* = R_{ij}^* = \frac{T_{ij}T_{ji}}{\sum_{u \in \mathcal{N}_i} T_{iu}T_{ui}} M_i. \tag{9.14}$$

9.4.5 Price of Anarchy Analysis

In the following we study the system efficiency at the prime Nash equilibrium compared with the social welfare solution. We use the price of anarchy as a metric to quantify the loss of efficiency as a result of decentralization. Let U_S be the social welfare of the network as the sum of the public utilities, that is, $U_S(\mathbf{r}, \mathbf{R}) = \sum_{i \in \mathcal{N}} \sum_{j \in N_i} T_{ij}T_{ji} \ln\left(1 + \frac{r_{ij}}{R_{ij}}\right)$, where $\mathbf{r} = \{\vec{r}_i\}_{i \in \mathcal{N}}, \mathbf{R} = \{\vec{R}_i\}_{i \in \mathcal{N}}$. A network planner optimizes the social welfare problem (SWP) as follows:

$$\text{(SWP)} \quad \max_{\mathbf{r},\mathbf{R}} \qquad\qquad U_S(\mathbf{r}, \mathbf{R})$$

$$\text{s. t.} \quad \sum_{j \in \mathcal{N}_i} r_{ij} \leq M_i, \quad r_{ij} \leq R_{ij}, \quad 0 \leq r_{ij} \leq \bar{r}_i.$$

Let $(\mathbf{r}^\circ, \mathbf{R}^\circ) := \{\vec{r}_i^\circ, \vec{R}_i^\circ\}_{i \in \mathcal{N}}$ be the optimal solution to the optimization problem (SWP) and the corresponding value is denoted as U_S°.

Definition 9.1 Let $(\mathbf{r}^*, \mathbf{R}^*) := \{\vec{r}_i^*, \vec{R}_i^*\}_{i \in \mathcal{N}}$ be a prime Nash equilibrium of the game **G2**, and $\mathcal{E}_P$ be the set of such a prime NE. Let U_S^* be the social welfare achieved under a prime NE $(\mathbf{r}^*, \mathbf{R}^*) \in \mathcal{E}_P$. The price of anarchy ρ_P of a prime NE is $\rho_P = \max_{(\mathbf{r}^*, \mathbf{R}^*) \in \mathcal{E}_P} \frac{U_S^*}{U_S^\circ}$

In the following theorem we show that prime NEs are efficient and the loss of efficiency is 0.

Theorem 9.3
The price of anarchy of a prime NE is 1.

Proof 9.2 The optimal value of Social Welfare Policy (SWP) is given by $U_S^\circ = \sum_{i \in \mathcal{N}} \sum_{j \in N_i} T_{ij}T_{ji} \ln 2$, and it is achieved when $r_{ij} = R_{ij}$ for all $i \in \mathcal{N}, j \in \mathcal{N}_i$. In addition, the property that $r_{ij} = R_{ij}$ of prime NE yields the same utility.

9.4.6 Knowledge Propagation

In this subsection we investigate from a macroscopic perspective the knowledge propagation over the collaborative intrusion detection network. Let $n_i = |\mathcal{N}_i|$ be the number of neighbors of node i, which is also referred to as the connectivity or degree. In general, the connectivity is different for every node. The network represented by the graph $\mathcal{G}$ can be characterized by the degree distribution $P_G(k), k = 0, 1, 2, \cdots, n - 1$, defined by $p_k = P_G(k) = \frac{1}{n}|\{i \in \mathcal{N}, \text{s. t. } n_i = k\}|$. A network is called an exponential network if its connectivity is distributed according to an exponential function (i.e., $P_G(k) \sim e^{-k}$). A scale-free network exhibits a power-law connectivity distribution (i. e., $P(k) \sim k^{\gamma}, \gamma \in (2,3)$). To study the property of knowledge propagation, we assume that $\mathcal{G}$ is a realization of a large random network, whose degree distribution is given by $P_G(k), k = 0, 1, \cdots$, and $\sum_{k=0}^{\infty} P_G(k) = 1$. For convenience, we define the generating function of the distribution $P_G(k)$ as $\Phi_0(z) = \sum_{k=1}^{\infty} p_k z^k$, where $0 \le z \le 1$. It is easy to verify the properties that $\Phi_0'(z) > 0, \Phi_0''(z) > 0$ and $p_k = \frac{\Phi_0^{(k)}}{k!}, k = 0, 1, 2, \cdots$. The mean degree of the network is $\bar{k} = \sum_{k=1}^{\infty} k p_k = \Phi_0'(1)$.

When a piece of knowledge is created at a node of degree k in the network, it starts to propagate to every individual to whom it is connected at the mean equilibrium rate $\tilde{r}_m$ once, which is the average propagation rate in the network at the equilibrium, that is, $\tilde{r}_m = \frac{1}{n} \sum_{i=1}^{n} \sum_{j=1}^{n} \frac{1}{n_i} r_{ij}^{\star}$. Let $Q_m^k = \{q_m^k, 0 \le m \le k, k = 0, 1, 2, \cdots\}$ be the distribution of the number of nodes connected to a node of degree k that receive the new knowledge. The probability of $m \le k$ nodes to receive new knowledge from a node of degree k is given by $q_m^k = \binom{k}{m} (\tilde{r}_m)^m (1 - \tilde{r}_m)^{k-m}$. Let $Q_m = \{q_m, m = 0, 1, \cdots\}$ be the distribution of the number of nodes who receive the knowledge in the network and q_m be the probability that m nodes receive the knowledge from a random node, which is given by $q_m = \sum_{k=m}^{\infty} p_k q_m^k = \sum_{k=m}^{\infty} p_k \binom{k}{m} (\tilde{r}_m)^m (1 - \tilde{r}_m)^{k-m}$. Let the generating function for the distribution $Q_{k,m}$ be $\Gamma_0(z, r^*) = \sum_{k=0}^{\infty} q_m z^m = \sum_{k=0}^{\infty} p_k [z\tilde{r}_m + (1 - \tilde{r}_m)]^k = \Phi_0(1 + (z - 1)\tilde{r}_m)$.

In the next round of propagation, as the new knowledge follows the connection between two nodes and reaches a new node, the connectivity of the node for further propagation or the *excess degree* of the node is one less. Assume that the probability of reaching a node of degree k is proportional to k. Then, the distribution of the number of nodes receiving the new knowledge is $Q_m^2 = \{q_m^e, m = 0, 1, \cdots\}$, where q_m^e is the probability that m nodes receive the knowledge in the second round, given by $q_m^e = \sum_{k=m}^{\infty} \frac{k p_k}{\bar{k}} q_m^k$. Hence, the corresponding generating function can be obtained as $\Gamma_1(z, \tilde{r}_m) = \sum_{k=0}^{\infty} q_m^e z^m = \Phi_1(1 + (z - 1)\tilde{r}_m)$, where $\Phi_1(z)$ is the generating function of the distribution $\{\frac{k p_k}{\bar{k}}, k = 1, 2, \cdots\}$, i.e., $\Phi_1(z) = \sum_{k=1}^{\infty} \frac{k p_k}{\bar{k}} = \frac{1}{\bar{k}} \Phi_0'(z)$. Let the mean excess degree in the second round of propagation be $D_1^e := \Gamma_1'(1, \tilde{r}_m) = \tilde{r}_m \Phi_1'(1) = \frac{\tilde{r}_m}{\bar{k}} \Phi_0''(1)$.

In the following we study the probability of persistence and extinction of new knowledge as a result of propagation in the network. We let $z_t, t = 0, 1, 2, \cdots$, denote the probability that a piece of knowledge will die out within the next t rounds of propagation. Suppose that a node i of degree k propagates information to a node j of degree k'. For the knowledge to die out in round t, the following round of propagation must die out at round $t - 1$. Note that the probability that the ensuing propagation from node i to j to die out is $q^e_{k'} z^{k'}_{t-1}$. Hence, the probability of the knowledge to die out in t rounds is the sum over all the possible degrees k', that is,

$$z_t = \sum_{k'=0}^{\infty} q^e_{k'} z^{k'}_{t-1} = \Phi_1(1 + (z_{t-1} - 1)\tilde{r}_m), \tag{9.15}$$

and the initial condition $z_0 = 0$. Because $\Phi_1(z)$ is an increasing function and $z \in [0, 1]$, the sequence $\{z_t, t = 0, 1, \cdots\}$ is an increasing sequence and has a limit z^*, and z^* is the solution to the algebraic equation $z^* = \Phi_1(1 + (z^* - 1)\tilde{r}_m)$.

Theorem 9.4
If $D^e_1 < 1$, the knowledge will die out with probability 1. If $D^e_1 > 1$, everyone in the network will receive the knowledge with probability 1.

Corollary 9.4.7 *There exists a threshold mean propagation rate r_c such that for $\tilde{r}_m > r_c$, the knowledge will persist in the network with probability 1; for $\tilde{r}_m < r_c$, the knowledge will die out with probability 1; and r_c satisfies the relation $r_c \Phi'_1(1) = 1$.*

Remark 9.4.8 *We can consider a random network distributed according to a Poisson distribution, that is, $p_k = \frac{e^{-\lambda} \lambda^k}{k!}$, for $\lambda \in \mathbb{R}_{++}$. The corresponding generating function is $\Phi_0(z) = e^{\lambda(z-1)}$ and $\Gamma'_0(z) = \lambda e^{\lambda(z-1)}$, $\Gamma'_0(1) = \lambda$. The generating function $\Phi_0(z) = \Phi_1(z)$ and $D^e_1 = \lambda r_c$. Hence, the threshold is $r_c = \frac{1}{\lambda}$.*

Remark 9.4.9 *Consider a power-law distributed network with $p_k = k^\alpha / \zeta(\alpha)$, known as a zeta distribution or discrete Pareto distribution [48, 111], where $\alpha > 1$ and $\zeta(\alpha) = \sum_{k=1}^{\infty} k^{-\alpha}$ is the Riemann zeta function. The power-law distribution has a finite mean $\bar{k} = \frac{\zeta(\alpha-1)}{\zeta(\alpha)}$ for $\alpha > 2$ and a finite variance for $\alpha > 3$. The generating function $\Phi_0(z) = Li_\alpha(z)/\zeta(\alpha)$, where $Li_\alpha(z)$ is the polylogarithm function, also known as Jonquière's function, defined by $Li_\alpha(z) = \sum_{k=1}^{\infty} \frac{z^k}{k^n}$. Note that $Li_\alpha(1) = \zeta(\alpha)$. Suppose that $\alpha > 3$. The mean excess degree can be obtained as $D^e_1 = \frac{\tilde{r}_m}{\zeta(\alpha-1)}(\zeta(\alpha-2) - \zeta(\alpha-1))$ and the threshold as $r_c = \frac{\zeta(\alpha-1)}{\zeta(\alpha-2)-\zeta(\alpha-1)}$.*

Remark 9.4.10 *Note that the mean propagation rate $\tilde{r}_m$ is dependent on the trust values $\mathbf{T}$. In general, higher trust values lead to higher mean propagation rates. Therefore, the threshold value r_c can be seen as a threshold on the trust values.*

9.5 Bayesian Learning and Dynamic Algorithms

In this section we describe a Bayesian learning approach to estimate the trust values used in Section 9.4 and establish a dynamic algorithm to find the prime Nash equilibrium that has been shown to exist in Theorem 9.2.

9.5.1 Bayesian Learning Model for Trust

In our P2P IDN context, the collaboration among IDSs tends to be long-term oriented compared to traditional file sharing P2P networks. This makes the evaluation of the trust values of collaborators based on personal experience suitable. In Section 9.4 we assumed that the trust values of all collaborators are given. In practice, they can be learned from past experience. In this section we introduce a Bayesian learning module for nodes to learn the trust of acquaintances. The learned trust value can be used for finding the equilibrium in Section 9.4 as well as for other applications and services in IDNs. This model extends our Dirichlet model for trust management [69, 74] with additional *credible bound* trust estimation.

9.5.1.1 Dirichlet Learning Model for Knowledge Quality

The quality of the knowledge propagated from IDS i to IDS j can be evaluated by node j after a certain time period. The quality assessment of a piece of knowledge results in classifying the knowledge into three categories: a) *effective detection, x_1*; b) *false alarm, x_2*; and c) *no detection, x_3*. Define the set of possible outcomes $\mathscr{X} = \{x_1, x_2, x_3\}$ and let X be the random variable described by the state space $\mathscr{X}$. Denote by $\vec{p} = \{p_1, p_2, p_3\}$ the vector whose components $p_l, l = 1, 2, 3$, satisfy $\sum_{l=1}^{3} p_l = 1$, each indicating the probability that the knowledge from IDS i to IDS j is classified in one of the categories x_l, that is, $P\{X = x_l\} = p_l$. Note that we have dropped the indices i and j in the notations for convenience in presentation. We use the vector of cumulative observations up to time n, $\vec{\gamma}^{(n)} = \{\gamma_1^{(n)}, \gamma_2^{(n)}, \gamma_3^{(n)}\}$, together with the initial beliefs of X to model $\vec{p}$ using a posterior Dirichlet distribution, that is, $\text{Dir}(\vec{p}|\vec{\gamma}) = \frac{\Gamma(\sum_{l=1}^{3} \gamma_l^{(n)})}{\prod_{l=1}^{3} \Gamma(\gamma_l^{(n)})} \prod_{l=1}^{3} p_l^{\gamma_l^{(n)} - 1}$, where $\Gamma(\cdot)$ is the gamma function. In order to give more weight to recent observations over old ones, $\vec{\gamma}^{(n)}$ is updated according to $\vec{\gamma}^{(n)} = \sum_{l'=1}^{n} \lambda^{t_{l'}} \vec{S}^{l'} + c_0 \lambda^{t_0} \vec{S}^0$, where n is the number of observations; $t_{l'}, l' = 1, \cdots, n$, is the time elapsed (age) since the l'-th outcome $\vec{S}^i$ was collected. $\vec{S}^0$ is the initial beliefs vector; $c_0 > 0$ is a priori constant, which puts a weight on the initial beliefs. Vector $\vec{S}^{l'}$ denotes the outcome of the knowledge at time $t_{l'} > 0$, which is a 3-tuple with one entry set to 1 corresponding to the selected category for that knowledge and the others being zero. Parameter $\lambda \in [0, 1]$ is the forgetting or discount factor. A small λ makes old observations quickly forgettable.

9.5.1.2 Credible-Bound Estimation of Trust

Let the random variable $Y = \sum_{l=1}^{3} p_l w_l$ be the expected knowledge quality from a sender, where $w_l, l = 1, 2, 3$, is the quality weight on knowledge in category x_l. The mean and the variance of Y can be obtained as $E[Y] = \sum_{l=1}^{3} w_l E[p_l] = \frac{1}{\gamma_0} \sum_{l=1}^{3} w_l \gamma_l$ and $\sigma^2[Y] = \frac{1}{\gamma_0^2 + \gamma_0} \sum_{k=1}^{3} w_k \gamma_k (w_k(\gamma_0 - \gamma_k) - 2 \sum_{l=k+1}^{3} w_l \gamma_l)$, where $\gamma_0 = \sum_{l=1}^{3} \gamma_l$. The trust values can be estimated through the *credible-bound* trust defined by $T = E[Y] - 2\sigma[Y]$. It has several properties, as follows. (P1) For each node i, increasing the knowledge sharing rate increases its trust value with others. (P2) When $\gamma_1, \gamma_2, \gamma_3$

are sufficiently large, Y can be approximated by a Gaussian distribution. Then T is approximately the 95% credential lower bound of Y.

9.5.2 Dynamic Algorithm to Find the Prime NE at Node

Algorithm 9.1 Dynamic Algorithm to Find the Prime NE at Node i

---

1: **Initialization** :
2: $\vec{R}^{in} \Leftarrow \{\varepsilon, \varepsilon, ..., \varepsilon\}$ // Small request rates for new collaborators.
3: $\vec{R}^{out} \Leftarrow$ **SendReceive**$(\vec{R}^{in})$ // Exchange requested sending rates with collaborators.
4: **set** new timer event$(t_u,$ "**SpUpdate**") // Update sending rates and request rates periodically.
5: **Periodic update:**
6: **at timer event** ev of type "SpUpdate" **do**
7: // Update the sending rate and the requested sending rates.
8: **for** $k = 0$ to B **do**
9: $\quad \vec{r}^{out} \Leftarrow$ **OptimizeSending**$(\mathbf{T}, \vec{R}^{out}, \mathbf{M}, \vec{r})$ // (PPi) optimization.
10: $\quad \vec{r}^{in} \Leftarrow$ **SendReceive**$(\vec{r}^{out})$ // Exchange sending rate with collaborators.
11: $\quad \vec{R}^{in} \Leftarrow$ **OptimizeRequest**$(\mathbf{T}, \vec{r}^{in}, \vec{R})$ // (Pi) optimization.
12: $\quad \vec{R}^{out} \Leftarrow$ **SendReceive**$(\vec{R}^{in})$
13: **end for**
14: **set** new timer event$(t_u,$ "**SpUpdate**")
15: **end timer event**

In this subsection we describe a distributed algorithm (Algorithm) for each node to determine its knowledge propagation rates to collaborators. The subscript i is removed for the convenience of presentation. The goal of the algorithm is to lead the system to converge to a prime NE that we introduced previously. In the beginning, nodes set a small requested sending rate for all new collaborators (line 2). An update process is triggered periodically where function **OptimizeSending** is used for the nodes to find their optimal sending rates $\vec{r}^{out}$ based on the trust matrix $\mathbf{T}$ and requested sending rate $\vec{R}^{out}$, which is informed by the collaborators in process **SendReceive** (line 3). $\mathbf{M}$ and $\vec{r}$ are the sending capacity and knowledge contribution rate of i, respectively. Function **OptimizeRequest** is for the node to find optimal $\vec{R}^{in}$ (**G2**), which gives the maximal private utility, given $\mathbf{T}$, the incoming sending rate $\vec{r}^{in}$, and $\vec{r}$. The update process is repeated B rounds to yield convergence.

The purpose of Algorithm 10.2 is to find the optimal numerical solution for (PPi) under general conditions. This algorithm is based on the fact that the marginal weighted satisfactions from all collaborators are continuous and monotonically decreasing, that is, $(T_{ji} S_{ij}'') < 0, \forall i, j$. $\mathscr{S}$ contains the sorted marginal weighted satisfactions of all collaborators at their boundaries $\{0, \min(\vec{r}_i, R_{ij})\}$. The idea is to find

---

Algorithm 9.2 Function OptimizeSending($\mathbf{T}, \vec{R}^{out}, M, \vec{r}$)

1: // Add to $\mathscr{S}$ the marginal satisfaction at lower bound and upper bound of all collaborators $\mathscr{N}$.

2: **AddMarginalSatisfactions**($\mathscr{N}, \mathscr{S}$) // $\mathscr{S}$ in descedant order.

3: $\mathscr{S}_H = \emptyset, \mathscr{S}_M = \emptyset, \mathscr{S}_L = \mathscr{N}$ // Sets containing collaborators taking upper-bound, medium value, and lower-bound at optimal.

4: **for each** $V \in \mathscr{S}$ **do**

5:     NextCutOff$\leftarrow$ **GetSat**(V) // Get marginal satisfaction.

6:     **if Resource**($\mathscr{S}_L, \mathscr{S}_M, \mathscr{S}_H$,NextCutOff) $< M$ **then**

7:         **if IsLowerBoundSat(V) then**

8:             move the associated collaborator of V from $\mathscr{S}_L$ to $\mathscr{S}_M$

9:         **else**

10:             move the associated collaborator of V from $\mathscr{S}_M$ to $\mathscr{S}_H$

11:         **end if**

12:     **else**

13:         go to **FinalStep:** // Determine the optimal cutoff marginal.

14:     **end if**

15: **end for**

16: **FinalStep:** // Assign sending rates to all collaborators.

17: **for** $j = 0$ to $|\mathscr{N}|$ **do**

18:     **if** $\mathscr{N}_j \in \mathscr{S}_H$ **then**

19:         $\vec{r}_j = \min(\vec{r}, \vec{R}_j^{out})$ // Nodes take upper-bounds.

20:     **else if** $\mathscr{N}_j \in \mathscr{S}_L$ **then**

21:         $\vec{r}_j = 0$ // Nodes take lower-bounds.

22:     **else**

23:         // Use Kuhn-Tucker condition to find inner solutions.

24:         $\vec{r}_j = \dfrac{\mathbf{T}_j(M - \sum_{k \in \mathscr{S}_H} \min(\vec{r}, \vec{R}_k^{out}) + \sum_{k \in \mathscr{S}_M} \vec{R}_k^{out})}{\sum_{k \in \mathscr{S}_M} \mathbf{T}_k} - \vec{R}_j^{out}$

25:     **end if**

26: **end for**

27: **return** $\vec{r}$

---

the "cutoff" marginal satisfaction, where collaborators with both marginals higher than the "cutoff" take their upper-bounds, collaborators with both marginals lower than the "cutoff" take their lower-bounds, and others take inner solutions with their marginals equal to the "cutoff." We start "cutoff" low, increase it step by step, and move nodes to $\mathscr{S}_H$ and $\mathscr{S}_M$ accordingly until the sending resource exceeds its capacity. The computational complexity of Algorithm 10.2 is $O(|\mathcal{N}|)$.

Algorithm 9.3 Function OptimizeRequest($\mathbf{T}, \vec{r}^{in}, \vec{R}^{in}, \bar{R}$)

1: **for** $i = 0$ to $|\mathcal{N}|$ **do**
2:   **if** $\vec{r}_i^{in} = 0$ **then**
3:     $\vec{R}_i^{in} \Leftarrow \vec{R}_i^{in}/2$ // Request to i is too high, cut in half.
4:   **else if** $\vec{r}_i^{in} < \vec{R}_i^{in}$ **then**
5:     $\vec{R}_i^{in} \Leftarrow \vec{r}_i^{in}$ // Tune down request to approach Prime NE.
6:   **else**
7:     $\mathscr{S} \Leftarrow \mathscr{S} \cup \{T_i, \mathcal{N}_i\}$ // $\mathscr{S}$ is sorted descending by T_i.
8:   **end if**
9: **end for**
10: // Increase the requested sending rate of the half collaborators with higher compatibility by a small amount.
11: **for** $j \in$ **TopHalf**$(\mathscr{S})$ **do**
12:   $\vec{R}_j^{in} \Leftarrow \vec{R}_j^{in} + \Delta$ // Increase the request rate by a small amount.
13: **end for**
14: $U = \sum_{k \in |\mathcal{N}|} \vec{R}_k^{in}$ // Total request rate.
15: **if** $U > \bar{R}$ **then**
16:   $\vec{R}^{in} \Leftarrow \frac{\bar{R}}{U}\vec{R}^{in}$ // Normalize into constraint $\bar{R}$.
17: **end if**
18: **return** $\vec{R}^{in}$

Algorithm 9.3 is used to adjust the requested sending rate of all collaborators according to their last status. We use a fast decrease and linear increase strategy for request adjustment. If the requested sending rate from the last cycle is not fully claimed, then the next request is adjusted to be the claimed amount; otherwise, increase the request by a small amount. The computational complexity of Algorithm 9.3 is $O(|\mathcal{N}|)$.

9.6 Evaluation

In this section we use a simulation network to demonstrate the appealing properties of the knowledge sharing system. All our experiments are based on the average of a large number of experiment replications with different random seeds. Confidence intervals are small enough to be neglected.

Table 9.2: Simulation Parameters

Parameter	Value	Description
M_i	10, 100	The propagation sending capacity of node i
$\bar{R}_i$	10, 100	The receiving capacity of node i
$\bar{r}_i$	1, 10	The rule contribution rate of node i
λ	0.97	Forgetting factor for Bayesian Trust hearing (Section 9.5.1)
B	10	Computation rounds for Algorithm 10.1

9.6.1 Simulation Setup

We simulate a network of n nodes. Each node $i \in \{1, 2, \cdots, n\}$ contributes intrusion detection knowledge to the network following a Poisson distribution with an average arrival rate $\bar{r}_i$. Trust values are learned through past experiences using the credible-bound estimation method described in Section 9.5.1.2. The knowledge sending rate follows the two-level game design described in Section 9.4. The sending capacity M_i and receiving capacity $\bar{R}_i$ for each node values are specified in each experiment. The weight vector w is $\{1, -0.5, 0\}$ (see Section 9.5.1.1). Forgetting factor λ is set to be 0.7. We evaluate the properties of scalability, efficiency, incentive compatibility, fairness, and robustness of the knowledge sharing system.

The parameters we used in our experiments are shown in Table 9.2.

9.6.2 Trust Value Learning

In this experiment we compare the credible-bound (CR) method with other commonly used learning methods such as simple average (SA) where a node takes the simple weighted average of past experiences, and moving average (MA) where the weights on past experiences discount exponentially with time.

We simulate a simple network of two nodes. Node 0 propagates knowledge to node 1 following a Poisson process with average rate $r_{01} = 10$ messages/day. The quality of the messages is randomly chosen from {"effective detection," "false alarm," "no detection"} with probability $\vec{p} = (0.5, 0, 0.5)$, respectively. At the beginning of day 50, node 0 turns dishonest and starts spamming node 1 with all false positive messages, that is, $\vec{p} = (0, 1, 0)$. Node 1 evaluates and compares T_{01} using three different methods.

Figure 9.13 shows that the trust value T_{01} converges after a few days and the CR method yields slightly lower value compared to the other two methods. From the 50-th day on, all methods observe a fast drop in T_{01}. However, the learning speeds of the MA and CR methods are faster than SA. This is due to the forgetting factor, which puts higher weights on new experiences. We then change r_{01} from 1 to 19 and observe T_{01} at the 50-th day using these three methods. From Figure 9.14 we see that T_{01} increases and approaches 0.5 asymptotically under the CR method, while T_{01} from the two other methods mostly stay at 0.5. Therefore, nodes with higher contributions

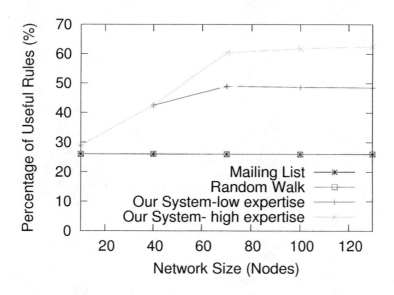

Figure 9.9: The comparison of information quality.

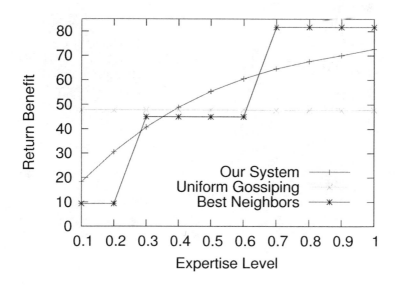

Figure 9.10: Incentive on expertise level.

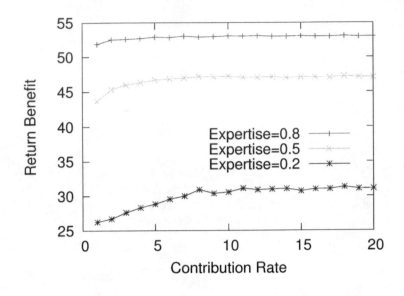

Figure 9.11: Incentive of contribution rate.

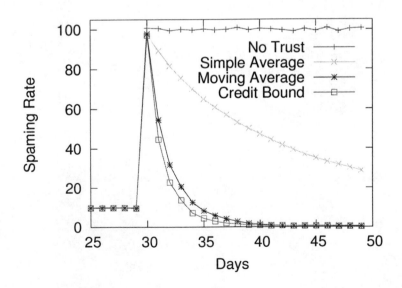

Figure 9.12: The influence from a betrayal attack.

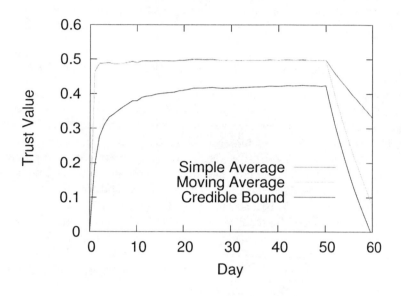

Figure 9.13: Compatibility under different learning methods.

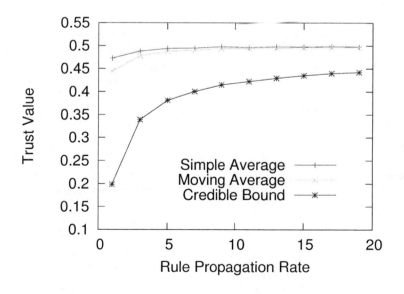

Figure 9.14: The credible-bound compatibility versus sample rate.

to the collaboration network have higher trust values when the CR method is used. Free-riders in this case will have low trust values because their contribution rate is low.

9.6.3 Convergence of Distributed Dynamic Algorithm

In this experiment, we evaluate the convergence speed of the dynamic algorithm (Algorithm 10.1) for the participants to achieve the *prime equilibrium*. We configure a network of four nodes sharing common interests in intrusion detection; the trust values of the four nodes to the others are $0.9, 0.8, 0.7$, and 0.5, respectively. We set $M_i = 10$ messages/day, $\bar{R}_i = 100$ messages/day, and $\bar{r}_i = 10$ messages/day for all i. All nodes start with small sending rates and small request rates to all collaborators, and adjust them following Algorithm 10.1. The number of updating and exchanging is controlled by parameter B. To make an appropriate parameter choice, we try different values of B and observe the sending rate from node 0 to other nodes after B rounds of optimal adjustment and information exchange. The result is shown in Figure 9.15. We can see that the sending rates have a fast convergence speed. Similar results occur under other parameter settings. We fix $B = 10$ in the remaining of the experiments.

9.6.4 Scalability and Quality of Information (QoI)

In this experiment we compare the scalability and QoI using our knowledge sharing and propagation system with (1) the traditional mailing list mechanism, where

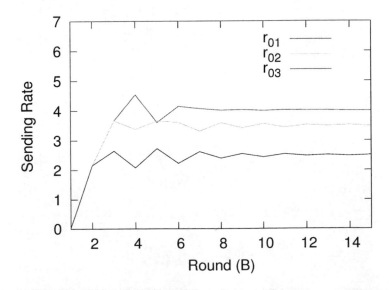

Figure 9.15: The convergence of dynamic algorithm.

detection knowledge is broadcast to all the other nodes in the system; and (2) with the random walk mechanism, where knowledge starts from a small set of nodes and each node randomly selects one neighbor to propagate the knowledge to unless the knowledge has been received before. We simulate a network with size starting from 10 nodes and we increase it by 30 nodes each round up to 130. Among all the nodes, 20% of them have high trust values of 0.9 and the remaining 80% nodes have low trust values of 0.1. All nodes have the same configuration, that is, $M_i = M := 20$ messages/day, $\bar{R}_i = \bar{R} := 20$ messages/day, and $\bar{r}_i = \bar{r} := 1$ messages/day for every $i \in \mathcal{N}$. The random walk mechanism starts with three initial nodes.

Figure 9.16 shows the average number of messages a node receives each day. We can see that when using the mailing list propagation, the receiving rate increases linearly with the network size. Assuming that the receivers can tolerate up to 30 messages/day, then the system is not scalable beyond 30 nodes because a large number of messages overwhelms the receivers. Under the random walk mechanism, the number of nodes receiving the messages increases slowly with network size so it is scalable up to around 200 nodes. Our system allows nodes to configure a receiving capacity $\bar{R}$, which ensures the received messages rate to be below $\bar{R}$ under all network sizes. Therefore, our system is scalable under any network size.

The *quality of information* (QoI) for all methods is plotted in Figure 9.9. We define QoI as the percentage of effective knowledge that nodes receive. We see that our system leads to significant improvements in QoI received by both the low-trust and the high-trust nodes in comparison to the mailing list method and the random walk method. This is because our system allows nodes to track the trust values of others, and therefore nodes only request knowledge from good ones. In addition, the high-trust nodes receive higher quality intrusion detection information than low-trust nodes, which also reflects the incentive compatibility of the system.

9.6.5   *Incentive Compatibility and Fairness*

Incentive compatibility is an important feature for a collaboration network because it determines the long-term sustainability of the system. In this experiment we vary the trust values and knowledge contribution rate of a participating node, and observe the output of its return benefit, which is the expected number of useful messages a node receives per day.

We configure a network with 30 nodes with random trust values uniformly chosen from $[0, 1]$, and we set $M = \bar{R} = 100$ messages/day and $\bar{r} = 10$ messages/day for all nodes. We change the trust value of node 0 from 0.1 to 1.0 and observe its return benefit. We compare our results with two other information propagation methods, namely uniform gossiping and best neighbor mechanism. In the uniform gossiping mechanism, knowledge is propagated uniformly to randomly selected nodes in the neighborhood. The receiver drops messages from less trustable collaborators when the total receiving rate hits its limit. In the best neighbor mechanism, messages are always propagated to a small number of fixed (most trusted) collaborators. The sending capacity and receiving capacity also apply to the uniform gossiping and best neigh-

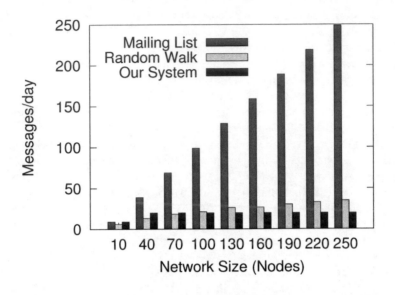

Figure 9.16: The comparison of scalability.

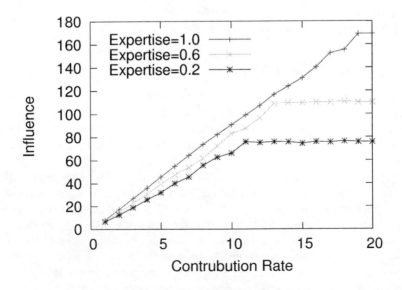

Figure 9.17: The influence versus sending rate.

bor propagation. Hence, we also configure their sending and receiving capacities to be 100 messages/day.

Figure 9.10 shows that uniform gossiping provides no incentive to nodes with higher trust values, while the best neighbor propagation scheme provides incentives but lacks fairness. It is easy to observe that even though nodes share the same trust values, they may end up with very different return benefits just because they may be involved in different groups. In comparison, our propagation mechanism is built upon an optimization framework with a continuous concave logarithmic utility on the return benefit with trust values taken into account. Hence, it leads to incentive compatibility as well as fairness. In Figure 9.11, we also change the knowledge contribution rate $\bar{r}_0$ of node 0 and observe the return benefits. We can observe that the benefit of collaboration increases with knowledge contribution rate. Contributing more to the collaboration network brings a higher return benefit. Our propagation system is incentive compatible for both contributions in quality and quantity.

9.6.6 Robustness of the System

The purpose of this experiment is to demonstrate the robustness of the system in the face of malicious attacks such as betrayal attacks and denial-of-service (DoS) attacks. Note that the DoS attack here means that the malicious node tries to send a large amount of spam messages to slow down the processing speed of the IDS or create a large number of false positives. It may create frustration for the users. To simulate a betrayal attack, we let an expert node (node 0) behave well in the beginning to gain high trust values and then start to propagate spam messages at day 30. We fix $\bar{R} = 100$ messages/day and $\bar{r} = 10$ messages/day for all nodes. We observe the number of spam messages that the malicious node is allowed to send in each day. In Figure 9.12, we can see that the number of spam messages sent by the malicious node increases quickly in the first day. However, under our system, the spam rate drops down quickly and approaches 0 after a short period of time. This is because the collaborators have perceived the spam messages and have lowered the requested sending rates to the malicious node. We compare the efficiency among different trust learning models, including our Bayesian credit bound model (CR). We can see that our CR model demonstrates the fastest reaction speed to the betrayal attack.

To simulate a DoS attack, we let the malicious node 0 increase its contribution rate $\bar{r}_0$ from 1 to 20 with an unlimited outbound sending rate, which is a typical strategy of a spammer. We observe the influence of the spammer node on all the other nodes, which is defined by the total number of spam messages received from the spammer node per day. The larger the influence of a node, the higher the potential of damage the node can cause when it turns into a malicious one. We can see from Figure 9.17 that the influence of a node is bounded in the system. This is because our system enforces propagation agreements between each pair of nodes. Each node sets a knowledge propagation constraint on all its collaborators in the two-level game framework (see Section 9.4). Therefore, when a node intends to launch a DoS attack, the amount of messages it is allowed to send to others is upper bounded by $\bar{R}$ set by its collaborators. Nodes sending message rate higher than what was mutually agreed upon can be considered malicious, and thus removed from the acquaintance lists of others.

9.7 Conclusion

This chapter presented the framework design of knowledge-based intrusion detection networks using P2P communications. In particular, we focused on the knowledge propagation mechanism design. We established a two-level game-theoretic model for nodes to control knowledge propagation rates to their collaborators. We have shown that the system possesses a prime Nash equilibrium, which is demonstrated to have the properties of incentive, fairness, and robustness to malicious attacks such as betrayal DoS attacks. Moreover, the system has also been shown to be scalable and inherently efficient in comparison to random gossiping and fixed neighbor sharing schemes. We also analyzed the macroscopic properties of knowledge propagation in a large IDN network at the Nash equilibrium of the system.

In addition, we have used the Bayesian learning approach to estimate the trust values between nodes based on empirical data. Using simulations, we have corroborated the important properties of the IDN. A possible extension of this work is to study the system robustness to other types of attacks, such as collusion attacks, sybil attacks, and newcomer attacks. In addition, a further study of the macroscopic behavior of this system arising from multi-hop rule propagations and analyzing the time evolution of the rule propagation at the system level may also be a possible extension.

Chapter 10

Collaborative Malware Detection Networks

CONTENTS

10.1   Introduction

In previous chapters we discussed the architecture and components design of efficient and trustworthy consultation-based intrusion detection networks. In this chapter we discuss a case study dedicated to a consultation-based malware detection IDN referred to in the following as CMDN (Collaborative Malware Detection Network). In CMDN, different antivirus software exchange expertise to help each other in malware detection. We will focus our discussion on the design of such a network so that the collaboration can be effective, privacy preserving, and robust to malicious insiders.

Undoubtedly, cyber intrusions have become a global problem. Attackers not only harvest private information from the compromised nodes, but also use the nodes to attack others. Cyber intrusions are typically accomplished with the assistance of *malware* (a.k.a. malicious code). Malware is a piece of software that is used to gather confidential information, exploit computing resources, or cause damage without the user's consent. Typical examples of malware include worms, viruses, trojan horses, spyware, and rootkits. Malware can spread through various routes, for example, email attachments, Internet downloads, worms, or removable media.

Millions of new malware instances appear every year [66] and the number has been growing at an exponential rate. Malware is used to not only to harvest private information from compromised hosts, but also to organize such compromised hosts to form botnets [5]. Many million-node botnets have been discovered in the past few years, such as BredoLab [6] and Conficker [21]. Bots can be used to attack other hosts, such as distributed-denial-of-services (DDoS) attacks. A DDoS attack in March 2013 targeting the largest spam filtering system, Spamhaus was one of the largest DDoS attacks in history [11]. The massive attacks generated traffic of 300 Gbps and slowed down the Internet globally for a week.

To protect computers against malware, antivirus systems (AVs) are used to detect, block, and remove malware from hosts. Two typical metrics are used to measure the quality of an AV: the *true positive* rate (TP) and the *false positive* rate (FP). The former means an AV raises an alarm when there is a real threat; while the latter means an AV raises a false alarm for benign software. The goal of an AV is to maximize the TP while minimizing the FP. The most common technique to detect malware is *signature-based* detection, which involves searching for known malicious patterns within suspicious files. Signature-based detection performs fast and usually has a low FP. However, it may not be able to detect new threats, for example, zero-day attacks. To mitigate such limitation, *behavior-based* detection [67, 89], *heuristics-based* detection [85, 90] and *reputation-based* detection [2] are employed to improve malware detection efficiency. The behavior approach analyzes a behavior log/graph of a suspicious file, such as a sequence of system calls, and matches them with known malware behavior patterns. The heuristic approach analyzes malware and seeks similar patterns with known malicious code. The reputation-based approach evaluates the reputation of each file based on several attributes, such as file publisher, popularity, age, and reputation of host machines [45]. All three approaches are considered a promising direction to detect new threats; however, heuristic matching without enough evidence of maliciousness can cause a high FP.

Although the primary goal of an AV is to detect and remove malware, it is also important that malware detection system is able to correctly classify benign files. AVs with low TP may not effectively protect hosts from malware, while the consequences of false positives can be disastrous. For example, a security vendor released a flawed signature database update in 2010 that removed a critical system file from Windows XP machines, causing the affected machines to be unable to boot up afterward. [16]. In a similar instance, TrendMicro spent $8 million reimbursing customers for reparation expenses [28].

Security vendors may not exchange information, for example, malware samples reported from their customers, with other vendors because of privacy issues and competition. Providing prompt signature update against the latest threats is important for dominating a market. A single AV vendor may not be able to obtain malware samples of zero-day threats to be analyzed in time, so that they may fail to protect their customers. However, if diverse security vendors collaborate with each other, by means of providing *feedback* regarding the legacy of suspicious files, they may achieve better malware detection accuracy and, in turn, better satisfy customers.

In this chapter we present a fully distributed collaborative malware detection network (CMDN) for AVs to exchange expertise; for example, AVs send suspicious files (original binaries or fingerprints) or their behavior logs to other AVs for scanning and decide whether or not to raise an alarm based on feedback from other AVs. This chapter focuses on the collaborative decision component design, for which our goal is to make *accurate* collaborative malware detection, that has acceptable runtime efficiency and is resistant to malicious insiders. We present a collaborative detection model named *RevMatch*, where the final malware decision is made based on looking up history with the same feedback combination. When such a match is not found or the number of matches is too small for a confident decision, then partial matching is sought instead. Our evaluation results, based on real-world malware data sets, demonstrate that our algorithm effectively improves the detection accuracy compared to other decision algorithms in the literature, while it also performs well in runtime efficiency and is robust to malicious insiders. Although our framework is designed for AV collaborations, it can be also used for collaboration between intrusion detection systems.

The highlights of this chapter can be summarized as follows: (1) a distributed framework design and architecture design for CMDN, where AVs consult each other to improve their malware detection efficiency; (2) a novel robust and efficient collaborative decision algorithm, named RevMatch, and compare it with other existing approaches based on real-world malware samples. The results reveal the limitation of the current method of using AVs and the importance of AV collaboration; and (3) our collected evaluation data can be used as a benchmark by other researchers in the collaborative malware detection domain.

This chapter is organized as follows. Section 10.2 discusses some existing collaborative malware detection systems and collaborative malware/intrusion detection decision methods. Section 10.3 discusses CMDN architecture design. The detailed design of collaborative decision model is described in Section 10.4. We present the evaluation results in Section 10.5 and further discuss the results in Section 10.6. Finally, we conclude this chapter in Section 10.7.

10.2   Background

10.2.1   Collaborative Malware Detection

Using a collaborative approach for malware detection was previously discussed in the literature. Oberheide et al. proposed CloudAV, a system [114] where end hosts send suspicious files to a central cloud-based antivirus service for scanning malware with a number of different AVs. A threshold approach is used to aggregate feedback from multiple AVs. An implementation of CloudAV is described in [102]. RAVE [127] is another centralized collaborative malware scanning system where emails are sent to several "replicas" for malware scanning. A replica consists of a *payload*, which is running on one version of an AV for malware scanning, and a *wormhole*, which is used for collecting scanning results from a payload and commuting between different replicas for decision making. A simple voting-based mechanism is employed to make final decisions.

Peer-to-peer communication overlay is also used for collaborative malware detection or intrusion detection [44, 73, 100]. Decentralized network architectures allow participants to share workload with others and thus avoid bottlenecks and single points of failure, which are common weaknesses of centralized systems.

10.2.2   Decision Models for Collaborative Malware Detection

Several different models of collaborative decision for malware/intrusion detection have been proposed in the literature. We list a few that can be easily adapted to CMDN.

10.2.2.1 Static Threshold

The static threshold (ST) model [114] raises an alarm if the total number of malware diagnoses in the result set is higher than a defined threshold. This model is straightforward and easy to implement. The tunable threshold can be used to decide the sensitivity in intrusion detection. However, the ST model considers the quality of all AVs equally, making the system vulnerable to attacks by colluded malicious insiders.

10.2.2.2 Weighted Average

The weighted average (WA) model [69, 105] takes the weighted average of all feedback from AVs. If the weighted average is larger than the threshold, then the system raises an alarm. The weight of each AV can be the trust value or quality score of the AV. The impact from high-quality AVs is larger than from low-quality AVs. The weighted average model also provides a tunable threshold for the sensitivity of detection.

10.2.2.3 Decision Tree

The decision tree (DT) model [60] uses a machine-learning approach to produce a decision tree, in order to maximize decision accuracy. The decision tree approach can provide a fast, accurate, and easy-to-implement solution to the collaborative malware detection problem. The training data with labeled samples is used to generate a binary tree and decisions are made based upon the tree. However, the decision tree approach does not work well with partial feedback, that is, when not all participants give feedback. It is also not flexible (no easy way to tune the sensitivity of detection) as decision trees are usually precomputed.

10.2.2.4 Bayesian Decision

The Bayesian decision (BD) model [75] is another approach for feedback aggregation in intrusion detection (or malware detection). In this approach, the conditional probability of malware/goodware given a set of feedback is computed using Bayes' Theorem and the decision with the least risk cost is always chosen. The BD model is based on the assumption that feedbacks from collaborators are independent, which is usually not the case.

10.3 Collaboration Framework

In this section we present CMDN, a framework for AVs to perform collaborative malware detection. We also present the architecture design of CMDN and describe its building blocks. Finally, we discuss some potential challenges such a system may encounter.

The topology of CMDN is shown in Figure 10.1, where computers with malware detection capabilities are logically connected, forming a peer-to-peer network. Each

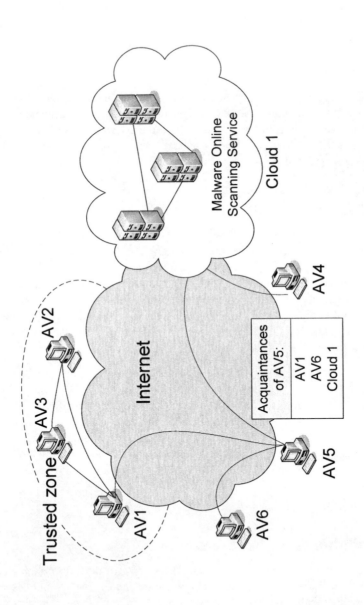

Figure 10.1: Topology design of collaborative malware detection network.

node maintains a list of collaborators to communicate with. We call the list of collaborators the *acquaintance list*. There are two different types of participating nodes in CMDNs: pure service nodes and trader nodes. *Pure service nodes* (e.g., cloud 1 in Figure 10.1) only provide malware scanning services for others and do not request service from others. A pure service node may be an online malware scanning service provided by some security vendor or a system similar to CloudAV [114]. *Trader nodes* (e.g., AV5 in Figure 10.1), on the other hand, request services from other nodes and can also provide services in exchange if needed. Trader nodes allow participants to benefit each other by exchanging malware scanning services with each other.

The CMDN described above requires participating nodes to have malware scanning capabilities. When a node in the CMDN has a suspicious file detected by a heuristic or anomaly detector, but cannot make a confident decision about whether the file is malicious (e.g., no matching malware signature is found), it may send the file or its fingerprint to its acquaintances for scanning. For acquaintances with behavior-based detection ability, the behavior log of the suspicious file can also be sent for consultation. When an acquaintance AV receives a malware scanning or behavior consultation request, it either searches its signature base to seek the matching records, or analyzes the behavior log using its behavior analysis engine, and replies with a *feedback* (malware or goodware) to the requester. Upon receiving feedbacks from its acquaintances, the requester AV needs to decide whether or not to raise a malware alarm based on the received feedbacks (Section 10.4).

10.3.1 Architecture Design

The architecture design of CMDN is illustrated in Figure 10.2. Each node is composed of six components used for collaboration activities, namely, AV scanner, collaborative decision, communication overlay, resource control, trust evaluation, and acquaintance management.

The *Communication Overlay* is the component that handles all the communications between the host node and other peers in the network. The messages passing through the communication overlay include test files from the host node to its acquaintances, malware consultation requests from the host node to its acquaintances, feedback from acquaintances; malware consultation requests from acquaintances; and feedback to acquaintances.

The *Collaborators Trust Evaluation* component allows AVs in the CMDN to evaluate the quality and trustworthiness of others. The host node can use test files to gain experience quickly. Indeed, the verified consultation results can also be used as experience.

The *Acquaintance Management* component decides who to collaborate with and manages different privileges for nodes with different trust levels. For example, nodes can send original files to trusted collaborators for scanning.

The *Resource Control* component is used to decide how much a host allocates resources to respond to the consultation requests from each of its acquaintances. An incentive-compatible resource management model can assist a node with an AV service to allocate resources to acquaintances in a fair manner. A node that abusively

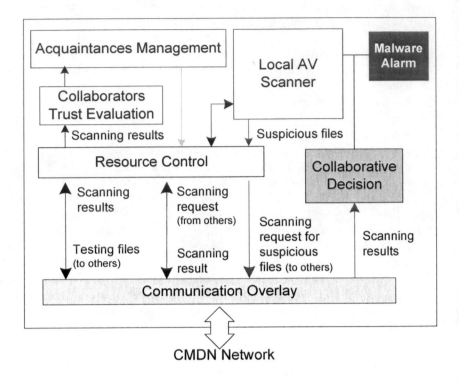

Figure 10.2: Architecture desgin of a trader node in CMDN.

uses the resources of others will be penalized by being removed from the acquaintance lists of other nodes.

The *Collaborative Decision* component has a direct impact on the accuracy of the collaborative malware detection. After the host node sends out consultation requests to its acquaintances, the collected scanning results are used to decide whether the host should raise an alarm or not. Both false positive and false negative decisions bring costs to the host node. In the next section we discuss a decision model that can effectively improve collaborative detection accuracy.

10.3.2 Communication Overhead and Privacy Issue

To reduce the communication overhead in CMDNs, nodes may send the digest (fingerprint) of suspicious files first. If collaborator AVs find the digest in their blacklist/whitelist, then they return the corresponding result. Otherwise, they can request the sender to forward the original file. For AVs with behavior-based malware detection capability, the behavior log can be sent to them for analysis.

When a host sends a file to its collaborators for scanning, the file receiver may hold the record and turn it against the sender. To reduce this privacy concern, original files are only sent to trusted peers for scanning in the CMDN. To avoid man-in-the-middle attacks, all communications among connected nodes in a CMDN are encrypted to prevent eavesdropping.

The system also uses "test files" to evaluate the quality of collaborators and to guard against dishonest/malicious collaborators in the CMDN. The real scanning files and test files are sent randomly and it should be difficult for recipients to distinguish test files from real files.

10.3.3 Adversaries and Free-Riding

Malicious insiders can be another issue in a CMDN because adversaries may disguise as an active CMDN participant and attack the CMDN. For example, adversaries may send false scanning/consultation results to other nodes or send excessive scanning/consultation requests to others to overload the system. CMDNs can handle these problems by means of admission control and trust management. Trust management evaluates the expertise level and the honesty of nodes. Admission control restricts the amount of requests from participating nodes. Some trust models for intrusion detection networks have been discussed in [59, 69].

Free-riding is another potential problem in CMDN because it discourages nodes from contributing to the network. An incentive-compatible resource management encourages active contributors and discourages free-riding. Nodes that do not contribute to a CMDN refrain from benefiting from other nodes in the network. A resource management model for intrusion detection networks was discussed in Chapter 7.

10.4 Collaborative Decision Model

In a CMDN, a collaborative malware detection decision model based on feedback is key to obtaining high detection accuracy. Robustness is highly important for such a decision model because adversaries have strong motivation to evade or compromise the system. However, robustness is not the focus of most machine-learning approaches. We present the design of a robust and efficient collaborative decision model named *RevMatch*, which can make accurate collaborative malware detection decisions based on the feedback from acquaintances, and is robust to malicious insiders. In this section we first formulate the collaborative decision problem and then discuss the corresponding solution.

10.4.1 Problem Statement and RevMatch Model

We formulate the decision problem as follows:

Given labeled history consisting of the feedback of n AVs on m files whose ground truth are known (malware or goodware), we decide whether a suspicious file is malware based on the feedback set **y** *from a subset of the AVs.*

Table 10.1: Summary of Notations

Symbol	Meaning
$\mathcal{N}$	Set of AVs in the CMDN
n	Total number of AVs in the network
AV_i	Antivirus i
$\mathcal{N}_i$	Set of acquaintances of AV_i
$|\mathcal{N}_i|$	The number of acquaintances of AV_i
$\mathbf{M}, \mathbf{G}$	Total number of malware and goodware in the labeled records database
$\mathbf{P}_M, \mathbf{P}_G$	Prior probability of malware and goodware in the real world
m	Total number of samples used for evaluation
Q_i	Quality score of AV_i
$\mathbf{y}_k$	Scanning results (feedback) from acquaintance AV_k
τ_s	The threshold for the static threshold method
τ_w	The threshold for the weighted average method
τ_c	Observation threshold for the RevMatch method
$M(\mathbf{y}), G(\mathbf{y})$	The number of malware and goodware in records with matching feedback set $\mathbf{y}$
FP, FN	The false positive and the false negative
C_{fp}, C_{fn}	Cost of false positive and false negative decisions
Δt	Minimum time gap for two adjacent updates on the same feedback
α	Discount factor
β	Weight on priors of malware and goodware

To solve this problem, we model the decision problem as follows: suppose a scenario where a set of AVs $\mathcal{N}$ are consulting each other for malware assessment. AV_i ($i \in \mathcal{N}$) sends a suspicious file to other AVs in its acquaintance list $\mathcal{N}_i$ for consultation. Let random variable $\mathbf{Y}_i := [Y_j]_{j \in \mathcal{N}_i}$ denote the feedback vector that contains the scanning results from its acquaintances. Note that $Y_j \in \{0, 1\}$, and $Y_j = 1$ and $Y_j = 0$ indicate the suspicious file is malware or goodware, respectively[1]. Suppose AV_i sends a suspicious file to its acquaintances for consultation and receives a feedback set $\mathbf{y} = \{\mathbf{y}_1, ..., \mathbf{y}_{|\mathcal{N}_i|}\}$ from its acquaintances, where $\mathbf{y}_j \in \{0, 1\}$ is the feedback from acquaintance j. AV_i needs to decide whether or not the suspicious file is malware based on the feedback $\mathbf{y}$. Table 10.1 summarizes the notations we use in this section for the readers' convenience.

We model the above decision problem as a utility optimization problem. Let random variable $X \in \{0, 1\}$ denote the outcomes of "goodware" and "malware." Let $\mathbf{P}_M(\mathbf{y})$ denote the probability of being "malware" given the feedbacks y from all acquaintance AVs. $\mathbf{P}_M(\mathbf{y})$ can be written as $\mathbf{P}_M(\mathbf{y}) = \mathbb{P}[X = 1 | \mathbf{Y} = \mathbf{y}]$. Let C_{fp} and C_{fn}

---

[1]For the convenience of presentation, we drop the subscript i in the notations appearing later in this chapter.

denote the average cost of a FP decision and a FN decision. We assume that there is no cost when a correct decision is made. We define a decision function $\delta(\mathbf{y}) \in \{0,1\}$, where $\delta = 1$ means raising a malware alarm and $\delta = 0$ means no alarm. The risk of decision $R(\delta)$ can be written as

$$R(\delta) = C_{fn}\mathbf{P}_M(\mathbf{y})(1-\delta) + C_{fp}(1-\mathbf{P}_M(\mathbf{y}))\delta$$
$$= (C_{fp} - (C_{fp}+C_{fn})\mathbf{P}_M(\mathbf{y}))\delta + C_{fn}\mathbf{P}_M(\mathbf{y})$$

To minimize the risk $R(\delta)$, we need to minimize $(C_{fp} - (C_{fp}+C_{fn})\mathbf{P}_M(\mathbf{y}))\delta$. Therefore, the AV raises malware alarm (i.e., $\delta = 1$) if

$$\mathbf{P}_M(\mathbf{y}) \geq \frac{C_{fp}}{C_{fp}+C_{fn}}. \tag{10.1}$$

To make the optimal decision, the key step is estimating $\mathbf{P}_M(\mathbf{y})$. Our solution (RevMatch) is to search in the labeled history for records that have the same feedback set as $\mathbf{y}$. Let $M(\mathbf{y})$ and $G(\mathbf{y})$ denote the number of malware and goodware in the labeled records with matching feedback set $\mathbf{y}$. If the number of observed matching records in history is larger than a threshold, that is, $M(\mathbf{y}) + G(\mathbf{y}) \geq \tau_c > 0$, then $\mathbf{P}_M(\mathbf{y})$ can be estimated using

$$\begin{aligned}
\mathbf{P}_M(\mathbf{y}) = \mathbb{P}[X=1|\mathbf{Y}=\mathbf{y}] &= \frac{\mathbb{P}[\mathbf{Y}=\mathbf{y}|X=1]\mathbb{P}[X=1]}{\mathbb{P}[\mathbf{Y}=\mathbf{y}]} \\
&= \frac{\mathbb{P}[\mathbf{Y}=\mathbf{y}|X=1]\mathbb{P}[X=1]}{\mathbb{P}[\mathbf{Y}=\mathbf{y}|X=1]\mathbb{P}[X=1]+\mathbb{P}[\mathbf{Y}=\mathbf{y}|X=0]\mathbb{P}[X=0]} \\
&= \frac{\mathbb{P}[\mathbf{Y}=\mathbf{y}|X=1]\mathbf{P}_M}{\mathbb{P}[\mathbf{Y}=\mathbf{y}|X=1]\mathbf{P}_M+\mathbb{P}[\mathbf{Y}=\mathbf{y}|X=0]\mathbf{P}_G} \\
&= \frac{1}{1+\frac{\mathbb{P}[\mathbf{Y}=\mathbf{y}|X=0]\mathbf{P}_G}{\mathbb{P}[\mathbf{Y}=\mathbf{y}|X=1]\mathbf{P}_M}} \\
&\simeq \frac{1}{1+\frac{G(\mathbf{y})\mathbf{M}\mathbf{P}_G}{M(\mathbf{y})\mathbf{G}\mathbf{P}_M}} \tag{10.2}
\end{aligned}$$

where $P[\mathbf{Y}=\mathbf{y}|X=1]$ is the probability that a feedback set $\mathbf{y}$ is received when the file is malware; and $P[\mathbf{Y}=\mathbf{y}|X=0]$ is the probability that diagnosis $\mathbf{y}$ is received when the file is goodware. $\mathbf{P}_M$ is the prior probability of malware; $\mathbf{P}_G$ is the prior probability of goodware. $\mathbf{M}, \mathbf{G}$ are the numbers of malware and goodware samples in the labeled history.

We use a simple example in Figure 10.3 to illustrate a use case of this decision model. When AV_0 receives a suspicious file s and cannot make a confident decision, it sends the file to its acquaintances AV_1, AV_2, AV_3 for scanning. The feedback set returned is $\{1,1,0\}$. AV_0 searches its labeled records database and finds two matches. Both matches are malware. If $\tau_c = 2$, AV_0 decides that file s is malware using the decision formula described in Equation (10.2).

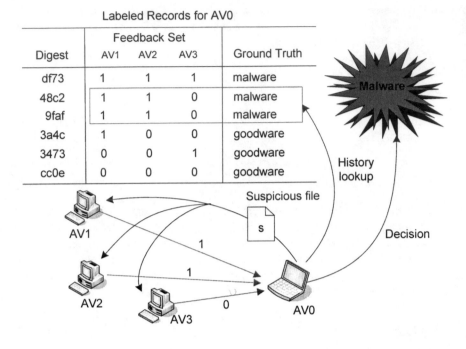

Figure 10.3: An example of the RevMatch decision algorithm for CMDNs.

10.4.2 Feedback Relaxation

The previous results are based on the condition that $M(\mathbf{y}) + G(\mathbf{y}) \geq \tau_c$, where $\tau_c > 0$ is a system parameter to specify the minimum number of matches in order to reach some "confidence" in decision making using Equation (10.2). In this subsection, we discuss how to deal with the case of $M(\mathbf{y}) + G(\mathbf{y}) < \tau_c$.

$M(\mathbf{y}) + G(\mathbf{y}) < \tau_c$ indicates there are not enough matches and thus no confident decision can be made. The RevMatch model handles this problem using *feedback relaxation*. That is, it ignores feedbacks from some acquaintances, intending to increase the number of matches by partial matching. The RevMatch model chooses to ignore the feedback from the least competent AV, as removing incompetent nodes can effectively increase the matching cases number while keeping valuable feedback from high-quality AVs. The competence level of an AV can be its trust value or quality score.

Algorithm 10.1 describes the process of removing incompetent AVs from the feedback set one by one until the number of matching samples exceeds the threshold τ_c. Then, a decision is made based on the remaining feedback set. Upon receiving a diagnosis set $\mathbf{y}$, it first checks if the number of matching cases in the records exceeds the threshold τ_c. If it does, it makes a decision based on the collected matches.

Otherwise, the least competent AV is removed from the feedback set in each round until the number of matching samples exceeds the threshold. After that, it returns the corresponding decision and the remaining feedback set.

Algorithm 10.1 Relaxation($\mathbf{y}$, l_a)

//This algorithm removes feedback from the least competent AVs until the ac-quaintances list until the number of matches reaches the threshold τ_c. It has two parameters, the feedback vector $\mathbf{y}$ and an ordered list of AVs l_a, which is sorted by the competence levels of AVs in ascending order.

$(\mathbf{M}(\mathbf{y}), \mathbf{G}(\mathbf{y})) \Leftarrow$ find matches for $\mathbf{y}$

if $\mathbf{M}(\mathbf{y}) + \mathbf{G}(\mathbf{y}) \geq \tau_c$ **then**

$\quad \delta \Leftarrow \max_{\delta \in \{0,1\}} R(\delta)$

$\quad$ return $(\mathbf{y}, \delta)$

end if

//Feedback relaxation

for each a in l_a **do**

$\quad \mathbf{y} \Leftarrow \mathbf{y}$ removes feedback of AV a

$\quad (\mathbf{M}(\mathbf{y}), \mathbf{G}(\mathbf{y})) \Leftarrow$ find matches for $\mathbf{y}$

$\quad$ **if** $\mathbf{M}(\mathbf{y}) + \mathbf{G}(\mathbf{y}) \geq \tau_c$ **then**

$\quad\quad \delta \Leftarrow \max_{\delta \in \{0,1\}} R(\delta)$

$\quad\quad$ return $(\mathbf{y}, \delta)$

$\quad$ **end if**

end for

10.4.3   Labeled History Update

The *labeled history* (ground truth set) is highly important because all decisions are based on the ground truth (GT) search for matches. As previously mentioned, AVs in CMDN collect labeled history by sending test files to acquaintances and recording their feedbacks and GT. Real consultation files can also be used when their GT are revealed afterward.

The GT set $\mathbf{T}$ is a collection of feedback records labeled with their GT (malware or goodware) as shown in Figure 10.3. To increase storage efficiency, a GT entry $\mathbf{T}_i$ can be represented with attributes $\{F_i, a_i, b_i, t_i\}$. F_i is the binary set representing the feedbacks from acquaintances, a_i and b_i are the number of malware and goodware in history with feedback F_i. t_i is the timestamp of the last GT sample recorded with feedback F_i. The purpose of recording the timestamp is to prevent history poison flooding attacks, where a malicious insider (probably a malware producer) accumu-lates credibility quickly by releasing a large number of zero-day malware that other

AVs may not be able to detect in the beginning, and then raises alarms on goodware to mislead others (see Section 10.6.6).

The labeled history update process is described in Algorithm 10.2. When a node has a new test file with GT $\bar{g} \in \{0, 1\}$, it sends the file to all collaborators for consultation and receives feedback $\bar{F}$. Suppose there exists an entry $F_j = \bar{F}$ in the labeled history and $t_j < currentTime() - \Delta t$, then update $a_j = \alpha a_j + \bar{g}$ and $b_j = \alpha b_j + (1 - \bar{g})$, and also reset t_j; otherwise if there is no entry with feedback $\bar{F}$, then create a new entry $\{F_{new}, a_{new}, b_{new}, t_{new}\}$. Δt is the minimum time gap that two adjacent updates have the same feedback. α is the discount factor on older data, and β is the weight on priors. $\mathbf{P}_M, \mathbf{P}_G$ are the priors for malware and goodware, respectively.

Algorithm 10.2 Ground Truth Update($\mathbf{T}, \bar{F}, \bar{g}$)

1: //This algorithm updates the ground truth set $\mathbf{T}$ when a new ground truth $\bar{g}$ with scanning feedback $\bar{F}$ arrives.
2: $j \Leftarrow$ search records in $\mathbf{T}$ with feedback $\bar{F}$
3: **if** $j \geq 0$ and $t_j < currentTime() - \Delta t$ **then**
4: $\quad a_j \Leftarrow \alpha a_j + \bar{g}$ // update the number of malware
5: $\quad b_j \Leftarrow \alpha b_j + (1 - \bar{g})$ // update the number of goodware
6: **else if** j is not found **then**
7: $\quad F_{new} = \bar{F}$ // create a new entry $F_{new} = \bar{F}$
8: $\quad a_{new} \Leftarrow \beta \mathbf{P}_M + \bar{g}$
9: $\quad b_{new} \Leftarrow \beta \mathbf{P}_G + (1 - \bar{g})$
10: $\quad \mathbf{T} \Leftarrow \mathbf{T} \cup \{F_{new}, a_{new}, b_{new}, currentTime()\}$
11: **end if**

10.5 Evaluation

In this section we use real data to evaluate the performance of the RevMatch model and compare it with four other decision models, namely, ST, WA, DT, and BD (described in Section 10.2). The metrics we use for the evaluation include detection accuracy, running time efficiency, and robustness against insider attacks. We use *quality score*, which is the combination of FP and FN, to measure detection accuracy; running time efficiency is the average running time for making a decision; robustness is the level of resistance to malicious insider attacks. We evaluate the performance of RevMatch and draw comparisons among different collaborative decision algorithms.

10.5.1 Data Sets

In order to evaluate the accuracies of the decision algorithms, we collected real-world malware and goodware samples. Our malware data sets were collected from Mal-

Table 10.2: Data Sets

Dataset ID	Data Set Description	Samples	Year	Malware Alarm Rate
S1	Old malware	58,730	2008–2009	84.8%
S2	New malware	29,413	2011–2012	59.5%
S3	Hybrid malware	50,000	2009–2012	69.7%
S4	Goodware (SourceForge)	56,023	2012	0.3%
S5	Goodware (Manual)	944	2012	7.9%
S6	Hybrid goodware	5,000	2012	1.6%

ware Analysis System (formerly CW-Sandbox)[2], Offensive Computing[3], and other antivirus vendors. In terms of the collection time, our malware data sets are divided into two groups: old malware data set (S1) collected in 2008–2009 and new malware data set (S2) collected in 2011–2012. We also mixed the two data sets and selected 50,000 of them to form a hybrid malware data set (S3).

In our evaluation, we also included goodware to measure false positive rates of the decision algorithms. We crawled the top 10,000 projects in SourceForge[4] and extracted PE (Portable Executable) binary files as goodware samples (S4). We also collected binary files (S5) manually as false positive samples, such as some driver files and computer games from reputable producers from various sources. We also selected a mixed combination of goodware samples to form a hybrid goodware data set (S6). Table 10.2 shows the size of each data set.

We used VirusTotal[5] to obtain scanning results from a variety of antivirus tools. Using the VirusTotal API, we uploaded our entire malware and goodware data sets and acquired scanning logs of forty different antivirus tools. Figure 10.4 shows both the TP and FP of each antivirus engine based on hybrid data sets S3 and S6. One caveat is that we do not intend to compare different AV engines' detection rates because VirusTotal is not designed for performance comparisons. VirusTotal's scanning results are based upon command-line versions of AV engines that may not be armed with more sophisticated techniques, for example, behavioral analysis. We replace the names of AVs with indexed labels (e.g., AV_i) and the full list of AVs used in our experiments can be found in alphabetical order in Table 10.3.

We collected the average percentage of AVs raising malware alarms to each data set based on VirusTotal's scanning results. We notice a higher percentage of AVs raise malware alarms on older malware samples than newer ones (see Table 10.2). The cause of the difference might be that antivirus vendors have more time to analyze and create more accurate antivirus signatures for older malware samples.

In our setting, we used VirusTotal's scanning results as domain knowledge or

---

[2] https://mwanalysis.org/.
[3] http://www.offensivecomputing.net/.
[4] http://sourceforge.net/.
[5] https://www.virustotal.com.

Table 10.3: Antiviruses Used for Evaluation (presented in alphabetical order)

AhnLab-V3	Comodo	Jiangmin	Rising
AntiVir	DrWeb	K7AntiVirus	Sophos
Antiy-AVL	Emsisoft	Kaspersky	SUPERAntiSpyware
Avast	eSafe	McAfee	Symantec
AVG	eTrust-Vet	Microsoft	TheHacker
BitDefender	Fortinet	NOD32Norman	TrendMicro
ByteHero	F-Prot	nProtect	VBA32
CAT-QuickHeal	F-Secure	Panda	VIPRE
ClamAV	GData	PCTools	ViRobot
Commtouch	Ikarus	Prevx	VirusBuster

previous observation on binary files. Given the same amount of information about binary files, our goal is to determine which decision algorithm (1) yields the best detection rate and (2) provides more resilience against manipulated information.

10.5.2 Experiment Setting

We emulate a CMDN composed of forty AVs from different vendors as trader nodes. Each node includes all other nodes in its acquaintance list.

The data collected in Section 10.5.1 is partially used for constructing labeled history for nodes in CMDN. The remaining data is used for testing/evaluation. In the next subsections, we evaluate and compare the efficiency of several different collaborative decision models.

10.5.3 Ranking of AVs

Both the WA model and RevMatch model require the ranking of AVs. In this section we evaluate the TP, FP, and quality scores of AVs based on hybrid data sets S3 and S6. Moreover, the false negative rate (FN) is the probability that a malware is not detected and the true negative (TN) is the probability that goodware is correctly classified as goodware. High TP and low FP reflects high quality on malware detection. We define *quality score* of AV_i, denoted by Q_i, using $Q_i = 1 - (C_{fn}FN_i + C_{fp}FP_i), \forall i \in \{1, 2, ..., n\}$, where C_{fn} and C_{fp} are the penalization factors on the false negative and false positive rates, respectively.

The FP, TP, and quality scores for all AVs are plotted in Figure 10.4, where AVs are sorted by their quality scores ($C_{fn} = C_{fp} = 1$). Complete data results can be found in Table 10.4. We can see that TP and FP from different AVs vary greatly, and high-quality AVs have both high TP and low FP. The highest quality score an AV can achieve is 0.851. Results also show that all AVs are more effective in detecting old malware (S1) than new malware (S2).

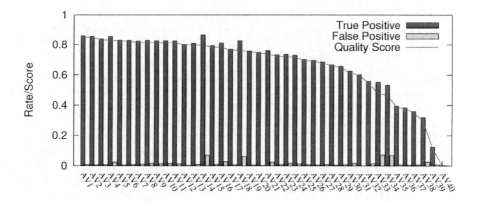

Figure 10.4: True positive rate and false positive rate of AVs.

10.5.4   Static Threshold

The static threshold (ST) model takes the total number of AVs that raises malware alerts. If the number is larger than a given threshold τ_s, then it raises a malware alarm. That is, if $\sum_{j \in \mathcal{N}_i} V_j \geq \tau_s$, where $V_j \in \{0, 1\}$ is the diagnosis result from AV_j, then it raises a malware alarm.

We implemented the ST model and plot the evaluation results in Figure 10.5. We can see that FP decreases and FN increases when threshold τ_s raises. When τ_s is 0, ST reports all files to be malware; when τ_s is 40 (the total number of AVs), ST reports all files to be goodware. The quality score of ST reaches the highest when τ_s is 5. In the rest of this section, we set $\tau_s = 5$ unless we specify otherwise.

10.5.5   Weighted Average

The weighted average (WA) model takes the weighted average of the decisions from all AVs and asserts the suspicious file to be malware when the weighted average is higher than a threshold τ_w. In our implementation, we use the quality scores computed in Section 10.5.3 as the weight of all AVs. That is, WA only raises a malware alarm if $\frac{\sum_{j \in \mathcal{N}_i} Q_j V_j}{|\mathcal{N}_i|} \geq \tau_w$, where $V_j \in \{0, 1\}$. As shown in Figure 10.6, WA yields optimal results when the threshold $\tau_w = 4/40$. Compared to ST, WA performs slightly better in malware detection quality. In the rest of the evaluation, we fix τ_w to $4/40$ unless we specify otherwise.

10.5.6   Decision Tree

The decision tree (DT) model uses machine learning to produce a tree-structured predictive tool to map feedback from different AVs to conclude that a suspicious file

Table 10.4: Quality Ranking for Antiviruses (AV1–AV40 correspond to the AVs listed in Table 10.3 with assigned nicknames)

Antivirus Alias	Detection Rate(S1)	Detection Rate(S2)	True Positive (malware S3)	False Positive (goodware S6)	Quality Score $C_{fn} = C_{fp} = 1$
AV1	0.951	0.800	0.859	0.008	0.851
AV2	0.944	0.797	0.855	0.006	0.849
AV3	0.925	0.787	0.840	0.007	0.833
AV4	0.961	0.783	0.855	0.024	0.831
AV5	0.939	0.759	0.831	0.005	0.826
AV6	0.939	0.757	0.830	0.007	0.823
AV7	0.940	0.747	0.824	0.011	0.813
AV8	0.946	0.752	0.830	0.017	0.813
AV9	0.952	0.742	0.827	0.014	0.813
AV10	0.932	0.755	0.827	0.016	0.812
AV11	0.936	0.752	0.825	0.013	0.812
AV12	0.914	0.733	0.802	0.002	0.800
AV13	0.931	0.726	0.809	0.009	0.799
AV14	0.947	0.813	0.866	0.070	0.796
AV15	0.863	0.753	0.795	0.010	0.785
AV16	0.935	0.726	0.812	0.027	0.784
AV17	0.931	0.654	0.770	0.006	0.764
AV18	0.908	0.779	0.826	0.062	0.764
AV19	0.911	0.648	0.758	0.005	0.753
AV20	0.891	0.653	0.750	0.002	0.748
AV21	0.890	0.679	0.761	0.024	0.737
AV22	0.927	0.594	0.734	0.008	0.725
AV23	0.938	0.607	0.737	0.017	0.720
AV24	0.929	0.592	0.731	0.013	0.718
AV25	0.903	0.562	0.702	0.007	0.695
AV26	0.907	0.556	0.697	0.005	0.692
AV27	0.897	0.544	0.686	0.009	0.677
AV28	0.849	0.546	0.667	0.005	0.663
AV29	0.882	0.513	0.657	0.007	0.651
AV30	0.861	0.461	0.626	0.016	0.610
AV31	0.755	0.494	0.603	0.000	0.603
AV32	0.771	0.421	0.560	0.014	0.545
AV33	0.814	0.377	0.553	0.072	0.481
AV34	0.746	0.416	0.534	0.069	0.465
AV35	0.525	0.330	0.395	0.008	0.387
AV36	0.754	0.141	0.385	0.005	0.380
AV37	0.474	0.283	0.360	0.007	0.353
AV38	0.473	0.221	0.320	0.025	0.295
AV39	0.204	0.062	0.124	0.009	0.116
AV40	0.022	0.001	0.003	0.002	0.001

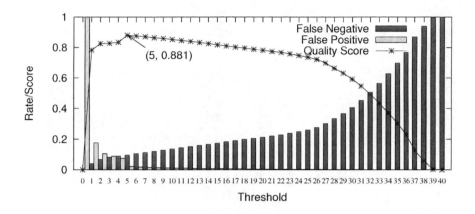

Figure 10.5: TP, FP, and quality scores of static threshold-based model with different thresholds (based on data set S3, S6).

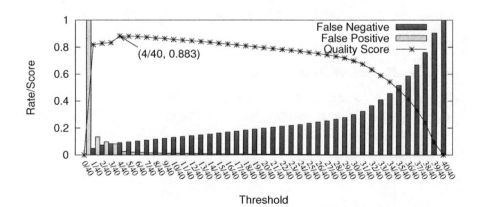

Figure 10.6: TP, FP, and quality scores of weighted average model with different thresholds (based on data set S3, S6).

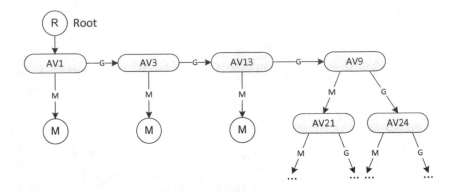

Figure 10.7: The optimal decision tree generated by Weka *J*48 Algorithm (top 5 levels).

is malware, or not. We used Weka[6], a datamining software, as the machine learning tool to produce decision trees for evaluation. We chose algorithm *J*48 for decision tree generation based on data set S3 and S6. We used 10-fold cross-validation to avoid overfitting. Figure 10.7 shows the partial outcome of the final decision tree. The entire decision tree includes twenty-six out of forty AVs in the decision loop. Our results show that the DT model achieves a high TP 0.956. However, it also has a higher FP of 0.077, which leads to a moderate quality score of 0.879 (see Table 10.5). We speculate the reason behind this is that the DT model focuses on reducing the overall number of false decisions, which does not necessarily produce optimal *quality score* when there is large discrepancy in training data set sizes of malware and goodware.

10.5.7 Bayesian Decision

The Bayesian decision (BD) model uses Bayes' Theorem to calculate the conditional probability $\mathbf{P}_M(\mathbf{y})$. A malware alarm is raised if $\mathbf{P}_M(\mathbf{y}) > \frac{C_{fp}}{C_{fp}+C_{fn}}$. However, the BD model is based on the assumption that all AVs are independent, which is not the case in reality. We also implemented the BD model and the detection accuracy is shown in Table 10.5.

10.5.8 RevMatch

The RevMatch model (Section 10.4) takes the feedback and does a history records lookup for decision. We implemented RevMatch and evaluated it using 10-fold cross-validation based on data sets S3 and S6. We fix parameters $\alpha = 1$, $\beta = 0$, and $\mathbf{P}_M = \mathbf{P}_G = 0.5$. In the first experiment, we fix parameters $C_{fp} = C_{fn} = 1$ and increase

---

[6]http://www.cs.waikato.ac.nz/ml/weka/.

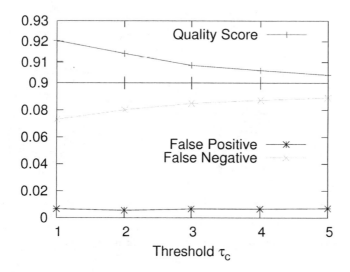

Figure 10.8: The iImpact from τ_c in RevMatch model.

threshold τ_c from 1 to 5. As shown in Figure 10.8, a higher τ_c leads to a slightly higher FN and lower quality score.

In the next experiment, we fix $\tau_c = 1$ and set different penalization weights on false negative rates C_{fn}. Figure 10.9 shows that a higher C_{fn} leads to a higher FP and a lower FN. We speculate the reason is that RevMatch automatically trades FP for a lower FN, since the penalization of FN is higher.

10.5.9 Comparison between Different Decision Models

In this experiment, we compare the quality scores of five different decision models: ST, WA, DT, BD, and RevMatch. The results are based on data set S3 and S6. We used fixed thresholds 5 for ST and 4/40 for WA. We used 10-fold cross-validation for both DT and RevMatch models. We set parameter $\tau_c = 1$ and $C_{fp} = C_{fn} = 1$. The results are shown in Table 10.5. We can see that RevMatch outperforms all other models in terms of overall quality score. Also, all collaborative detection models have higher quality scores than any single AV.

Next, we increase C_{fn} from 1 to 13 and plot the quality score of all decision models. The results are shown in Figure 10.10. We can see that RevMatch is superior to all others in all cases. BD performs the worst on higher C_{fn}. An interesting observation is that ST starts to perform better than WA when C_{fn} is sufficiently large. We speculate the reason is that when it is costly to miss malware, then the system con-

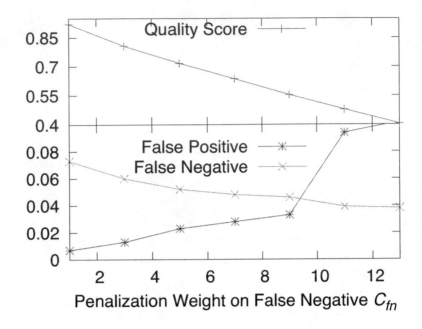

Figure 10.9: The impact from C_{fn} in RevMatch model.

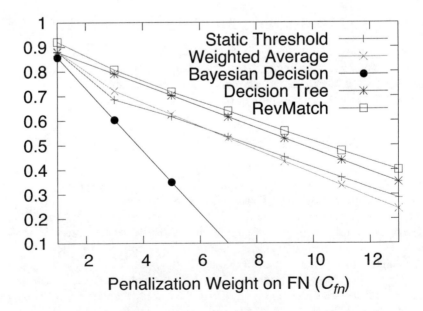

Figure 10.10: Quality scores of all models with different C_{fn}.

Table 10.5: Quality Scores among Different Decision Models

Method	True Positive TP	False Negative FN	False Positive FP	Quality Score $1 - C_{fp}FP - C_{fn}FN$
Static threshold	0.903	0.097	0.022	0.881
Weighted threshold	0.908	0.092	0.025	0.883
Decision tree	0.956	0.044	0.077	0.879
Bayesian decision	0.871	0.129	0.013	0.858
RevMatch	0.927	0.073	0.007	0.920
Best single AV	0.859	0.141	0.008	0.851

siders the opinion from all AVs rather than focusing on some high-quality AVs. Note that in this experiment, ST and WA both re-select their optimal decision thresholds for each C_{fn}.

10.5.10 Robustness against Insider Attacks

In an open CMDN, adversaries may join the network and serve as CMDN members in the beginning and then suddenly turn around and send incorrect feedback. The tasks of quickly identifying and removing malfunctioning or malicious insiders are the responsibilities of trust management and acquaintance management. However, in this subsection, we are interested in knowing the maximal impact malicious nodes can bring to the system if such a malicious node identification and removal mechanisms do not exist. We evaluate the impact of malicious insiders on the four decision models by intentionally injecting attacks into the experimental data.

In the first experiment, we start from the lowest ranking AV and replace its feedback by a malicious one, and gradually increase the number of malicious attackers by replacing feedback of other low quality AVs. We emulate three types of attacks, namely the *alarmer attack*, the *dormant attack*, and the *random attack*. Attackers launching an alarmer attack always report malware whenever a scanning request is received; attackers launching a dormant attack always report goodware for all scanning requests; whereas in a random attack, nodes report random decisions (either malware or goodware). Figure 10.11 shows the impact of these three different attacks on RevMatch model with different numbers of attackers. The alarmer attack has the highest impact and the dormant attack is the least effective. With the alarmer attack, the quality score drops down significantly when the number of attackers is higher than 5.

In another experiment, we investigate the impact of alarmer attacks on different decision methods. Figure 10.12 shows that the decision tree was least durable to colluded alarmer attacks. Its quality score had no change with the first two attackers, but dropped quickly after the third attacker joined in. We investigated the reason and found that the first two AVs were not included in the decision tree while the third attacker AV was. The results also show that ST can endure at most four attackers be-

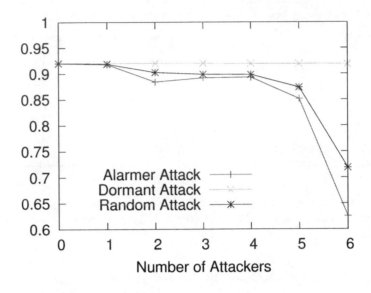

Figure 10.11: RevMatch model under three different attacks.

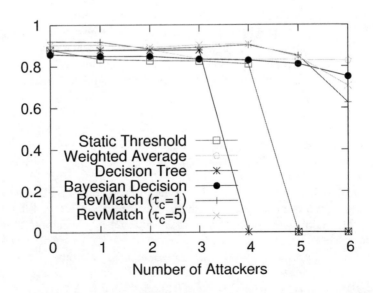

Figure 10.12: The quality scores versus the number of attackers.

cause the decision threshold is 5. The RevMatch, BD, and WA models are relatively more robust to colluded alarmer attacks. We also notice that using a higher decision threshold τ_c on RevMatch increases the resistance against attackers while decreasing the detection quality when there is no insider attack.

10.5.11 Acquaintance List Length and Efficiency

In the previous experiments, we showed that collaboration can effectively improve the intrusion detection accuracy for all participating IDSs. In this experiment, we study the impact of collaboration network size on the overall detection quality in the network. We start with five AVs with the lowest ranking and gradually increase the network size by adding more competitive AVs until it reaches forty, and we observe the malware detection quality score with different network sizes. We repeat the above process by starting from the top ranking AVs and add lower ranking ones in the second experiment, and by adding randomly picked AVs in the third experiment. The results (Figure 10.13) show that collaboration significantly improves the detection accuracy for nodes with low detection capability and nodes with high detection accuracy also benefit from it. We can see that although the collaboration between the top five AVs already yields good results, recruiting more AVs with lower ranking can further improve the overall accuracy. In all cases, a network with twenty-five AVs can achieve high malware detection quality. The drawback of collaborating with many AVs is the maintenance overhead because the participating AVs need to allocate resources to assist their collaborators. A host should select an appropriate acquaintance list size depending on the amount of resources it can reserve for AV collaboration.

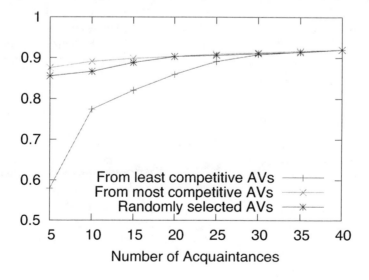

Figure 10.13: The quality scores versus number of collaborators.

Table 10.6: Performance Summary of Collaborative Decision Models

Decision Model	Decision Quality	Runtime	Attacker Tolerance	Partial Feedback	Flexibility
Static threshold	Medium	very fast	4 attackers	No	Yes
Weighted average	Medium	very fast	5+ attackers	Yes	Yes
Decision tree	Medium	very fast	3 attackers	No	No
Bayesian decision	Low	very fast	5+ attackers	Yes	Yes
RevMatch	High	fast	5+ attackers	Yes	Yes

10.6 Discussion

In Section 10.5 we evaluated the performance of the RevMatch model and compared it with four other collaborative decision models namely, ST, WA, DT and BD. The criteria we have used for evaluation are quality score and resistance to insider attacks. Quality score is a combination of FP and FN of the decisions, and the resistance to insider attacks is the maximum number of alarmer attackers it can endure before the quality score of the decision model drops significantly. In this section we discuss other criteria that may be also important for choosing the right decision model for CMDN. They are runtime efficiency, partial feedback adaption, and tuning flexibility.

10.6.1 Runtime Efficiency on Decision

Runtime efficiency is an important criterion since it may not be acceptable for the system to take too long to make a decision. We evaluate the running time of all four decision models on a Ubuntu machine equipped with 2.13 GHz Intel Xeon and 3X4GB RAM. The ST, WA, BD, and DT models all take less than 1 millisecond in processing the decision algorithm. RevMatch takes less than 15 milliseconds on average to make a decision.

10.6.2 Partial Feedback

In a CMDN, some collaborators may not respond to scanning requests all the time, especially when they are overloaded. Therefore, it is important for AVs to be able to make effective decisions based on the feedback from a subset of collaborators. ST may not work effectively with partial feedback because the fixed thresholds may be too high when the number of feedback participants is small. DT also does not work well with partial feedback, as it requires the inputs that can form a decision path in the tree. WA, BD, and RevMatch can work well with partial feedback.

10.6.3   Tuning Flexibility

Tuning flexibility allows the system administrator to tune the sensitivity of malware detection. For example, the system can become more or less sensitive to malware by changing a parameter. Both ST and WA can be tuned for the sensitivity of the system by setting their thresholds. DT, however, does not have a parameter that can be tuned for detection sensitivity. BD has tuning parameters C_{fp}, C_{fn}. RevMatch can be tuned using the penalization factors (i.e., C_{fp}, C_{fn}) for sensitivity, and τ_c for the robustness of the system.

10.6.4   Comparison

Table 10.6 provides a qualitative performance summary of the five collaborative decision models based on the metrics we selected. We can see that RevMatch is superior in terms of detection accuracy, flexibility, and adaptability to partial feedback. It also performs well in terms of runtime efficiency and resistance against insider attacks. Our results provide a reference for decision makers regarding which collaborative decision method to employ in their CMDNs.

10.6.5   Zero-Day Malware Detection

In CMDN, behavior-based malware detection techniques might be employed by some AV vendors. Zero-day malware can be possibly detected by some AVs that have sophisticated behavior analysis engines. Collaboration makes it possible for AVs to exchange information on zero-day malware. Our collaborative approach can provide significant benefit to users of AV products who do not have the capability to detect zero-day malware.

10.6.6   Historical Data Poisoning Attack

Because RevMatch uses history data for decision, adversaries may try to poison the history data to benefit themselves. For example, an adversary knows about a type of zero-day malware (it might release them), so it always identifies this zero-day malware while the other AV engines miss it. After that, it suddenly reports all goodware to be malware, intending to cause its collaborators to raise a large number of false alarms. However, RevMatch is resistant to this type of attack because the ground truth update mechanism design prevents the adversary from poisoning the history data quickly, by using the minimum recording time gap Δt. It is difficult for the adversary to constantly create new types of zero-day malware to boost its credits. Also, nodes in the network only consult others when the received file is detected as suspicious by the anomaly approach, and goodware usually does not raise any concern by anomaly detection.

10.7 Conclusion and Future Work

In this chapter we presented a collaborative malware detection framework (CMDN) and its architecture design. We particularly focused on the design of its collaborative decision mechanism. We presented a decision model named RevMatch, which makes collaborative malware detection decisions based on looking up the historical records with the same feedback set. We discussed several evaluation metrics and compared the RevMatch model with other decision models in the literature based on real data sets. Our evaluation results showed that RevMatch outperforms all others in terms of detection accuracy, flexibility, and tolerance of partial feedbacks, while achieving satisfactory running time efficiency and robustness to insider attacks. In general, collaborative malware detection techniques improve detection quality in comparison to single AVs. In our future work, we plan to further improve the robustness of the decision system by introducing more sophisticated insider attacks in addition to those we discussed in this chapter, and devise corresponding defense mechanisms. We also intend to further improve the efficiency of the decision algorithm by integrating the confidence level in detection from all participating AVs.

CONCLUSION

Intrusion detection networks (IDNs) are collaboration networks interconnecting intrusion detection systems (IDSs) to exchange information, knowledge, and expertise, in order to collectively achieve higher intrusion detection accuracy. However, building an IDN is a challenging task. Intrusion detection efficiency, robustness against malicious insiders, incentive compatibility, and scalability are four desired features of IDNs. This book focused on a distributed consultation-based IDN architecture design, where IDSs are connected to their collaborators in a peer-to-peer overlay, and send consultation messages to their collaborators when they do not have enough confidence to make an accurate intrusion assessment. The consultation feedbacks from collaborators are then aggregated to make a final intrusion decision. A typical IDN architecture includes several components essential for IDS collaboration (Chapter 3), four of which were discussed extensively throughout this book, namely *trust management, collaborative intrusion decision, resource management*, and *acquaintance management.*

As part of trust management, we discussed in Chapter 4 the design of the trust component—a Dirichlet-based Bayesian trust learning model used to calculate the trust values of collaborators based on past experiences. We showed that this model not only provides an efficient way to estimate trust values, but also provides the confidence levels in trust estimations. Chapter 5 discussed how the collaborative intrusion decision problem can be formulated as a Bayes optimization problem. It also showed how optimal decision rules that minimize Bayes risks can be obtained using hypothesis testing methods and real-time efficient, distributed, and sequential feedback aggregation can be achieved using a data-driven mechanism. As part of resource management, a continuous-kernel noncooperative game model was described in Chapter 6 and used to solve the problem of fair and incentive-compatible resource allocation. Finally, for acquaintance management, we presented in Chapter 7 a statistical model to evaluate the trade-off between the maintenance cost and intrusion cost, and an effective acquaintance management method to minimize the overall cost for each IDS in the network by appropriately selecting acquaintances.

In addition to consultation-based IDNs discussed in Section II, we also discussed a different type of IDN design, namely knowledge-based IDNs in Chapter 8, particularly focusing on its knowledge propagation mechanism design. In Chapter 9 we described an application of consultation-based IDNs to malware detection, where antiviruses collaborate together to improve the detection accuracy of the overall network.

We have established a set of metrics to evaluate the performance of collaborative IDNs, namely intrusion detection accuracy, robustness against malicious insiders, incentive compatibility in resource allocation, and scalability in network size. In addition, a case study of collaborative malware detection using real malware and goodware data was presented to show antivirus detection rate, malware detection accuracy, and robustness of decision models.

Overall, the results showed that consultation-based IDN design and IDN architecture components presented in this book are indeed efficient, incentive compatible, scalable, and robust. In particular and to evaluate collaborative IDN robustness, we have considered various attack models and corresponding defense mechanisms.

Finally, it is worth mentioning that, the collaboration management framework for intrusion detection networks discussed in this book can be useful for other types of networks with untrusted nodes such as mobile ad hoc networks, sensor networks, vehicular networks, and social networks.

APPENDICES

Appendix A

Examples of Intrusion Detection Rules and Alerts

CONTENTS

A.1   Examples of Snort Rules

Snort is a network-based intrusion detection system (NIDS). Its detection system is based on rules that are shared publicly by users and Snort administrators. Snort rule and updates are open source and free for public use and modification.

Users can configure which interface Snort listens to and what action Snort performs when a packet is detected by Snort rules. Snort rules are statements that define what to do with the sniffed packets. Each rule should be one single line. A Snort rule is composed of a Rule Header and Rule Options. The header part identifies the traffic based on IP address and port and the action to be done; for example, should it be logged, escalated or ignored? The rule options further narrow down traffic to fit into some particular event.

Figure A.1 shows the structure of a typical Snort rule. The Rule Header is the first part of a Snort rule and the rule options is the second part of the rule. The header contains the following fields: Action field, Protocol field, Source and Destination IP, Source and Destination Port, Direction. The Rule Options can contain several pairs

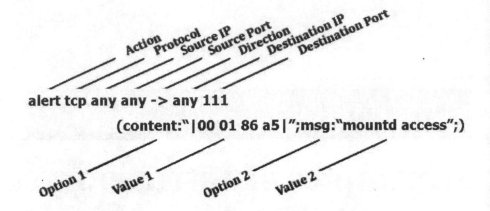

Figure A.1: Structure of a Snort Rule.

of option fields and value fields. In the example shown in figure A.1, The *content* option specifies the signature of an attack and the *msg* option specifies which message should be printed out when a suspicious packet is detected.

Snort rules can be customized by users and administrators on top of the base rules downloaded from the rule deposit center. Effective customized rules can be shared between Snort communities and adopted by users with similar interests. An efficient rule-sharing mechanism can effectively distribute Snort rules to peers who are most likely adopt the rule and therefore improve the intrusion efficiency of the entire community.

A.2   Example of an Intrusion Alert in IDMEF Format

Figure A.2 shows an example of an intrusion detection alert in IDMEF format.

```
<?xml version="1.0" encoding="UTF-8"?>
<idmef:IDMEF-Message xmlns:idmef="http://iana.org/idmef"
version="1.0">
  <idmef:Alert messageid="123456789abc">
    <idmef:Analyzer analyzerid="sensor01">
      <idmef:Node category="dns">
        <idmef:name>sensor.abc.com</idmef:name>
      </idmef:Node>
    </idmef:Analyzer>
    <idmef:CreateTime
ntpstamp="0xbc89f6f9.0xef669437">2012-09-09T10:01:25.93464Z</
idmef:CreateTime>
    <idmef:Source ident="a0b2" spoofed="yes">
     <idmef:Node ident="a0b2-1">
        <idmef:Address ident="a1a2-2" category="ipv4-addr">
          <idmef:address>192.0.1.100</idmef:address>
        </idmef:Address>
      </idmef:Node>
    </idmef:Source>
    <idmef:Target ident="b5b6">
      <idmef:Node>
        <idmef:Address ident="b5b6-1" category="ipv4-addr">
          <idmef:address>192.0.1.10</idmef:address>
        </idmef:Address>
      </idmef:Node>
    </idmef:Target>
    <idmef:Target ident="c7c8">
      <idmef:Node ident="c7c8-1" category="nisplus">
        <idmef:name>hipo</idmef:name>
      </idmef:Node>
    </idmef:Target>
    <idmef:Target ident="d1d2">
      <idmef:Node ident="d1d2-1">
        <idmef:location>Waterloo B10</idmef:location>
        <idmef:name>Cisco.router.b10</idmef:name>
      </idmef:Node>
    </idmef:Target>
    <idmef:Classification text="Ping-of-death detected">
      <idmef:Reference origin="cve">
        <idmef:name>CVE-1999-128</idmef:name>
        <idmef:url>http://www.cve.mitre.org/cgi-bin/cvename.cgi?
name=CVE-1999-128</idmef:url>
      </idmef:Reference>
    </idmef:Classification>
  </idmef:Alert>
</idmef:IDMEF-Message>
```

Figure A.2: Example of an intrusion alert in IDMEF format.

Appendix B

Proofs of Theorems

CONTENTS

B.1 Proof of Proposition 9.4.3

Proof B.1   In **G1**, for each $i \in \mathcal{N}$, the feasible set $\mathscr{F}_i$ is a closed, bounded, and convex subset of $\mathbb{R}^{n_i}$. The public utility function U_i^r is jointly continuous in its arguments and strictly convex in $\vec{r}_i$. Hence, using Theorem 4.3 in [38], we can show that **G1** admits a Nash equilibrium in pure strategies.

In **G2**, without relaxation, the convex program (PPi) admits a solution $\tilde{r}_{ij}$, which is continuous in $\vec{R}_i$ [165]. The feasible set of (Pi) is compact and convex, and the U_i^b is jointly continuous in its arguments and strictly convex in $\vec{R}_i$. Hence, **G2** has a Nash equilibrium at the level of private optimization. We can determine $r_{ij}^{\star}$, which yields an equilibrium at the level of public optimization. Therefore, **G2** admits a Nash equilibrium in pure strategies of $\{(\vec{r}_i, \vec{R}_i), i \in \mathcal{N}\}$.

B.2 Proof of Theorem 9.2

We first introduce a few definitions and then prove Proposition B.2.1, which will be used in the proof of Theorem 9.2.

Definition B.1 Let $\vec{R}_i^*, \vec{r}_i, i \in \mathcal{N}$, be an NE. The non-prime degree $\overline{D}$ of an equilibrium is the number of distinct pairs $\{i, j\}, j \in \mathcal{N}_i$, such that $R_{ij}^* \neq r_{ij}^*$. Note that a prime NE has non-prime degree 0.

Proof B.2 In the proof of Theorem 9.2, we show that any non-prime NE can be reduced to a prime NE with $\overline{D} = 0$. From Proposition 9.4.3 we know there exists at least one NE for **G2**. Let $\mathbf{R}^* = [\vec{R}_i^*]_{i \in \mathcal{N}}$ and $\mathbf{r}^* = [\vec{r}_i^*]_{i \in \mathcal{N}}$ be a NE. Suppose it is not a prime NE. Hence, there must exist at least one pair that satisfies $r_{uv}^* < R_{uv}^*$ for some pair $\{u, v\}$. Construct a feasible solution $(\mathbf{R}', \mathbf{r}^*)$ from $(\mathbf{R}^*, \mathbf{r}^*)$ such that $R_{ij}' = R_{ij}^*$, for every $\{i, j\} \in \bigcup_{i \neq j, j \in \mathcal{N}_i, i \in \mathcal{N}} \{i, j\} \backslash \{u, v\}$, and $R_{ij}' = r_{ij}^*$, for $\{i, j\} = \{u, v\}$. From Proposition B.2.1 we can show that $(\mathbf{R}', \mathbf{r}^*)$ also constitutes an NE, whose non-prime degree becomes $\overline{D}_i - 1$. By an iterative process, a non-prime NE $(\mathbf{R}*, \mathbf{r}^*)$ can be reduced to a prime NE. Hence, there exists a prime NE in **G2**.

Proposition B.2.1 *Let $(\mathbf{R}^*, \mathbf{r}^*)$ be a NE with $\overline{D} \neq 0$ and $\{u, v\}$ be a pair of nodes such that $r_{uv}^* < R_{uv}^*$. Let $(\mathbf{R}', \mathbf{r}')$ be a constructed feasible solution such that $\mathbf{r}' = \mathbf{r}^*$, $R_{ij}' = R_{ij}^*$, for every $\{i, j\} \in \bigcup_{i \neq j, j \in \mathcal{N}_i, i \in \mathcal{N}} \{i, j\} \backslash \{u, v\}$, and $R_{ij}' = r_{ij}^*$, for $\{i, j\} = \{u, v\}$. Then $(\mathbf{R}', \mathbf{r}^*)$ is an NE of **G2**.*

Proof B.3 We need to show that $\mathbf{r}^*$ is an optimal response to $\mathbf{R}'$, and then nodes have no incentive to deviate from $\mathbf{R}'$. For a feasible solution $(\mathbf{R}, \mathbf{r})$, we say that r_{ij} is a boundary allocation if $r_{ij} = \min(\vec{r}_i, R_{ij})$; otherwise, we say that r_{ij} is an internal allocation. At an NE solution, the marginal gains $\frac{\partial U_i^p}{\partial r_{ij}}, j \in \mathcal{N}_i$, are equal for internal allocation points. In addition, the marginal gain of i at boundary allocations is no less than the marginal gains of i at internal allocations.

Because $\mathbf{R}^*$ is a **G2** NE, node v has no incentive to move by changing R_{uv}. If a node v decreases its request to u from value R_{uv}^* to value r_{uv}^*, then the allocation from node u will not increase. This can be easily shown by contradiction as follows.

Suppose the reverse is true; then there must exist an internal allocation r_{um} to m whose marginal gain is higher than the marginal gain at R_{uv}'. However, from (9.2) and (9.5) we can see that by understating the requests, nodes can increase their marginal gains. Hence, the marginal gain at r_{um}^* is larger than the marginal gain at r_{uv}^*. Therefore, we can conclude that $\mathbf{r}^*$ is not an optimal solution of configuration $\mathbf{R}^*$, which contradicts the property of NE.

We also observe that node v cannot gain from u by either decreasing or increasing its request at R_{uv}'. Decreasing the request results in decreasing the allocation from u, because the resource is bounded by the request. On the other hand, increasing the request at R_{uv}' shall not increase the allocation from u, because it will otherwise contradict the properties of NE $\mathbf{R}^*$ that nodes v cannot gain better utility by changing its request at an NE.

Therefore, after the node v decreases R_{uv}^* to $R_{uv}' = r_{uv}^*$, we arrive at $\mathbf{r}' = \mathbf{r}^*$. The constructed solution $\mathbf{R}'$ and $\mathbf{r}'$ is another NE of $\mathbf{G2}$.

B.3   Proof of Proposition 9.4.4

Proof B.4   For each pair of nodes i, j, we have $\mathbf{r}_{ij} = \mathbf{A}_{ij}\mathbf{r}_{ij} + \mathbf{b}_{ij}$, where $\mathbf{r}_{ij} = [r_{ij}, r_{ji}]^T$, and

$$\mathbf{b}_{ij} = \left[\begin{array}{c} \lambda_{ij}\left(M_i + \sum_{v \neq j, v \in \mathcal{N}_i} q_{iv}r_{vi}\right) \\ \lambda_{ji}\left(M_j + \sum_{v \neq i, v \in \mathcal{N}_j} q_{jv}r_{vj}\right) \end{array} \right],$$

$$\mathbf{A}_{ij} = \left[\begin{array}{cc} 0 & (\lambda_{ij}-1)q_{ij} \\ (\lambda_{ji}-1)q_{ji} & 0 \end{array} \right].$$

Given the existence of Nash equilibrium and the assumption on q_{ij} and q_{ji}, the uniqueness of the Nash equilibrium is ensured only when $\mathbf{A}_{ij}$ is nonsingular.

B.4   Proof of Proposition 9.4.5

Proof B.5   From (9.13), we can find that the optimal response $R_{ij}^\star$ to other nodes is given by

$$R_{ij}^\star = \frac{\lambda_{ij}}{2 - \lambda_{ij}}\left(M_i + \sum_{u \neq j, u \in \mathcal{N}_i} R_{iu}\right).$$

Because $R_{ij}^\star$ is linear in $R_{iu}, u \in \mathcal{N}_i$, we can build it into a linear system of equations with the variables $R_{ij}, i, j \in \mathcal{N}$ stacked into one vector. The linear system has a unique solution if the condition of diagonal dominance holds, leading to the condition.

B.5   Proof of Proposition 9.4.6

Proof B.6   From Remark 9.4.1 we learn that $r_{ij}^\star$ is a monotonic decreasing function with respect to R_{ij}. Because the utility function in (Pij) is monotonically increasing with $r_{ji}^{\star}$, increasing R_{ji} will decrease the utility. Hence, IDS i seeks to lower R_{ji} until the optimal utility is achieved. In other words, an optimal solution $R_{ji}^{\star}$ is achieved at $R_{ji}^{\star} = r_{ji}^{\star} = \bar{r}_{ji}$. Assuming that $\bar{r}_i$ is sufficiently large, we have $\bar{r}_{ji} = R_{ji}$. Under the NE, we have $r_{ij}^{*} = r_{ij}^{\star} = R_{ij}^{\star} = R_{ij}^{*}$, $\forall i, j \in \mathcal{N}$ and $i \neq j$. Then from (9.13), r_{ij}^{*} solves

$$r_{ij}^{*} = r_{ij}^{\star} = \frac{T_{ij}T_{ji}}{\sum_{u \in \mathcal{N}_i} T_{iu}T_{ui}} \left(M_i + \sum_{v \in \mathcal{N}_i} r_{iv}^{*} \right) - r_{ij}^{*}, \tag{B.1}$$

which yields (9.14). It is easy to see that any requests $0 < R_{ji} < R_{ji}^{*}$ will lower the optimal allocation r_{ij}^{*} and hence its utility. For the case where constraint (9.3) becomes active, the solution (9.15) already satisfies the condition and hence remains optimal.

References

[1] http://news.netcraft.com/archives/2009/06/22/faster_actions_needed_against _phishingconficker domains.html [Last accessed on Feb. 15, 2013].

[2] Antivirus vendors go beyond signature-based antivirus. http://searchsecurity. techtarget.com/magazineContent/Antivirus-vendors-go-beyond-signature-based- antivirus [Last accessed on April 5, 2013].

[3] Avast. http://www.avast.com.

[4] Avira. http://www.avira.com [Last accessed on Feb. 15, 2013].

[5] Bots and botnetsa growing threat. http://us.norton.com/botnet/promo [Last accessed on Feb. 15, 2013].

[6] Bredolab Bot Herder Gets 4 Years for 30 Million Infections. http://www.wired .com/threatlevel/2012/05/bredolab-botmaster-sentenced [Last accessed on April 5, 2013].

[7] Bro. http://www.bro-ids.org/ [Last accessed on Feb. 15, 2013].

[8] CAIDA: The Cooperative Association for Internet Data Analysis. http://www.caida.org [Last accessed on Feb. 15, 2013].

[9] Common intrusion detection signatures standard. http://tools.ietf.org/html/ draft-wierzbicki-cidss-04 [Last accessed on Feb. 15, 2013].

[10] Cyber-attacks batter Web heavyweights. http://archives.cnn.com/2000/TECH/ computing/02/09/cyber.attacks.01/index.html [Last accessed on Feb. 15, 2013].

[11] DDOS attack on Spamhaus: Biggest cyber-attack in history slows down Internet across the world. http://www.mirror.co.uk/news/world-news/ddos-attack-spamhaus-biggest-cyber-attack-1788942 [Last accessed on April 5, 2013].

[12] Evolving DDOS Attacks Provide the Driver for Financial Institutions to Enhance Response Capabilities. http://www.alston.com/Files/Publication/dc282435-c434-42a2-afe7-38af660dc82a/Presentation/PublicationAttachment/2c3bb5d8-b035-4d03-8e3c-390c2da3751d/Cyber-Alert-Evolving-DDOS-Attacks.pdf [Last accessed on April 5, 2013].

[13] Fksensor. "http://www.keyfocus.net/kfsensor/download" [Last accessed on Feb. 15, 2013].

[14] Honeyd. "http://www.honeyd.org" [Last accessed on Feb. 15, 2013].

[15] Intrusion detection message exchange format. http://www.ietf.org/rfc/rfc4765.txt [Last accessed on Feb. 15, 2013].

[16] McAfee antivirus to reimburse consumers for bad update. http://news.techworld.com/security/3221657/mcafee-antivirus-to-reimburse-consumers-for-bad-update/ [Last accessed on April 5, 2013].

[17] myNetWatchman. http://www.mynetwatchman.com [Last accessed on Feb. 15, 2013].

[18] National vulnerability Database. http://nvd.nist.gov [Last accessed on Feb. 15, 2013].

[19] OSSEC. http://www.ossec.net/[Last accessed on Feb. 15, 2013].

[20] Protecting against the Rampant Conficker Worm. http://www.pcworld.com/article/157876/protecting_against_the_rampant _conficker_worm.html [Last accessed on Feb. 15, 2013].

[21] Protecting against the Rampant Conficker Worm. http://www.pcworld.com/article/157876/protecting_against_the_rampant_conficker_worm.html [Last accessed on April 5, 2013].

[22] Request for comments. http://newrfc.itms.pl/?mod=yes&range=4765 [Last accessed on Feb. 15, 2013].

[23] SANS Internet Storm Center (ISC). http://isc.sans.org/ [Last accessed on Feb. 15, 2013].

[24] Snort. http://www.snort.org/[Last accessed in Feb 15, 2013].

[25] Spector. http://www.specter.com [Last accessed on Feb. 15, 2013].

[26] Symantec. http://www.symantec.com/ [Last accessed on Feb. 15, 2013].

[27] The Honeynet Project. http://www.honeynet.org/[Last accessed on Feb. 15, 2013].

[28] Trend glitch costs 8 million. http://news.cnet.com/Trend-glitch-costs-8-million/2110-1002_3-5789129.html [Last accessed on April 5, 2013].

[29] TripWire. http://www.tripwire.com/ [Last accessed on Feb. 15, 2013].

[30] US-CERT. http://www.kb.cert.org [Last accessed on Feb. 15, 2013].

[31] What is SmartScreen Filter? http://www.microsoft.com/security/filters/smartscreen.aspx [Last accessed on Feb. 15, 2013].

[32] Why 2012 will be cybercrime's 'hell year'. http://www.nbcnews.com/technology/technolog/why-2012-will-be-cybercrimes-hell-year-196836 [Last accessed on Feb. 15, 2013].

[33] ZDnet. http://www.zdnet.com/blog/security/confickers-estimated-economic-cost-91-billion/3207 [Last accessed on Feb. 15, 2013].

[34] The honeynet project. know your enemy: Fast-flux service networks, 13 July, 2007. http://www.honeynet.org/book/export/html/130 [Last accessed on Feb. 15, 2013].

[35] Apples app store downloads top three billion, 2010. http://www.apple.com/pr/library/2010/01/05Apples-App-Store-Downloads-Top-Three-Billion.html [Last accessed on Feb. 15, 2013].

[36] K. G. Anagnostakis, M. B. Greenwald, S. Ioannidis, A. D. Keromytis, and D. Li. A cooperative immunization system for an untrusting Internet. In *Networks, 2003. ICON2003, The 11th IEEE International Conference on*, pages 403–408. IEEE, 2003.

[37] T. Başar and G. J. Olsder. *Dynamic Noncooperative Game Theory*. SIAM, Philadelphia, 2nd edition, 1999.

[38] T. Başar and G. J. Olsder. *Dynamic Noncooperative Game Theory*. SIAM Series in Classics in Applied Mathematics, Philadelphia, 1999.

[39] A. Berman and R. J. Plemmons. *Nonnegative Matrices in Mathematical Sciences*. SIAM, Philadelphia, 1994.

[40] D. Bertsekas. *Network Optimization: Continuous and Discrete Models*. Athena Scientific, Nashua, NH, 1998.

[41] M. Bishop. *Computer Security: Art and Science*. Addison-Wesley, 2003.

[42] S. Boyd and L. Vandenberghe. *Convex Optimization*. Cambridge University Press, 2004.

[43] A. Broder and M. Mitzenmacher. Network applications of bloom filters: A survey. *Internet Mathematics*, 1(4):485–509, 2004.

[44] M. Cai, K. Hwang, Y. K. Kwok, S. Song, and Y. Chen. Collaborative Internet worm containment. *IEEE Security & Privacy*, 3(3):25–33, 2005.

[45] D. Chau, C. Nachenberg, J. Wilhelm, A. Wright, and C. Faloutsos. Polonium: Tera-scale graph mining and inference for malware detection. In *Proccedings of SIAM International Conference on Data Mining (SDM) 2011*, 2011.

[46] S. Chen, D. Liu, S. Chen, and S. Jajodia. V-cops: A vulnerability-based cooperative alert distribution system. In *Computer Security Applications Conference, 2006. ACSAC'06. 22nd Annual*, pages 43–56. IEEE, 2006.

[47] R.A. Clarke and R. Knake. Cyber war: The next threat to national security and what to do about it. Ecco, 2010.

[48] National Research Council Committee on Network Science for Future Army Applications. *Network Science*. The National Academies Press, 2005.

[49] F. Cuppens and A. Miege. Alert correlation in a cooperative intrusion detection framework. In *2002 IEEE Symposium on Security and Privacy, 2002. Proceedings*, 2002.

[50] D. Dagon, X. Qin, G. Gu, W. Lee, J. Grizzard, J. Levine, and H. Owen. Honeystat: Local worm detection using honeypots. *Lecture Notes in Computer Science*, pages 39–58, 2004.

[51] A. Dal Forno and U. Merlone. Incentives and individual motivation in supervised work groups. *European Journal of Operational Research*, 207(2):878–885, 2010.

[52] D. Dash, B. Kveton, J. M. Agosta, E. Schooler, J. Chandrashekar, A. Bachrach, and A. Newman. When gossip is good: Distributed probabilistic inference for detection of slow network intrusions. In *Proceedings of the National Conference on Artificial Intelligence*, volume 21, page 1115. Menlo Park, CA; Cambridge, MA; London; AAAI Press; MIT Press; 1999, 2006.

[53] N. Daswani, C. Kern, and A. Kesavan. *Foundations of Security: What Every Programmer Needs to Know*. Dreamtech Press, 2007.

[54] C. Davies. iphone spyware debated as app library phones home, 2009. http://offerpia.com/won/link/?item_no=23887 [Last accessed on Feb. 15, 2013].

[55] H. Debar, M. Becker, and D. Siboni. A neural network component for an intrusion detection system. In *Research in Security and Privacy, 1992. Proceedings., 1992 IEEE Computer Society Symposium on*, pages 240–250. IEEE, 1992.

[56] H. Debar and A. Wespi. Aggregation and correlation of intrusion-detection alerts. In W. Lee, L. M, and A. Wespi, editors, *Recent Advances in Intrusion Detection*, Lecture Notes in Computer Science, pages 85–103. Springer, 2001.

[57] D. E. Denning. An intrusion-detection model. *Software Engineering, IEEE Transactions on*, (2):222–232, 1987.

[58] J. R. Douceur. The sybil attack. *Proceedings of the 1st International Workshop on Peer-to-Peer Systems (IPTPS '02)*, 2002.

[59] C. Duma, M. Karresand, N. Shahmehri, and G. Caronni. A trust-aware, p2p-based overlay for intrusion detection. In *International Conference on Database and Expert Systems Applications*, 2006.

[60] Y. Elovici, A. Shabtai, R. Moskovitch, G. Tahan, and C. Glezer. Applying machine learning techniques for detection of malicious code in network traffic. *KI 2007: Advances in Artificial Intelligence*, pages 44–50, 2007.

[61] E. Fehr and H. Gintis. Human motivation and social cooperation: Experimental and analytical foundations. *Annual Reviews in Sociology*, 33:43–64, 2007.

[62] M. Feldman, C. Papadimitriou, J. Chuang, and I. Stoica. Free-riding and whitewashing in peer-to-peer systems. *Selected Areas in Communications, IEEE Journal on*, 24(5):1010–1019, 2006.

[63] M. Fitzpatrick. Mobile that allows bosses to snoop on staff developed, 2010. "http://news.bbc.co.uk/2/hi/8559683.stm" [Last accessed in Feb 15, 2013].

[64] M. Fossi, G. Egan, K. Haley, E. Johnson, T. Mack, T. Adams, J. Blackbird, M. K. Low, D. Mazurek, D. McKinney, et al. Symantec Internet security threat report trends for 2010. *Volume XVI*, 2011.

[65] M. Fossi, E. Johnson, D. Turner, T. Mack, J. Blackbird, D. McKinney, M. K. Low, T. Adams, M. P. Laucht, and J. Gough. Symantec report on the underground economy: July 2007 to June 2008. Technical report, Technical Report, Symantec Corporation, 2008.

[66] M. Fossi, D. Turner, E. Johnson, T. Mack, T. Adams, J. Blackbird, S. Entwisle, B. Graveland, D. McKinney, J. Mulcahy, et al. Symantec global Internet security threat report. *XV, April*, 2010.

[67] M. Fredrikson, S. Jha, M. Christodorescu, R. Sailer, and X. Yan. Synthesizing near-optimal malware specifications from suspicious behaviors. In *Security and Privacy (S&P), 2010 IEEE Symposium on*, pages 45–60. IEEE, 2010.

[68] C. Fung, Q. Zhu, R. Boutabai, and T. Başar. Poster: SMURFEN: A Rule Sharing Collaborative Intrusion Detection Network. In *Proceedings of the 18th ACM Conference on Computer and Communications Security (CCS)*, pages 761–764, 2011.

[69] C. J. Fung, J. Zhang, I. Aib, and R. Boutaba. Dirichlet-based trust management for effective collaborative intrusion detection networks. *Network and Service Management, IEEE Transactions on*, 8(2):79 –91, June 2011.

[70] C. J. Fung, J. Zhang, and R. Boutaba. Effective acquaintance management for collaborative intrusion detection networks. In *16th International Conference on Network and Service Management (CNSM 2010)*, 2010.

[71] C. J. Fung, J. Zhang, and R. Boutaba. Effective acquaintance management based on Bayesian learning for distributed intrusion detection networks. *Network and Service Management, IEEE Transactions on*, 9(3):320–332, Sept. 2012.

[72] C. J. Fung, O. Baysal, J. Zhang, I. Aib, and R. Boutaba. Trust management for host-based collaborative intrusion detection. In *19th IFIP/IEEE International Workshop on Distributed Systems*, 2008.

[73] C. J. Fung and R. Boutaba. Design and management of collaborative intrusion detection networks. In *15th IFIP/IEEE Intl. Symposium on Integrated Network Management*, 2013.

[74] C. J. Fung, J. Zhang, I. Aib, and R. Boutaba. Robust and scalable trust management for collaborative intrusion detection. In *Proceedings of the Eleventh IFIP/IEEE International Symposium on Integrated Network Management (IM)*, 2009.

[75] C. J. Fung, Q. Zhu, R. Boutaba, and T. Barsar. Bayesian decision aggregation in collaborative intrusion detection networks. In *12th IEEE/IFIP Network Operations and Management Symposium (NOMS10)*, 2010.

[76] A. Gelman. *Bayesian Data Analysis*. CRC Press, Boca Raton, FL, 2004.

[77] A. Ghosh and S. Sen. Agent-based distributed intrusion alert system. In *Proceedings of the 6th International Workshop on Distributed Computing (IWDC04)*. Springer, 2004.

[78] S. J. Grossman and O.D. Hart. Takeover bids, the free-rider problem, and the theory of the corporation. *The Bell Journal of Economics*, pages 42–64, 1980.

[79] C. Grothoff. An excess-based economic model for resource allocation in peer-to-peer networks. *Wirtschaftsinformatik*, 45(3):285–292, 2003.

[80] D. Halder and K. Jaishankar. Cyber Crime and the Victimization of Women: Laws, Rights and Regulations. Information Science Reference, 2012.

[81] M. T. T. Hsiao and A. A. Lazar. Optimal decentralized flow control of Markovian queueing networks with multiple controllers. *Performance Evaluation*, 13(3):181–204, 1991.

[82] F. IAO. "Iloveyou" virus lessons learned report. 2003.

[83] Gartner Inc. Gartner survey shows phishing attacks escalated in 2007; more than 3 billion lost to these attacks. Press release, 2007.

[84] R. W. Janakiraman and M. Q. Zhang. Indra: a peer-to-peer approach to network intrusion detection and prevention. *WET ICE 2003. Proceedings of the 12th IEEE International Workshops on Enabling Technologies*, 2003.

[85] J. Jang, D. Brumley, and S. Venkataraman. Bitshred: feature hashing malware for scalable triage and semantic analysis. In *Proceedings of the 18th ACM conference on Computer and communications security*, pages 309–320. ACM, 2011.

[86] T. Jiang and J. S. Baras. Trust evaluation in anarchy: A case study on autonomous networks. In *INFOCOM*. IEEE, 2006.

[87] A. Jøsang and R. Ismail. The Beta Reputation System. In *Proceedings of the Fifteenth Bled Electronic Commerce Conference*, 2002.

[88] J. H. Keppler and H. Mountford. *Handbook of Incentive Measures for Biodiversity: Design and Implementation*. OECD, 1999.

[89] C. Kolbitsch, P. M. Comparetti, C. Kruegel, E. Kirda, X. Zhou, and X. F. Wang. Effective and efficient malware detection at the end host. In *Proceedings of the 18th Conference on USENIX Security Symposium*, pages 351–366. USENIX Association, 2009.

[90] D. Komashinskiy and I. Kotenko. Malware detection by data mining techniques based on positionally dependent features. In *Parallel, Distributed and Network-Based Processing (PDP), 2010 18th Euromicro International Conference on*, pages 617–623. IEEE, 2010.

[91] Y. A. Korilis and A. A. Lazar. On the existence of equilibria in noncooperative optimal flow control. *Journal of the ACM (JACM)*, 42(3):584–613, 1995.

[92] A. Le, R. Boutaba, and E. Al-Shaer. Correlation-based load balancing for network intrusion detection and prevention systems. In *Proceedings of the 4th International Conference on Security and Privacy in Communication Network*. ACM, New York, NY, 2008.

[93] B. C. Levy. *Principles of Signal Detection and Parameter Estimation*. Springer-Verlag, 2008.

[94] Z. Li, Y. Chen, and A. Beach. Towards scalable and robust distributed intrusion alert fusion with good load balancing. In *Proceedings of the 2006 SIGCOMM Workshop on Large-Scale Attack Defense*, pages 115–122. ACM New York, NY, 2006.

[95] Z. Li, Y. Chen, and A. Beach. Towards scalable and robust distributed intrusion alert fusion with good load balancing. In *Proceedings of the 2006 SIGCOMM Workshop on Large-Scale Attack Defense*. ACM, 2006.

[96] W. Lin, L. Xiang, D. Pao, and B. Liu. Collaborative Distributed Intrusion Detection System. In *Future Generation Communication and Networking, 2008. FGCN'08. Second International Conference on*, volume 1, 2008.

[97] M. E. Locasto, J. J. Parekh, A. D. Keromytis, and S. J. Stolfo. Towards collaborative security and P2P intrusion detection. In *Information Assurance Workshop, 2005. IAW'05. Proceedings from the Sixth Annual IEEE SMC*, pages 333–339, 2005.

[98] T. F. Lunt, D. E. Denning, R. R. Schell, M. Heckman, and W. R. Shockley. The seaview security model. *Software Engineering, IEEE Transactions on*, 16(6):593–607, 1990.

[99] R. T. B. Ma, S. C. M. Lee, J. C. S. Lui, and D. K. Y. Yau. A game theoretic approach to provide incentive and service differentiation in P2P networks. In *Sigmetrics/Performance*, 2004.

[100] M. Marchetti, M. Messori, and M. Colajanni. Peer-to-peer architecture for collaborative intrusion and malware detection on a large scale. *Information Security*, pages 475–490, 2009.

[101] S. Marsh. *Formalising Trust as a Computational Concept*. Ph.D. thesis, Department of Mathematics and Computer Science, University of Stirling, 1994.

[102] C. A. Martínez, G. I. Echeverri, and A. G. Castillo Sanz. Malware detection based on cloud computing integrating intrusion ontology representation. In *Communications (LATINCOM), 2010 IEEE Latin-American Conference on*, pages 1–6. IEEE, 2010.

[103] L. Mekouar, Y. Iraqi, and R. Boutaba. Peer-to-peers most wanted: Malicious peers. *Computer Networks*, 50(4):545–562, 2006.

[104] L. Mekouar, Y. Iraqi, and R. Boutaba. A recommended scheme for [eer-to-peer systems. In *International Symposium on Applications and the Internet (SAINT)*. IEEE, 2008.

[105] P. Miller and A. Inoue. Collaborative intrusion detection system. In *Fuzzy Information Processing Society, 2003. NAFIPS 2003. 22nd International Conference of the North American*, pages 519–524. IEEE, 2003.

[106] J. Mo and J. Walrand. Fair end-to-end window-based congestion control. *IEEE/ACM Transactions on Networking (ToN)*, 8(5):556–567, 2000.

[107] D. Moore, C. Shannon, D. J. Brown, G. M. Voelker, and S. Savage. Inferring internet denial-of-service activity. *ACM Transactions on Computer Systems (TOCS)*, 24(2):115–139, 2006.

[108] D. Moren. Retrievable iphone numbers mean potential privacy issues, 2009. http://www.macworld.com/article/1143047/phone_hole.html [Last accessed on Feb. 15, 2013].

[109] B. Morin and H. Debar. Correlation of intrusion symptoms: An application of chronicles. In G. Vigna, E. Jonsson, and C. Krgel, Editors, *RAID*, Lecture Notes in Computer Science, pages 94–112. Springer, 2003.

[110] Atlas Arbor Networks. http://atlas.arbor.net/ [last accessed in feb 15, 2013], 2008.

[111] M. E. J. Newman, A. L. Barabasi, and D. J. Watts. *The structure and dynamics of networks*. Princeton Univ Pr, 2006.

[112] K. C. Nguyen, T. Alpcan, and T. Başar. A decentralized Bayesian attack detection algorithm for network security. In *Proceedings of the 23rd International Information Security Conference*, 2005.

[113] P. Ning, Y. Cui, and D. S. Reeves. Constructing attack scenarios through correlation of intrusion alerts. In Vijayalakshmi Atluri, Editor, *ACM Conference on Computer and Communications Security*, pages 245–254. ACM, 2002.

[114] J. Oberheide, E. Cooke, and F. Jahanian. CloudAV: N-version antivirus in the network cloud. In *Proceedings of the 17th USENIX Security Symposium*, 2008.

[115] Pandalabs. Annual report Panda Labs 2010. http://press.pandasecurity.com/wp-content/uploads/2010/05/PandaLabs-Annual-Report-2010.pdf.

[116] A. G. P. Rahbar and O. Yang. Powertrust: A robust and scalable reputation system for trusted peer-to-peer computing. *IEEE Transactions on Parallel and Distributed Systems*, 18(4):460–473, 2007.

[117] V. Ramasubramanian, R. Peterson, and E. G. Sirer. Corona: A high performance publish-subscribe system for the World Wide Web. In *NSDI'06*.

[118] P. Resnick, K. Kuwabara, R. Zeckhauser, and E. Friedman. Reputation systems. *Communications of the ACM*, 43(12):45–48, 2000.

[119] M. Roesch and C. Green. Snort users manual. *Snort Release*, 1(1), April 2010.

[120] S. Russell and P. Norvig. *Artificial Intelligence: A Modern Approach*. Second Edition, Prentice Hall, Englewood Cliffs, NJ, 2002.

[121] J. Sabater and C. Sierra. Regret: A reputation model for gregarious societies. In *Proceedings of the Fifth International Conference on Autonomous Agents Workshop on Deception, Fraud and Trust in Agent Societies*, 2001.

[122] A.-D. Schmidt, R. Bye, H.-G. Schmidt, J. Clausen, O. Kiraz, K. A. Yuksel, S. A. Camtepe, and S. Albayrak. Static analysis of executables for collaborative malware detection on android. In *Communications, 2009. ICC'09. IEEE International Conference on*, pages 1–5. IEEE, 2009.

[123] W. Schwartau. *Information Warfare: Chaos on the Electronic Superhighway*. Thunder's Mouth Press, 1994.

[124] P. Sen, N. Chaki, and R. Chaki. HIDS: Honesty-rate based collaborative intrusion detection system for mobile ad-hoc networks. *Computer Information Systems and Industrial Management Applications. CISIM'08*, pages 121–126, 2008.

[125] T.C. Shelling. *The Strategy of Conflict*. Harvard University Press, 1980.

[126] O. Sheyner, J. W. Haines, S. Jha, R. Lippmann, and J. M. Wing. Automated generation and analysis of attack graphs. In *IEEE Symposium on Security and Privacy*, pages 273–284, 2002.

[127] C. Silva, P. Sousa, and P. Verissimo. RAVE: Replicated antivirus engine. In *Dependable Systems and Networks Workshops (DSN-W), 2010 International Conference on*, pages 170–175. IEEE, 2010.

[128] L. Spitzner. Honeypots: Definitions and value of honeypots. Available from: www. tracking-hackers. com/papers/honeypots. html, 2003.

[129] R. Srikant. *The Mathematics of Internet Congestion Control*. Birkhäuser, 2004.

[130] M. Srivatsa, L. Xiong, and L. Liu. TrustGuard: Countering vulnerabilities in reputation management for decentralized overlay networks. In *Proceedings of the 14th International Conference on World Wide Web*, 2005.

[131] I. Stoica, R. Morris, D. Karger, M. F. Kaashoek, and H. Balakrishnan. Chord: A scalable peer-to-peer lookup service for Internet applications. *ACM SIG-COMM Computer Communication Review*, 31(4):149–160, 2001.

[132] Y. L. Sun, Z. Han, W. Yu, and K. J. R. Liu. A trust evaluation framework in distributed networks: Vulnerability analysis and defense against attacks. In *INFOCOM*. IEEE, 2006.

[133] W. T. L. Teacy, J. Patel, N. R. Jennings, and M. Luck. Coping with inaccurate reputation sources: Experimental analysis of a probabilistic trust model. In *Proceedings of Fourth International Autonomous Agents and Multiagent Systems (AAMAS)*, 2005.

[134] T. Tran and R. Cohen. Improving user satisfaction in agent-based electronic marketplaces by reputation modeling and adjustable product quality. In *Proceedings of the Third International Joint Conference on Autonomous Agents and Multiagent Systems (AAMAS)*, 2004.

[135] J. N. Tsitsiklis. Decentralized detection. *Advances in Statistical Signal Processing*, pages 297–344, 1993.

[136] D. Turner, M. Fossi, E. Johnson, T. Mack, J. Blackbird, S. Entwisle, M. K. Low, D. McKinney, and C. Wueest. Symantec global Internet security threat report–trends for July-December 07. *Symantec Enterprise Security*, 13:1–36, 2008.

[137] J. Ullrich. D. Shield. http://www.dshield.org/indexd.html [Last accessed on Feb. 15, 2013].

[138] A. Valdes and K. Skinner. Probabilistic alert correlation. In W. Lee, M. Ludovic, and A. Wespi, editors, *Recent Advances in Intrusion Detection*, volume 2212 of *Lecture Notes in Computer Science*, pages 54–68. Springer, 2001.

[139] F. Valeur, G. Vigna, C. Krgel, and R. A. Kemmerer. A comprehensive approach to intrusion detection alert correlation. *IEEE Trans. Dependable Security Computational*, 1(3):146–169, 2004.

[140] P. B. Velloso, R. P. Laufer, D. de O. Cunha, O. C. M. B. Duarte, and G. Pujolle. Trust Management in Mobile Ad Hoc Networks Using a Scalable Maturity-Based Model. *IEEE Transactions on Network and Service Management (TNSM)*, 7(3):172–185, 2010.

[141] R. Vogt, J. Aycock, and M. Jacobson. Army of botnets. In *ISOC Symposium on Network and Distributed Systems Security*, 2007.

[142] A. Wald. *Sequential Analysis*. John Wiley and Sons, 1947.

[143] N. Weaver, V. Paxson, S. Staniford, and R. Cunningham. A taxonomy of computer worms. In *Proceedings of the 2003 ACM Workshop on Rapid Malcode*, pages 11–18. ACM New York, NY, 2003.

[144] A. Whitby, A. Jøsang, and J. Indulska. Filtering out unfair ratings in bayesian reputation systems. *The Icfain Journal of Management Research*, pages 48–64, February 2005.

[145] P. Wood, M. Nisbet, G. Egan, N. Johnston, K. Haley, B. Krishnappa, T.-K. Tran, I. Asrar, O. Cox, S. Hittel, et al. Symantec Internet Security Threat Report Rrends for 2011. Volume XVII, 2012.

[146] Y. S. Wu, B. Foo, Y. Mei, and S. Bagchi. Collaborative intrusion detection system (CIDS): A framework for accurate and efficient IDS. In *Proceeding of 19th Annual Computer Security Applications Conference*, 2003.

[147] H. Man Y. Liu, and C. Comaniciu. A Bayesian game approach for intrusion detection in wireless ad hoc networks. *Valuetools*, October 2006.

[148] Y. Yan, A. El-Atawy, and E. Al-Shaer. Ranking-based optimal resource allocation in peer-to-peer networks. In *Proc. of the 26th Annual IEEE Conference on Computer Communications (IEEE INFOCOM 2007)*, May, 2007.

[149] V. Yegneswaran, P. Barford, and S. Jha. Global intrusion detection in the DOMINO overlay system. In *Proceedings of Network and Distributed System Security Symposium (NDSS04)*, 2004.

[150] B. Yu and M. P. Singh. Detecting deception in reputation management. *Proceedings of the Second International Joint Conference on Autonomous Agents and Multiagent Systems*, 2003.

[151] G. Zhang and M. Parashar. Cooperative detection and protection against network attacks using decentralized information sharing. *Cluster Computing*, 13(1):67–86, 2010.

[152] J. Zhang and R. Cohen. Trusting advice from other buyers in e-marketplaces: the problem of unfair ratings. In *Proceedings of the 8th International Conference on Electronic Commerce: The new e-commerce: innovations for conquering current barriers, obstacles and limitations to conducting successful business on the internet*, 2006.

[153] Y. Zhang and Y. Fang. A fine-grained reputation system for reliable service selection in peer-to-peer networks. *IEEE Transactions on Parallel and Distributed Systems*, pages 1134–1145, 2007.

[154] Z. Zhong, L. Ramaswamy, and K. Li. ALPACAS: A large-scale privacy-aware collaborative anti-spam system. In *Proceedings IEEE INFOCOM*, 2008.

[155] C. V. Zhou, C. Leckie, and S. Karunasekera. Collaborative detection of fast flux phishing domains. *Journal of Networks*, 4:75–84, February 2009.

[156] C. V. Zhou, C. Leckie, S. Karunasekera, and T. Peng. A self-healing, self-protecting collaborative intrusion detection architecture to trace-back fast-flux phishing domains. In *The 2nd IEEE Workshop on Autonomic Communication and Network Management (ACNM 2008)*, April 2008.

[157] C. V. Zhou, S. Karunasekera, and C. Leckie. A peer-to-peer collaborative intrusion detection system. In *Proceedings of the IEEE International Conference on Networks*, pages 118–123, November 2005.

[158] Q. Zhu and T. Başar. Indices of power in optimal ids default configuration: theory and examples. In *Proc. of 2nd Conference on Decision and Game Theory for Security (GameSec 2011), College Park, MD, USA.*, November 2011.

[159] Q. Zhu, C. J. Fung, R. Boutaba, and T. Barsar. A Distributed Sequential Algorithm for Collaborative Intrusion Detection Networks. In *IEEE International Conference on Communications (ICC2010)*, 2009.

[160] Q. Zhu and L. Pavel. Enabling osnr service differentiation using generalized model in optical networks. *IEEE Transactions on Communications*, 57(9):2570–2575, September 2009.

[161] Q. Zhu, C. Fung, R. Boutaba, and T. Başar. A game-theoretic approach to knowledge sharing in distributed collaborative intrusion detection networks: Fairness, incentives and security. In *Proc. of the 50th IEEE Conference on Decision and Control (CDC) and European Control Conference (ECC), Orlando, USA*, December 2011.

[162] Q. Zhu, C. Fung, R. Boutaba, and T. Başar. GUIDEX: A game-theoretic incentive-based mechanism for intrusion detection networks. *IEEE Journal on Selected Areas in Communications (JSAC) Special Issue on Economics of Communication Networks & Systems, to appear*, 2012.

[163] Q. Zhu, C. Fung, R. Boutaba, and T. Başar. A game-theoretical approach to incentive design in collaborative intrusion detection networks. In *Proceedings of the International Symposium on Game Theory for Networks (GameNets)*, May, 2009.

[164] Q. Zhu and L. Pavel. End-to-end DWDM optical link power-control via a Stackelberg revenue-maximizing model. *Int. J. Netw. Manag.*, 18(6):505–520, November 2008.

[165] S. Zlobec. *Stable Parametric Programming*. Springer, 1st edition, 2001.

Index